To my beloved family of New Orleans,
Ladies Mia, Ruby, Beatrice, and Evangeline

the new orleans kitchen

classic recipes and
modern techniques for
an unrivaled cuisine

Justin Devillier

with Jamie Feldmar

Photographs by Dennis Culbert

LORENA JONES BOOKS
An imprint of **TEN SPEED PRESS**
California | New York

contents

introduction

New Orleans is in my blood, but my story starts two thousand miles away from here, in Dana Point, California. That's where I grew up, the son of a fourth-generation Louisiana father and a Philadelphia-bred Irish Polish mother. My mom was a healthcare professional, but she also had a catering company on the side, and she was a total kitchen work-horse, plowing through prep for five hundred stuffed mushrooms like it was no big deal. She let me play around in the kitchen from the time I was very young, teaching me how to fry eggs and make grilled cheese before I even went to elementary school.

My dad was an electrical engineer for the Department of Defense and, to be honest, he wasn't much of a cook. My parents split up when I was young, and I spent weekends at his house, where he had a few old Paul Prudhomme cookbooks—not because he wanted to master the art of Cajun cooking, but because he missed the food of his childhood and wanted to re-create some of those dishes in Southern California. I spent a lot of time flipping through those books, which were filled with crazy-long ingredient lists and super-specific instructions on how to do things like darken roux and brown meat.

I loved how detailed Prudhomme's recipes were, and as I got a little older, I started applying some of his techniques to my own culinary experiments. My mom's house was two minutes from the ocean, and I was the quintessential beach rat as a kid, surfing and fishing nonstop with a motley crew of other teens. We'd haul our fishing bounty back to shore to cook over a bonfire on the beach. At first it was really basic, but soon I started paying closer attention to recipes, following instructions to a T and learning more about how flavors and techniques interacted. As I cooked more and grew more confident, I started playing around a little, improvising with sauces and cooking techniques to prepare our catch.

All through high school I worked in restaurants, washing dishes and making pizzas, and loving every second of it. When I graduated, I moved a few hours north and enrolled in culinary school. I also got a job cooking at Disneyland—not in the park itself, but on the tourist-heavy promenade, which had themed restaurants as far as the eye could see. I landed at Ralph Brennan's Jazz Kitchen, a New Orleans–style restaurant, which I specifically sought out because of my dad's influence. We'd gone to New Orleans to visit his side of the family when I was kid, and I'd always loved the Creole and Cajun food, rich in French and Spanish traditions, but mixed with West African and Southern influences. I was intrigued by this fluid cuisine, which seemed rooted in classic techniques but also open to—if not reliant on—improvisation.

The Jazz Kitchen was a great education because it did fifteen hundred covers a day. I ripped through the line every night, cranked to eleven at all times, loving every second of the intensity. Once, one of my coworkers asked me, "Why are you going to culinary school? You'll learn more here than you'll ever learn there," and I knew he was right—my cooking school classmates were largely amateurs pursuing cooking as a hobby. So I dropped out of culinary school and got a kitchen job working the overnight shift at a hotel near my mom's house.

At this point, all I thought about and read about was food—I tore through cookbooks and food magazines, and watched a lot of *Great Chefs* on PBS; loving the lo-fi production—just a cook preparing three dishes with clear instructions and no showmanship. I was obsessed with learning classic techniques, and I'd practice making the same dishes dozens of times until I mastered them. I had a copy of *The Food Lover's Companion* and knew it cover to cover—I wanted to be able to look through cookbooks and know what everything was.

It was important for me to learn this stuff because I wanted to make a career out of cooking, and I had big professional ambitions. But I learned a lot about home cooking during this period, too. By following all these recipes word for word, I started to understand how and why flavors and techniques work, and how they come together to create a great dish. Once that groundwork was laid, I was able to start improvising a bit, while still adhering to the essential methods I'd mastered. In a way, it was like New Orleans cuisine itself, which relies on just a few fundamental techniques and ingredients but thrives on the creativity of its chefs.

That's when it all started to click for me, and that's what I want to do for you now. Instead of showing you how to re-create dishes like the ones you've had in my restaurants, I want to teach you the fundamentals behind these classic recipes. I want you to begin to understand how an ingredient might affect flavor, or why one technique in New Orleans cooking is called for over another. Once you start to understand cooking as something beyond the rote following of instructions, you will become more confident in your ability, and that's when things really start to get fun.

Cooking is about a combination of thoughtfulness and intuition. Once you have the techniques in place, you can start to go off script. It's okay to play around a little—and in fact, it's encouraged—once you start to understand how things work. In some ways, the purpose of this book is twofold: first, to get you to understand more, and then, to let go and simply enjoy applying what you know.

It took me a long time to learn these lessons. First, I had to spread my wings and get out of California. I chose New Orleans for many reasons—the family connection, the cost of living, and because I'd read an article about a local chef named Anne Kearney, whose restaurant, Peristyle, served exactly the kind of food I wanted to make—very Creole but very French, with lots of demi-glace and butter sauces and seasonal produce. Her food felt so perfectly New Orleans to me—rooted in tradition, but constantly evolving, depending on what was fresh and available. I wanted in.

I arrived in New Orleans in 2003, at the tender age of twenty-two. I emailed my old friends at Ralph Brennan's Jazz Kitchen, and they set me up with a line cook job at their fine-dining Italian restaurant in town. But one day, I went to Peristyle to meet Anne and tell her I wanted to work for her. I remember her opening the door, me introducing myself, and her immediately giving me a written test, right then and there, with questions about how to cook a piece of fish and the names of three mother sauces. Finally! Payoff for all my obsessive reading and practicing.

It took a few months, but eventually, a line cook position opened at Peristyle and I started working there full-time. I was in heaven—I had read about the kinds of techniques and flavors Anne used, but it wasn't until I worked with her that I finally got to dive deep into that style of cooking. I'd found my place. Working there exposed me to tons of ingredients for the first time—foie gras, sweetbreads, wild mushrooms, and baby fennel—and techniques I use to this day, like how to make mayonnaise and clean an artichoke.

I would have stayed at Peristyle forever, but Anne eventually decided to sell to a new owner, and it was time for me to move on. I was on the market when one of my Peristyle colleagues called and offered me a job

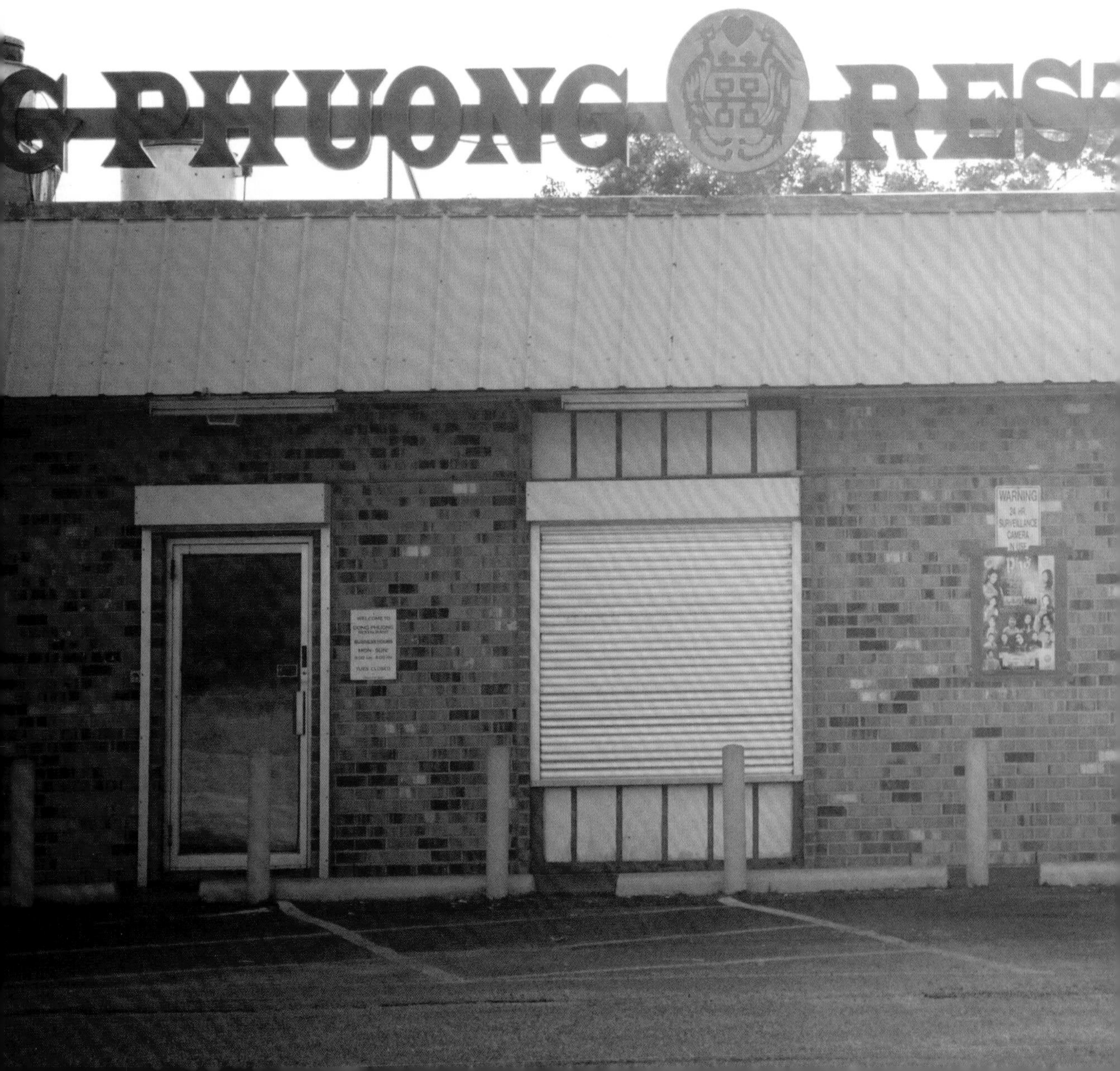
G PHUONG
REST
WARNING
24 HR.
SURVEILLANCE
CAMERA

at his new restaurant, La Petite Grocery. I took him up on it, and the gig was great. At the time, it was the hottest new restaurant in town, with a kind of French bistro–meets–Louisiana kitchen vibe. I worked there for about a year before leaving in early 2005 with the goal of becoming a sous-chef at one of the high-end new restaurants in the city. Things were going according to plan for a few months, until Hurricane Katrina hit, and everything changed.

It's painful for me to dwell on that period—it was a dark chapter, with a lot of heartbreak and loss. My house was flooded and my personal possessions destroyed, and the restaurant I was working at was totally out of commission. When the storm happened, I'd been dating my now-wife and business partner, Mia, for a few months. We evacuated and spent two weeks driving across the South, eventually winding up in Charleston, South Carolina, where Mia is from. The one upside from the storm was that it gave me a chance to get out of the kitchen and experience dining from the other side, as a customer, at some of the best restaurants in the South. That was eye-opening for me, to eat out and really start to understand what chefs were trying to say with their food. It all comes back to that idea of mastering fundamental techniques and flavors and then getting creative with them. I could finally see it in action, from outside the kitchen.

Mia and I came back to New Orleans three weeks after the storm, and we both ended up working at one of the only restaurants open in the French Quarter, cooking for first responders and emergency workers. It was rough—the restaurant put us up in a hotel nearby since we couldn't go home. I was only doing recovery cooking. We had a lot of long days and late nights, holed up and drinking with the handful of people who had been allowed inside the city limits, all of us bonded by the worry of what would become of our battered city. Things moved forward bit by bit—the lights came back on, trash got picked up, other services were being addressed. We moved out of the hotel, to the neighborhood known as Uptown, and I rode my bike to the Quarter every day at 6 AM to cook breakfast for the troops. After a few weeks of living in a PTSD-induced daze, I realized I needed to get back on track, and so I decided to leave the cafe and resume my pursuit of cooking higher-end food. That's when I returned to La Petite Grocery.

I returned as soon as it reopened after the storm, in October 2005. We had a lot of work to do to rebuild the infrastructure of the restaurant, which for decades had housed a beloved neighborhood grocery store, Von der Haar's Fine Foods. There were only two of us on staff, and I did everything in the kitchen, working every station and just cranking it out. We were packed—this was during a period when the few restaurants in New Orleans that were open were becoming real community meeting spots, as people began to return to the city after the storm. La Petite Grocery was very much a community gathering place, delivering a small sense of normalcy that people desperately craved. We worked hard and tried to make it fun.

In 2007, I took over as executive chef, at the ripe old age of twenty-six. Mia and I married the following year, and she left her accounting job to come on as general manager full-time in 2009. Having her onboard really helped smooth all the rough edges—the aesthetics improved, along with the wine list and the service. Soon thereafter, Mia and I were offered the opportunity to purchase the majority stake in the restaurant. It wasn't an immediate yes—I still had plans of cooking my way across Europe like the chefs of years past. But I listened to my gut, and my gut said that the chance to take the restaurant and truly make it our own was too good to pass up.

Once we owned the restaurant, we really changed things—we revamped the layout of the menu, branding, staff uniforms, and more. Before we took over, the restaurant felt a little closed off—the big windows looking out onto Magazine Street were covered in red velvet curtains, giving the space a dark and mysterious vibe. We wanted to open up to the city, both physically and metaphorically. Down came the curtains, and in came natural light, a more contemporary soundtrack, and an updated menu (more on that in a minute). We put up vintage photographs taken when the space was Von der Haar's grocery, to preserve the legacy of the place. We continued to maintain the classic ambiance and food that attracted longtime customers, but we also wanted to attract a new generation of diners who would appreciate our youthful energy.

I spent time making the menu feel more my own, going all the way back to what I'd learned in my Peristyle days, creating what I like to think of as a French restaurant wearing New Orleans clothes. I introduced dishes that are now considered signatures, like the turtle Bolognese, Blue Crab Beignets (page 88), and Abita Root Beer–Braised Short Ribs (see page 293). But we also started running seven daily specials, depending on what was in at the market and we were in the mood to cook. I loved having the consistency of a regular menu and the challenge of reinventing ourselves every day; that flexibility and willingness to experiment is what New Orleans cuisine is all about.

Shortly after we officially took over, influential local critic Brett Anderson gave us a perfect "four beans" rating in the New Orleans *Times-Picayune*, writing "the La Petite of the current era generates the excitement you only find when chefs are starting to hit their stride." He said that I belonged "to a generation of chefs intent on cooking food that conveys the hunger of its creator," which pretty much nailed it. All I've ever really wanted to do is cook well and make people happy with my cooking.

It was amazing and totally humbling to get a review like that, and things started snowballing from there. In 2011, I was nominated for my first James Beard award, as I was every year thereafter, until I won Best Chef: South in 2016. Words can't properly describe my feelings on that occasion, so I'm going to quit while I'm ahead and just say it was a huge honor.

We haven't slowed down businesswise, either. In 2015, Mia and I opened a second restaurant, Balise, in an 1832 Creole townhouse in the Warehouse District of New Orleans, a slightly more casual, tavern-style sister property to La Petite Grocery. And now we have a third restaurant, a French brasserie, Justine.

Restaurants are a huge part of my life, but what I do at the restaurants isn't the focus of this book. For me, the true art of cooking comes from mastering certain fundamental principles, then having the confidence to riff off of them. That's how I taught myself to cook, and it's how I cook when I'm off-duty at home with Mia and our three daughters or I'm out on a hunting trip in rural Louisiana with my buddies. I don't cook restaurant-style food when I'm not at my restaurants, but I do take the lessons I've learned as a professional chef and adapt them to whatever I'm working with. It's not about dumbing things down—it's being thoughtful about how and why I put a dish together, and having the confidence to apply the same principles to a meal at home.

That's really what this book is about: teaching you to find the true pleasure of cooking, New Orleans–style, at home.

about this book

When I decided I wanted to write a cookbook, I spent a lot of time thinking about the books that have shaped me at different stages of my journey as a chef. I realized that the ones that have had the biggest impact on me were the ones I read when I was just starting out, a super-curious twenty-one-year-old cook who wanted to absorb every bit of information I could. No chef I worked for would have allowed me to develop dishes and experiment in their professional kitchen, so I was most creative at the stove of the underequipped crash pad that I called home. Late nights feeding hungry coworkers or Sundays spent cooking all day and drinking beer with our small group of friends were the norm. The books I consulted during this time became key in helping me understand the techniques and processes that shaped my own style of cooking, and eventually became the backbone of my cuisine. I hope this book will do the same for you.

getting started

The book is organized by course, starting with stocks and sauces, as they provide the foundation for many of the recipes in the book, then moving to appetizers, vegetable-based side dishes, salads, soups, seafood, poultry, meat, desserts, and a pantry section with staples like pickles, jellies, compound butters, and more.

The structure is intentionally straightforward, as I believe this is the best way for home cooks to learn to improve their technique. Many of the stand-alone recipes in the early chapters will be used as part of a composed dish in later chapters. I think it's important to have a chapter in the beginning dedicated to stocks and sauces—as many cookbooks do—because starting with them relates to the way a cook should think. A recipe is a sum of its parts, and its parts are separate things. They don't all fit together because they have to—they fit together because the person who created the recipe built it intentionally. So learning the fundamentals of sauce making is important on its own, as a separate art form. You must understand how they work across many different recipes, so that you can eventually go forth and apply them as you see fit.

For example, that same herbaceous green Salsa Verde (page 54) you'll learn to make in the Stocks, Sauces & Dressings chapter will be called for later, alongside a perfectly grilled skirt steak in the Meat chapter. But I also give examples for ways to tweak a sauce's taste and texture, depending on what you're making it for. The idea is to encourage you to think about different ways to combine flavor profiles, textures, and techniques—to build a plate with an understanding of why all of the components fit together.

When you're cooking your way through this book, try to master the techniques and notice when they appear in various recipes. Some recipes repeat the same technique, and that's intentional—I want to show how you can use one technique to get to two totally different places, by modifying the cooking method or the ingredients and, therefore, the flavor.

Take the Aioli on page 65, for example. Once you master the fundamental technique of emulsifying an oil into a mixture of egg yolks and acid, you can take it anywhere you want, flavorwise. If you're serving aioli with shellfish, you might steep saffron in the lemon juice. If you're serving it with fried green tomatoes, you might want to puree basil into it. You can also dilute it with buttermilk and turn it into dressing, or make a homemade Ranch-style sauce by adding dill and other fresh herbs. Or take the Cornbread on page 371, which can be used as a batter to make the pancakes on page 87, baked into crumbs to top the mac-and-cheese on page 146, or used in the stuffing for the quail on page 263. It's a simple foundational recipe, but I apply it differently across other recipes, and once you have it down, you'll find even more ways to use it.

Finally, study the photos, especially the step-by-step technique shots. I can spend all day telling you what caramelized onions are supposed to look like, but there's a reason people say a picture is worth a thousand words.

key ingredients

These are the ingredients I recommend stocking your pantry and refrigerator with in order to successfully cook the recipes in this book (and many others). I cannot overemphasize the importance of investing in high-quality ingredients, even basic ones. They are the foundation of everything you will cook, so start strong by sourcing well.

Acid: Acid from vinegars, citrus juice, and pickle brine are used to balance the flavors of a variety of dishes. I use them primarily at the end, to finish a plate with a final spike of brightness just before serving. (Add acid too early in the cooking process, and its flavor becomes muted.) Deciding which to use comes down to the flavor profile of the dish. I reach for fresh lemon juice the most, to finish everything from pasta to butter sauce to a piece of grilled meat. I might use lime or orange juice in a butter sauce or broth, and vinegar (usually white or red wine, balsamic, or apple cider) in something cold, like chilled vegetables or shellfish. (And, of course, in vinaigrettes.) I like to use the juice from Pickled Jalapeños (page 353) in something with a peppery flavor, like braised or smothered beans. Understanding the balance between salt, acid, and fat is really important when you're tasting a dish. Get in the habit of tasting everything, and asking yourself which of those three things a dish might need more of.

Butter: All recipes in this book call for unsalted butter. Remember, you can always add salt, but you can't take it out. You don't have to buy the most expensive European brand, but buy quality butter from a reputable source, ideally with more than 80 percent butterfat—not the stuff that keeps in plastic tubs for years. If you can buy it from a local farm, even better.

Cheese: Notes on specific types of cheeses are given in recipes that call for them, but a general note about Parmesan is needed: Take the extra five minutes required to grate your own. The preshredded stuff looks and tastes like wood chips. Invest in real Parmesan from Italy (Parmigiano-Reggiano)—it's available at warehouse clubs!

Cream, heavy: Again, shop for high-quality dairy, and lucky you if you have access to farm-fresh heavy cream.

Cured pork: Cured pork is historically the backbone of Louisiana cooking. I'm talking about things like tasso, ham hocks, salt pork, bacon, andouille, chaurice (another hot sausage), and more. Walk around southern Louisiana on a Sunday afternoon, and that's what you'll smell wafting through the air, probably mixed with beans or greens.

Cured pork goes into a lot of the classic one-pot wonders of Louisiana. I really enjoy the smokiness of tasso, andouille, bacon, and ham hocks. But I also enjoy the pure porky flavor of unsmoked, salt-cured, and seasoned pork, like the Cured Pork Belly (Pancetta) on page 375. You can use that interchangeably with any of the products mentioned above; just know that it will lack a distinguishable smoky flavor. That doesn't make it lesser-than, though—in fact, I find that using the unsmoked version in things like simmered beans allows you to impart more pork flavor without overpowering the dish.

Eggs: All eggs called for in the book are large. Buy good eggs from hens that are pastured.

Fish sauce: Fish sauce is the liquid collected from salted, fermented anchovies, which (unsurprisingly) has a funky, salty, fishy flavor, and is used as a seasoning. At first, you might want to use it sparingly, but as your palate adjusts, you'll wind up putting it in everything, and in large amounts. It adds a rich umami flavor to sauces, soups, vinaigrettes, and more. *Colatura di alici* is the Italian version, and *garum* is the Greco-Roman version, but when I refer to it in this book, I mean the Vietnamese stuff, preferably from Three Crabs, Red Boat, or Squid brands.

Flour: The recipes in this book call for all-purpose flour. I like to use organic unbleached all-purpose, ideally made with 100 percent American wheat (King Arthur has a nice version). As its name implies, all-purpose flour can be used just about anywhere. To measure flour for the recipes in this book, take a dry measuring cup or spoon, dip it right into a container of flour, give it a few gentle taps on the table, and then run the back of a butter knife across the top to make sure it's even.

Herbs: Everything called for in my recipes should be fresh, unless otherwise noted. Fresh herbs have long been a big part of my cooking style. They make such a difference in the brightness and complexity of what you're eating, making every bite much more interesting. Dry herbs can be useful for soups, stews, and braises, but for garnishing or finishing, the fresh version is much quicker to release its oils and aromas. I call for a variety of fresh herbs throughout my recipes, but three of the most common are chives, parsley, and tarragon.

Chives have a light, herbaceous, oniony flavor, much more delicate than other members of the allium family. I rarely add them to something hot unless it's right before serving, lest they lose their structure and bright green color (and in turn, flavor). I usually finely chop chives and use them to finish anything that could use a bright, aromatic touch.

Fresh parsley has a very light citrus minerality, with an oh-so-slightly-earthy flavor. I sometimes finely chop it and cook it into soups and sauces, but I use it most often as a garnish, leaving the leaves whole or coarsely chopping them. Parsley's flavor is versatile—you can put it on just about anything, and it will make that thing taste just a little bit better. I prefer flat-leaf parsley over curly.

Tarragon has a lemony, anise-y flavor and an herbaceous grassiness, which lends itself well to eggs and shellfish. If you cook with tarragon, it tends to get muddy and muted, so I like to add it at the end to keep it as bright and fresh as possible. (You can build a similar flavor during cooking with fennel, or even a touch of Pernod or another type of pastis.)

The combination of chives, parsley, and tarragon, with the addition of chervil, if available, constitutes the classic French combo of fines herbes, a fresh herb mixture that brightens dishes from bouillabaisse to soupe au pistou to all kinds of vegetables. It's a classic for a reason, and I love to use this combination as often as possible.

Hot sauce: Here in New Orleans, we use a lot of hot sauce. I generally stick to the classic Southern-style pepper vinegar hot sauces, like Tabasco or Louisiana "Red Dot." Making your own is easy and very gratifying (see page 62), and it keeps more or less forever, so I highly encourage you to try it at home. I also like to use hot pepper vinegar (see the Duck and Andouille Gumbo on page 201, for example), by which I mean the pickling liquid from a jar of pickled jalapeños (see page 353) or other pickled peppers. When I want a sharp, peppery acidity without the richness and body of a sauce, this is my go-to.

Oils for high-temperature cooking: Grapeseed is my oil of choice for high-temperature cooking, like frying. Some oils take on a weird flavor when they're heated over high (I'm looking at you, canola), but grapeseed stays neutral. It has a relatively high smoke point and a light taste, so it's also perfectly suitable for making emulsions and aioli.

Oils for mid-temperature cooking: When I want to benefit from the high-heat tolerance of grapeseed oil but impart the flavor of olive oil, I choose an 80/20 blend that is 80 percent grapeseed oil (it's available bottled, or make your own). I use it when I'm braising or searing meat, and when I make salad dressings in a blender, as I find that the spinning and agitation from the motorized blade gives extra-virgin olive oil a bitter flavor. (If you're whisking a dressing by hand, extra-virgin is okay, though.)

Oils for low-temperature cooking: I use extra-virgin olive oil when I'm cooking things that require a gentle, low-temperature touch. I reach for it when sweating vegetables and I'm trying to avoid browning, or poaching fish. I sometimes sauté vegetables in extra-virgin olive oil, but I don't sear meat in it, because when it hits its smoke point, its naturally fruity, grassy flavor becomes bitter and muted. You could sear with it, but it's not a good idea—the reason you spend extra on extra-virgin olive oil is because it has been treated carefully to retain its nice fruity, fresh-pressed olive flavor, and a hot pan will destroy that. Extra-virgin olive is also my oil of choice for finishing cooked dishes, and using in most uncooked dressings and sauces. I like California Olive Ranch, which makes affordable, high-quality oils; they are available across the country.

Olives: I use three kinds of olives—Nicoise or Arbequina, when I want black olives, and green Castelvetranos. When it comes to olives, it's more important to use the highest quality than to use the exact type called for in a recipe. Don't buy jarred or canned olives—they're flavorless (though useful for sticking on your fingers and torturing your siblings). Turn, instead, to the olive bar, if your market has one. High-quality olives have a very briny flavor and natural saltiness, without any metallic taste or acidity from the brine. The brine should take on the color of the olive, and the olive itself should be meaty, with a slightly floral, fruity note from the oil in its flesh.

Red chile: Most of my recipes call for seasoning with basic salt and pepper, but I also like to use a lot of red chile. Classic dried red chile flakes have their place (primarily on top of pizza), but I don't keep them around at home because they have seeds. I love gochugaru, a Korean red chile flake, for everyday use. It has a finer texture, is more fragrant, and is slightly hotter and sweeter than the standard version. It's an awesome ingredient, and you can see it do its work. If you make a sauce with it, for example, it stains the liquid a lovely red hue, which tells me it still has potency, and its flavor will be well dispersed in the final dish. Gochugaru is available at many Asian markets and online.

My other favorite form of dried red chile is piment d'Espelette, which is made of sun-dried red peppers from the Basque region of France. This one is even more fragrant than gochugaru (and is usually more expensive). It has an orange hue, feels a little softer, and applies its incredible fragrance to everything it touches. I add it at the very end of cooking, because it's so aromatic and adds a nice floral flavor. A little goes a long way here. Piment d'Espelette is available at many gourmet specialty stores.

Rice: Rice is another staple ingredient of Louisiana cooking. If you live in a region where rice is grown, buy local. If you don't, look around—there's a lot of good rice available in grocery stores today, ideally domestically grown. I prefer medium-grain with a neutral flavor. Avoid parboiled rice. That stuff is the worst.

Salt: I never use iodized table salt for anything. For cooking, I use kosher for general seasoning, and call for it throughout this book. I like Diamond Crystal brand, because as you rub it between your fingers, it breaks down into finer pieces, so you can control the density of the flakes. I do occasionally call for fleur de sel (sea salt) to finish a handful of recipes. For that I like Maldon, which has a perfect flaky, crisp texture and a triangular shape. The thing to remember about Maldon is that it dissolves fast, so a little goes a long way.

Shellfish: Because this is a New Orleans cookbook, many of my recipes involve shellfish, some of which might be tough to find fresh unless you live on a coast. I have provided notes in the recipes on where to find ingredients, like crawfish and octopus, but in general, use what you have access to. If you're in the Pacific Northwest, use Dungeness crab instead of blue. If you're in Maine, use local oysters instead of Gulf ones. (This holds true for fish as well—if you're near the Great Lakes and you have great walleye, use it instead of the Gulf fish I call for.) If you're land-locked, try to find something frozen in the shell, or you can always mail order fresh Gulf seafood. It's worth the expense for something like the Blue Crab Beignets on page 88. Shrimp freezes particularly well—my advice is to buy American wild-caught shrimp that's been individually quick-frozen (IQF) if you can.

Spices: I occasionally call for whole spices in brines and marinades, but I love to make my own spice rub or mix with ground spices, as well. As many cookbook authors suggest, toasting and grinding your own spices in small amounts is the way to go—you get a much richer, fresher flavor this way (assuming you're using spices that you've purchased in the recent past, because they do go stale and lose flavor after months on the shelf). You can use a coffee grinder reserved for this purpose, which also allows you to control the coarseness of the grind. Wipe it out with a damp paper towel after using. It's also nice to have a small mesh strainer that you can sift spices through if they must be very fine.

core techniques

Some books have special sections dedicated to the equipment you will need. This book isn't one of them. Make sure you have decent knives that you can sharpen, some good spoons, one really nice stockpot, and one nice sauté pan; from there, you can make pretty much every one of the recipes in this book. I will occasionally call for other tools to help you make faster work of some kitchen prep, but none of them are mandatory. With just a handful of basic kitchen tools, you can master all of the following skills.

Emulsifying: This is a word that comes up a lot in my recipes, particularly in vinaigrettes, sauces, and some soups. Technically speaking, an emulsion is a suspension of two liquids that wouldn't naturally mix, such as oil and vinegar. If you pour vinegar on top of oil, it will sit in a separate layer on top of the oil, until you whisk them together. After whisking, the two will eventually separate (or "break"), unless they are bound together permanently by an emulsifying agent, such as an egg yolk. Learning how to make proper emulsions is one of the most important skills any cook can acquire, and I have provided detailed instructions in recipes that call for them, such as Aioli (page 65) and Bacon Vinaigrette (page 59).

Ice water baths: For a standard ice water bath, simply fill a large container (like a mixing bowl) three-quarters full with ice and add just enough water to make a slush. Sometimes you'll need to season it with salt to keep the cooking seasoning from washing away. (I have provided specific instructions per recipe when this is necessary.) For vegetables, such as the broccoli in Broccoli Caesar (see page 165), an ice water bath helps maintain their vibrant green color after they are blanched. For the Ricotta Dumplings (see page 141), a quick dip in icy water helps set the soft, delicate pillows in an easy-to-handle shape.

Knife cuts: In a home kitchen, no one will judge you for imperfectly chopping vegetables, but it's still important to cut them into uniform sizes to ensure even cooking. Here are the sizes I refer to:

Small dice: ¼-inch cubes

Medium dice: ½-inch cubes

Large dice: ¾-inch cubes

Mashing garlic: Some of my recipes, particularly vinaigrettes and sauces, call for "mashed" garlic. To mash garlic, peel it, mince it very finely, sprinkle a little salt over, and mash the tiny pieces into a paste with the flat side of your knife. It's similar to using a mortar and pestle. I do this to help disperse the garlic flavor more evenly into what I'm cooking.

Searing and deglazing (creating and then loosening the fond): These are techniques that come up a lot, particularly when making pan sauces. The first step, searing, involves cooking a piece of meat or fish in hot oil to form an even, golden, caramelized crust. Bits of that crust fall off the meat into the pan, where they mingle with evaporated meat juices and stick to the bottom, becoming the fond. Fond is a very good thing—those little bits are packed full of concentrated meat flavor, which will enrich a sauce. When you deglaze a pan, you pour in liquid (such as stock, wine, or water), scrape off everything adhering to the bottom with your spatula, and quickly stir the fond into the liquid. This is another fundamental technique for building flavor, and once you have it mastered, you'll be able to apply it to countless recipes.

Seasoning: Sometimes I call for exact amounts of salt and pepper, and sometimes I don't. Here's why: Ingredients like bacon, pancetta, shrimp, and some cheeses already have salt in them, so it's better to cook with them, taste what you cook, and season accordingly. It's important for you to explore your own palate, and learn how to truly season to taste. In professional kitchens, the number-one lesson is "taste your food." That is the underlying philosophy in all of cooking. Even when I give an exact measurement for seasoning, I still want you to taste and adjust the amount accordingly. When seasoning meats or a whole pan of vegetables, season them from 12 inches above. This technique, which you've probably seen on cooking shows, evenly disperses the salt and pepper.

Supreming citrus: This is a technique for serving citrus in neat slices, without rind, pith, or membrane. To do it, cut both ends off the citrus—the top and bottom—so the citrus has a flat, even base to sit on and doesn't roll or wobble. Using the end of your knife, gently slice down, following the curvature of the fruit, cutting away the peel, including the membrane and the pith, so you see only the fruit. Gently cut between each rib to release the segments in neat wedges.

Vegetable measurements: In recipes where an exact volume of a vegetable ingredient is essential, I call for a volume measurement rather than a total number of said vegetable (for example, 2 cups sliced onion, instead of 1 medium onion, sliced). Here's a quick cheat sheet to help with your shopping list:

Beets: 1 tennis ball–size = 1 cup sliced

Bell pepper: 1 medium = 2 cups small-diced

Cabbage: 1 medium head = 16 cups thinly sliced

Carrots: 1 medium = 1 cup small-diced

Celery: 2 stalks = 1 cup sliced

Celery root: 1 medium = 2½ cups medium-diced

Chile: 1 medium = 1½ tablespoons small-diced

Fennel: 1 medium bulb, greens removed = 1½ cups small-diced

Leek: 1 medium, white and green parts = 1 cup small-diced

Onion: ½ medium onion = 1 cup sliced

Parsnip: 1 medium = 1 cup medium-diced

Potato: 1 medium Yukon gold = 1½ cups medium-diced

Shallot: 1 small = ¼ cup small-diced

Tomato: 1 medium = 1½ cups medium-diced

stocks, sauces & dressings

Stocks and sauces are the backbone of the food I like to cook, and in this chapter you'll learn to make some of the most important recipes in the book. Specifically, look at the recipes for roux and stock at the beginning of the chapter, and aioli on page 65, as fundamental techniques. Focus on memorizing the techniques and then ultimately mastering them.

As you get more experienced in the kitchen, you'll want to pair dishes with sauces to enhance both. You will also become better at utilizing the vegetables and meats you cook. Stock, for example, is the foundation of many sauces, and a handy way to use up the leftover parts of a protein that may otherwise be discarded. Think about it: When you make a nice chicken stock with the roasted carcasses of the bird you cooked, you're breaking down a single ingredient into its most basic elements, developing the best flavor from each piece, and then using it in another way. That's a big part of the craft of cooking.

An understanding of how to make roux is fundamental to cooking Louisiana food. It's an old-school technique rooted in classic French cookery, mixed with Cajun grandma cooking.

In this chapter, I detail the steps for making three kinds of roux—blond, brown, and dark (pages 42, 45, and 46)—but before I get to the roux recipes, a few words about fats: I like to use clarified butter in lighter (blond) roux, and peanut or other high-temperature-friendly oils for darker roux. Blond roux are often used in velvety, creamy, béchamel-based dishes, to which the flavor and texture of butter are well suited. And because blond roux cooks briefly, there is less risk of burning the butter, as you might during the longer cooking times required for a brown or dark roux. It is possible to take a roux beyond the dark point, to get an even deeper, darker, richer flavor—this is called a black roux, and it has the approximate color of dark chocolate. But you must be very careful not to scorch it, or it won't emulsify properly with the liquid. I recommend stopping at dark roux until you have roux-making fully mastered.

Play around in this chapter and pay attention to what happens when you tweak the recipes—adding more or less oil to an aioli, for example, to make it runnier or thicker. The instructions are there to guide you, but experiment as you learn how these techniques work to develop your own style and preferences. In professional kitchens, where consistency is key, cooks are taught to make things the same way every time. When you're in a creative, research-and-development mode at home, be flexible—that's how you learn new things.

blond roux

Blond roux is the foundation for the French mother sauce béchamel, which is responsible for delicious cream-based soups, chowders, mornay sauce, mac-and-cheese, and more. I use clarified butter for blond roux for its, well, buttery flavor and velvety texture. It's important to use clarified butter, because regular butter is filled with water, which will leave you with an unappealing slurry. It's more efficient to evaporate the moisture out of the butter before adding the flour, helping hold your roux together tightly, with a richer butter flavor. If you don't want to make your own, you can use ghee, which you'll find in a South Asian or specialty food market.

makes 2 cups

1 cup unsalted butter

1 cup all-purpose flour

Clarify the butter by melting it completely in a large saucepan over medium heat, 6 to 8 minutes. Decrease the heat to low and cook until all the water evaporates and the milk solids that were carried by the water have separated and floated to the top, 20 to 25 minutes. Skim off the solids and discard, reserving the clear yellow butterfat. You should have about ⅔ cup of clarified butter. It will keep in the refrigerator for up to 3 weeks.

In a medium heavy-bottomed pot (I like ceramic or enamel-coated cast iron) over high heat, melt the clarified butter for 1 to 1½ minutes. Do not allow it to smoke; avoid even tiny plumes. Whisk in the flour and break up any clumps to form a smooth paste—it should look like a thin batter.

Decrease the heat to medium-low, and using a wooden spoon, preferably with a flat top, move the roux around—stirring, but also turning it, so the butter and flour cook evenly, about 5 minutes. The roux should start to smell like popcorn as the flour toasts in the butter. Continue cooking and stirring for another 5 to 7 minutes, until the mixture is even and smooth in color and texture. The goal here is to gently toast the flour just enough to remove its raw taste without browning it. If you see the color start to deepen as you stir, decrease the heat. The total cooking time for a blond roux is 10 to 12 minutes. When it is ready, it should resemble cake batter, and the color should be off-white (that is, blond).

The roux will keep in an airtight container for up to 2 weeks in the refrigerator and should be dissolved into hot liquid when reheating.

brown roux

This is my go-to roux for spicy and zesty seafood and meat dishes made with tomatoes, peppers, chiles, and the like. You see it in things like étouffée (see page 222) or poached gulf fish (see page 239). One of my favorite things about roux is that its uses change as it gets darker—the blond roux is good for making velvety sauces but doesn't add much flavor beyond butteriness, whereas this darker roux becomes a flavor agent in its own right, lending a rich, toasty Louisiana flavor to anything it touches.

makes 2 cups

⅔ cup peanut oil

1 cup all-purpose flour

In a medium heavy-bottomed pot (I like ceramic or enamel-coated cast iron) over high heat, heat the oil until shimmering. Do not allow it to smoke; avoid even tiny plumes. Whisk in the flour and break up any clumps to form a smooth paste—it should look like a thin batter.

Decrease the heat to medium-low, and using a wooden spoon, preferably with a flat top, move the roux around—stirring, but also turning it, so the oil and flour cook evenly, about 5 minutes. Continue cooking and stirring for another 5 to 7 minutes, until the mixture is even and smooth in color and texture. The goal here is to gently toast the flour just enough to remove its raw taste without browning it. If you see the color start to deepen as you stir, decrease the heat.

After 10 to 12 minutes of total cooking time, you should have a blond roux. Continue cooking for an additional 5 to 10 minutes, stirring often to evenly distribute the roux over the pot, until there is a noticeable color change from off-white to peanut-butter brown. Brown roux should take a total of 15 to 20 minutes to cook, and have the same batterlike viscosity as blond roux.

dark roux

Out of all three roux, this is the most quintessentially southern Louisiana in flavor. Dark roux is one of the most important components of Louisiana cooking. It reflects the myriad cultures that have played a role in forming Creole and Cajun cuisine. No one else in the world uses dark roux, and mastering its technique is the mark of a true Louisiana cook.

makes 2 cups

⅔ cup peanut oil

1 cup all-purpose flour

In a medium heavy-bottomed pot (I like ceramic or enamel-coated cast iron) over high heat, heat the oil until shimmering. Do not allow it to smoke; avoid even tiny plumes. Whisk in the flour and break up any clumps to form a smooth paste—it should look like a thin batter.

Decrease the heat to medium-low, and using a wooden spoon, preferably with a flat top, move the roux around—stirring, but also turning it, so the oil and flour cook evenly, about 5 minutes. Continue cooking and stirring for another 5 to 7 minutes, until the mixture is even and smooth in color and texture. The goal here is to gently toast the flour just enough to remove its raw taste without browning it. If you see the color start to deepen as you stir, decrease the heat.

After 10 to 12 minutes of total cooking time, you should have a blond roux. Continue cooking for an additional 5 to 10 minutes, stirring often to evenly distribute the roux over the pot, until there is a noticeable color change from off-white to peanut-butter brown.

Once the roux is brown, continue cooking for an additional 5 to 10 minutes, stirring often to evenly distribute the roux over the pot, until there is a noticeable change from a peanut-butter shade of brown to a milk chocolate hue. Cook, stirring continuously to avoid burning, until the roux becomes a dark chocolate color. A dark roux should take a total of 25 to 30 minutes to cook, and have a batterlike viscosity.

beef stock and demi-glace

Beef stock is an all-purpose liquid backbone, and one of the most important recipes in this book. As a stock, it's far richer than chicken—the protein you extract from beef bones reduces differently, so you get a lot more volume, and a much richer flavor. It can be used as is for soups and braises, or reduced to a thick, meaty demi-glace sauce. Beef stock is a foundational recipe that I call for throughout this book, from the broth in the brisket and kale stew on page 205 to the demi-glace in the Riesling jus for the pan-roasted pork porterhouse steak on page 282.

What's so great about beef stock is that it can also serve as a vehicle for other flavors—I like to use the viscosity and structure of beef to carry the flavors of lamb, venison, or chicken. I might, for example, roast lamb bones and then simmer them in beef stock, and reduce that to a lamb-beef demi-glace to make a sauce. Or I might make a red wine reduction and combine it with beef stock to change its acidity, sweetness, and complexity. This stock just delivers flavor—it's rich yet neutral, giving you a magical result that is difficult to match with many other ingredients. This stock takes about 12 hours to make, so plan ahead.

makes about 3 quarts stock or 1 quart demi-glace

2½ pounds beef bones, such as knuckle, oxtail, and marrow bones (see Note)

1 cup coarsely chopped onion

½ cup coarsely chopped peeled carrots

½ cup coarsely chopped celery

¾ cup red wine

3 tablespoons tomato paste

3 sprigs thyme

2 dried bay leaves

5 black peppercorns

1 whole clove

5 cloves garlic

Water to cover

NOTE

If you have access to veal bones, you can use them in lieu of beef bones.

Preheat the oven to 325°F.

Spread out the bones in an even layer in a roasting pan, and roast in the oven until they're a dark, rich brown color (go beyond golden), 1½ to 2 hours. Transfer the bones to a large stockpot and set aside.

Increase the oven temperature to 400°F.

Spread out the onion, carrots, and celery in the same roasting pan in which you roasted the bones, and place in the oven. After about 10 minutes, remove the pan, stir the vegetables, and scrape up the fond (caramelized bits of meat and evaporated juices on the bottom of the pan), using the moisture from the vegetables to release any meaty bits stuck to the pan. Roast for an additional 15 to 20 minutes, until the vegetables are light brown, about 30 minutes in total. Set aside.

Meanwhile, in a medium saucepan over high heat, combine the red wine and tomato paste and bring to a boil. Decrease the heat to medium-low and simmer for 10 to 15 minutes to dissolve the paste and cook out the alcohol in the wine, stirring often with a spatula or wooden spoon to

CONTINUED

shellfish stock

makes about 2 quarts

2 tablespoons olive oil

8 ounces shrimp, lobster, crab, or crawfish shells, or a combination, rinsed

1 tablespoon tomato paste

2½ quarts water

¾ cup coarsely chopped onion

½ cup coarsely chopped celery

¼ cup coarsely chopped fennel bulb (optional, but delicious)

2 dried bay leaves

2 cloves garlic

5 black peppercorns

Where I live, shellfish stock is used almost as often as chicken stock—it's a staple in Louisiana kitchens. I find myself with oh so many shrimp heads, so I use them to meet the endless need for shellfish stock—and to avoid wasting any part of the shellfish. Empty shells from other dishes can be bagged and stored in the freezer until you have enough to make a batch. I love giving all those heads and shells a second life.

Toasting shellfish shells in a pan with some oil before adding water helps release all of their naturally sweet, nutty flavors, and builds a deep, rich aroma, which is exactly what we want to flavor our stock. Use either cooked or raw shellfish shells—both work. If you have fennel on hand, it adds a subtle layer of sweet anise flavor, which I find quite lovely, though nonessential.

In a stockpot over high heat, combine the oil and shellfish shells, stirring often. At first, the shells will steam and release some water, which will evaporate, creating steam, which will settle down. Once this happens, the shells will begin to cook in the oil and deepen to a dark red color, and the aroma of roasting shellfish will fill the air. This whole process should take 15 to 20 minutes.

When the shells are toasty and the oil has taken on a red color, there should be little bits of protein stuck to the bottom of the pan. Add the tomato paste and stir to coat the shells, scraping up the bits on the bottom of the pan and allowing the tomato paste to cook slightly in the oil, about 2 minutes.

Add the water, onion, celery, fennel, bay leaves, garlic, and peppercorns. Bring to a boil over medium-high heat, then immediately decrease the heat to low and simmer for 1 hour. Remove from the heat and let cool slightly, about 20 minutes. Strain the stock into a clean pot and discard the solids. Let the stock cool, uncovered, until room temperature.

The stock will keep for up to 5 days in the refrigerator or up to 6 months in the freezer.

chicken stock

So many cookbooks include a chicken stock recipe because it's a versatile liquid that adds flavor and richness. It doesn't always add chicken flavor, and therein lies its beauty.

In a professional kitchen, I use backbones and other parts left over after cutting up chickens, but at home I use this easier method. After roasting a chicken and serving the meat, I save the carcass for stock. My default recipe is a dark stock, made with bones that have been roasted, but you can make a light version, which will have a clear, lightly flavored broth, ideal for seafood and vegetable soups.

Finally, you can also use separate chicken bones in lieu of using a whole intact carcass—just roast the raw bones from the legs, breasts, and so forth until they're dry and golden brown before proceeding.

makes about 2 quarts

1 chicken carcass (cooked and all meat picked off), or about 1 pound raw chicken bones

¾ cup coarsely chopped onion

½ cup coarsely chopped celery

⅓ cup coarsely chopped peeled carrots

2 sprigs thyme

2 cloves garlic

10 black peppercorns

About 2¼ quarts water

Preheat the oven to 375°F.

Using your hands, pull apart the bones of the bird and break the backbone in half. Arrange the bones in an even layer in a large roasting pan or an ovenproof skillet. Roast in the oven until golden brown, about 35 minutes, and let cool slightly. (Alternatively, if you prefer a lighter stock, preheat the oven to 325°F and roast the chicken bones until slightly dry, about 20 minutes.)

Place the bones in a small stockpot—the trick here is to use one that will hold the chicken bones and vegetables snugly, so you don't need too much water in order to cover them. Crowd the bones into the pot and place the onion, celery, and carrots on top of the bones. Place the thyme, garlic, and peppercorns on top of the vegetables. The contents of the pot should be about 2 inches below the rim.

Add the water just to cover the bones and vegetables, and place over high heat. Bring to a boil, then decrease the heat to low and cook gently, uncovered, for 4 hours. The stock should not be bubbling at all. Think of it like making tea: you're steeping the bones to extract their flavor. If you notice any evaporation of the liquid, replenish with fresh water. The goal is to end up with the same volume of water that you began with.

Remove the pot from the heat and let cool slightly, about 20 minutes. Strain the stock into a clean pot and discard the solids. Let the stock cool, uncovered, until room temperature.

The stock will keep for up to 5 days in the refrigerator or 6 months in the freezer.

beef stock and demi-glace

Beef stock is an all-purpose liquid backbone, and one of the most important recipes in this book. As a stock, it's far richer than chicken—the protein you extract from beef bones reduces differently, so you get a lot more volume, and a much richer flavor. It can be used as is for soups and braises, or reduced to a thick, meaty demi-glace sauce. Beef stock is a foundational recipe that I call for throughout this book, from the broth in the brisket and kale stew on page 205 to the demi-glace in the Riesling jus for the pan-roasted pork porterhouse steak on page 282.

What's so great about beef stock is that it can also serve as a vehicle for other flavors—I like to use the viscosity and structure of beef to carry the flavors of lamb, venison, or chicken. I might, for example, roast lamb bones and then simmer them in beef stock, and reduce that to a lamb-beef demi-glace to make a sauce. Or I might make a red wine reduction and combine it with beef stock to change its acidity, sweetness, and complexity. This stock just delivers flavor—it's rich yet neutral, giving you a magical result that is difficult to match with many other ingredients. This stock takes about 12 hours to make, so plan ahead.

makes about 3 quarts stock or 1 quart demi-glace

2½ pounds beef bones, such as knuckle, oxtail, and marrow bones (see Note)

1 cup coarsely chopped onion

½ cup coarsely chopped peeled carrots

½ cup coarsely chopped celery

¾ cup red wine

3 tablespoons tomato paste

3 sprigs thyme

2 dried bay leaves

5 black peppercorns

1 whole clove

5 cloves garlic

Water to cover

NOTE

If you have access to veal bones, you can use them in lieu of beef bones.

Preheat the oven to 325°F.

Spread out the bones in an even layer in a roasting pan, and roast in the oven until they're a dark, rich brown color (go beyond golden), 1½ to 2 hours. Transfer the bones to a large stockpot and set aside.

Increase the oven temperature to 400°F.

Spread out the onion, carrots, and celery in the same roasting pan in which you roasted the bones, and place in the oven. After about 10 minutes, remove the pan, stir the vegetables, and scrape up the fond (caramelized bits of meat and evaporated juices on the bottom of the pan), using the moisture from the vegetables to release any meaty bits stuck to the pan. Roast for an additional 15 to 20 minutes, until the vegetables are light brown, about 30 minutes in total. Set aside.

Meanwhile, in a medium saucepan over high heat, combine the red wine and tomato paste and bring to a boil. Decrease the heat to medium-low and simmer for 10 to 15 minutes to dissolve the paste and cook out the alcohol in the wine, stirring often with a spatula or wooden spoon to

CONTINUED

avoid scorching. The mixture will thicken as it simmers, becoming like a swampy bog.

Add the red wine–tomato paste mixture to the pot with the bones. Add the vegetables, and then the thyme, bay leaves, peppercorns, clove, and garlic. Add enough water to cover the vegetables by about 4 inches.

Bring to a boil over high heat, then decrease the heat to very low. Make sure the heat is low enough to prevent rapid evaporation but hot enough to create small percolating bubbles for the duration of the steeping and extracting process. Simmer, skimming often to remove any fat or foam rising to the top, for 12 hours. It's important to simmer the stock for this long or longer, because you want to extract all of the collagen, marrow, and flavor from the bones. The proteins you pull out during a slow simmer give the stock that sticky, delicious texture. If you notice any evaporation of the liquid, replenish with fresh water. The goal is to end up with the same volume of water you began with.

Strain the stock into a clean pot and discard the solids. Let the stock cool to room temperature and then chill overnight in the refrigerator. In the morning, skim off any solidified fat on the surface.

The stock will keep for up to 5 days in the refrigerator or 6 months in the freezer.

To make the stock into demi-glace, in a large stockpot over medium-high heat, bring the finished beef stock to a boil and continue to boil until reduced to 1 quart, 1½ to 2 hours. Demi-glace will keep for up to 5 days in the refrigerator or 6 months in the freezer.

brown butter vinaigrette

We use this vinaigrette as a dressing for the warm spinach and frisée salad on page 159, but it's actually quite versatile. You can use it as a dressing for a warm potato salad or shaved Brussels sprouts, for example, and as a sauce for fish or seared scallops. The technique of browning butter appears throughout this book—it's one of my favorite ways to add a dimension and depth of flavor to dishes. I am of the opinion that almost anything that calls for melted butter can be improved by substituting brown butter; it brings everything it touches up a level.

makes about 1½ cups

¼ cup sherry vinegar

2 tablespoons Dijon mustard

1 tablespoon honey

½ teaspoon kosher salt

2 tablespoons minced shallots

1 clove garlic, finely chopped

1½ teaspoons thyme leaves

¾ cup plus 2 tablespoons unsalted butter

In a mixing bowl, whisk together the vinegar, Dijon, honey, salt, shallots, garlic, and thyme. Set aside.

In a small saucepan over medium-high heat, melt the butter and allow the water to cook out of it. As the butter melts, and the water escapes in the form of steam, the butter will turn from a cloudy yellow to a clear translucent yellow. At this point, the butter should gradually start browning and developing a nutty aroma, and bits of it will begin to stick to the bottom of the pan. The whole process should take 5 to 7 minutes.

Remove the brown butter from the heat and let it cool slightly in the saucepan. Gently whisk the brown butter into the vinegar-mustard mixture to combine. Scrape any butter solids on the bottom of the saucepan into the vinaigrette as well. Stir to combine. Transfer to a serving dish.

The vinaigrette will keep for up to 2 days in the refrigerator.

salsa verde

I love salsa verde for its versatility. You can use it as the base for a dressing for a chilled seafood salad or drizzle it over grilled skirt steak (see page 301) or Serrano-wrapped cobia (see page 236). It's also fantastic coated on grilled or raw vegetables, or even as a dip for French fries. It adds an acidic, herbaceous punch to everything it touches.

Make this a few hours in advance to give the flavors time to mellow. Salsa verde is usually still good on the second day, but if it has started to oxidize, use it in a marinade instead of as a sauce. Play around with the herbs. You'll probably want to leave the parsley because it provides a neutral base, but you could omit the oregano and add tarragon and chervil, for example. Avoid sturdy herbs, like sage, rosemary, and thyme, which have a twiggy texture that's unpleasant in a sauce.

makes about 1½ cups

2 tablespoons red wine vinegar

1 tablespoon freshly squeezed lemon juice

1 tablespoon Dijon mustard

2 cloves garlic, finely chopped

3 tablespoons finely chopped shallots

3 anchovies, finely chopped

¾ cup extra-virgin olive oil

½ cup finely chopped flat-leaf parsley

¼ cup finely chopped chives

2 tablespoons finely chopped oregano

2 tablespoons finely chopped cilantro

2 teaspoons dried red chile flakes, ideally piment d'Espelette or Korean gochugaru (see page 32)

Kosher salt

Freshly cracked black pepper

In a mixing bowl, combine the vinegar, lemon juice, Dijon, garlic, shallots, and anchovies. Let sit for 20 minutes so the acids can soften the sharp taste of the garlic and shallots and help them blend better into the sauce.

Gently whisk in the oil. Fold in the parsley, chives, oregano, cilantro, and chile flakes and season with salt and pepper. Transfer to a serving dish.

The salsa verde will keep in the refrigerator for up to 2 days.

herb pistou

Pistou is similar to pesto (both generally translate to "paste"). It's a nice way to add more fresh herbaceous flavor to a dish in sauce form. The parsley and the process are the backbone of the recipe, but you can add whatever herb you want to direct the flavor. Here, I use basil, though you could swap it out for tarragon or oregano, for example. Pistou is at its best and brightest when freshly made (because it oxides), but you can use leftovers in a marinade or rub for chicken, meat, and vegetables. This recipe appears in Pan-Seared Goat Cheese Dumplings (see page 81) and Garlic-and-Herb-Crusted Snapper with Oven-Dried Tomatoes (see page 231).

makes about 2 cups

2 cups loosely filled flat-leaf parsley, coarsely chopped (stems and all)

10 large basil leaves

1½ teaspoons kosher salt

Grated zest and juice of 1 lemon

1 clove garlic, mashed (see page 37)

1⅓ cups 80/20 blended oil (see page 30)

Extra-virgin olive oil

Combine the parsley, basil, salt, lemon zest and juice, garlic, and blended oil in a blender and blend for 1 to 2 minutes, until the mixture is smooth and bright green. Transfer to a serving dish.

Store leftover pistou, covered with a thin layer of olive oil (to prevent oxidation), for up to 4 days in the refrigerator.

crushed-olive vinaigrette

This is an extremely solid salad dressing (just ask the Shaved Summer Squash Salad on page 164), but it also makes a nice condiment—a rustic tapenade that is almost an olive salad. I like to serve it with crisp raw vegetables that can stand up to the brininess of olives, but you could also mix it with fresh tomatoes for a simple pasta dish, or offer it as an accompaniment for a mixed meat and cheese platter.

makes about 1 cup

2 tablespoons red wine vinegar

1 tablespoon Dijon mustard

1 large clove garlic, very finely chopped

1 teaspoon kosher salt

½ cup vegetable oil

¼ cup Castelvetrano olives, with pits

¼ cup small black olives, such as Arbequina or Nicoise, with pits

¼ cup chopped flat-leaf parsley leaves

Freshly cracked black pepper

In a mixing bowl, whisk together the vinegar, Dijon, garlic, and salt and add the oil in a slow stream, whisking constantly to combine.

Gently crush each olive with the back of a knife—don't mash them into a paste, just crack them open a bit and remove the pits.

Add the olives and parsley to the vinaigrette and fold to combine. Season with a few grinds of black pepper and fold again. Refrigerate for 1 hour to let the flavors to meld.

The vinaigrette will keep in the refrigerator for up to 2 days.

bacon vinaigrette

As delicious as vegetables are on their own, they're even better with a bacon-flavored dressing. This vinaigrette is particularly well suited to the roasted turnips on page 119, and to many Southern vegetables and greens. Other smart ideas: spoon it over cooked potatoes for a German-style potato salad, use it as a dressing on a warm spinach salad, or drizzle it over roasted fish for a smoky flavor.

makes about 2 cups

2 slices thick-cut bacon, cut crosswise into matchsticks (about ¼ cup)

½ cup sherry vinegar

2 tablespoons minced shallot

1 tablespoon Dijon mustard

2 teaspoons honey

1 cup canola oil

Line a plate with paper towels. Heat a small sauté pan over medium heat. Add the bacon and cook, stirring slowly as it releases its fat and becomes crispy and dark red in color, about 10 minutes. Using a slotted spoon, transfer to the prepared plate to drain, and set aside. Measure ¼ cup of the bacon fat in the pan and discard the rest.

Whisk together the vinegar, shallot, Dijon, and honey. Slowly whisk in the oil and reserved bacon fat and continue whisking until emulsified (see page 35).

The vinaigrette will keep in the refrigerator for up to 2 days.

bagna cauda

Bagna cauda is an Italian hot condiment from the Piedmonte region with anchovies, garlic, and olive oil or butter (or both) as its backbone. I love all of those flavors, and I started making it because I'm always trying to find a way to add a little piquancy to the vegetable sides we make at the restaurants. I've messed around with a lot of variations of bagna cauda through the years, and this one, featuring brown butter, might not be traditional, but it is the best. In addition to serving as a dressing for crudités or cooked vegetables, bagna cauda is fantastic on baked clams, basted over grilled chicken, or even spread on a loaf of bread, split and baked like garlic bread.

makes about ½ cup

⅓ cup unsalted butter

¼ cup extra-virgin olive oil

4 or 5 cloves garlic, mashed (see page 37)

2 teaspoons fish sauce (preferably Three Crabs or Red Boat; see page 28), or 4 to 6 anchovy fillets, very finely chopped (see Note)

Kosher salt

1 to 2 teaspoons freshly squeezed lemon juice

NOTE
It is traditional to use anchovy fillets here, but I highly recommend using a high-quality fish sauce if you can find one, as its fermented aged flavor adds incredibly concentrated umami when cooked in butter.

In a small saucepan over medium-high, melt the butter and allow the water to cook out of it. As the butter melts, and the water escapes in the form of steam, the butter will turn from a cloudy yellow to a clear translucent yellow. At this point, the butter should gradually start browning and developing a nutty aroma, and bits of it will begin to stick to the bottom of the pan. The whole process should take 5 to 7 minutes.

Transfer the butter to a dry, heatproof bowl and set aside. Scrape any solid bits from the bottom of the pot into the bowl as well, and wipe the pot clean to ensure no solid bits remain.

Pour the oil into the same pot and warm over medium-low heat for about 1 minute. Decrease the heat to low and add the garlic, stirring to distribute it evenly. The garlic shouldn't be sizzling or frying—you might see a few small bubbles percolating, but any more than that and your heat is too high. The idea is for the garlic to get soft and melty, not crispy, which should take about 15 minutes.

Stream the brown butter into the pot, add the fish sauce or anchovies, and let the mixture cook slowly, stirring occasionally, until the garlic is very soft and the sauce is toasty brown in color, another 15 minutes. Taste the sauce. (A good way to taste it is to cut a few sticks of raw celery on a plate and drizzle a little sauce over them; they should be amazingly delicious.) Adjust the seasoning by adding more salt and lemon juice as necessary.

The bagna cauda will keep covered in the refrigerator for up to 2 days.

fish sauce caramel

I like to use this as a marinade—the longer the meat sits in it, the better the marinade is able to penetrate. And when you grill that meat, the sugars in the sauce help form a beautiful char. It reminds me of the sweet-salty, deliciously charred flavors at some of the amazing Vietnamese restaurants in New Orleans, and it tastes great on everything from pork to poultry to shrimp.

In a small saucepan over medium-high heat, combine the sugar and ½ cup of the water. Cook, stirring occasionally, until the sugar is dissolved and the mixture is clear and rapidly bubbling, about 5 minutes. Increase the heat to high and cook, without stirring, until the syrup has reached a deep amber color, 8 to 10 minutes. You don't want to cook the syrup any longer than necessary to achieve the right color, or the water in the mixture will evaporate, causing the sugar in it to recrystallize.

Remove the pot from the heat and very carefully add the remaining ½ cup water and the fish sauce (the syrup will bubble and give off steam). Stir to ensure that the sugar is fully dissolved, and add the ginger and cilantro. Return the pot to high heat, bring to a full boil, and cook for 5 seconds. Remove from the heat.

Steep the ginger and cilantro in the caramel, as though you are brewing tea, for 25 to 30 minutes. Strain out the ginger and cilantro and discard.

The sauce will keep in an airtight container in the refrigerator for up to 6 months.

makes about 1½ cups

2 cups sugar

1 cup water

¼ cup fish sauce (preferably Three Crabs or Red Boat; see Note)

3 tablespoons coarsely chopped ginger

3 sprigs cilantro

NOTE

In New Orleans, many of the Vietnamese restaurants use Three Crabs brand fish sauce. It's available online, though Red Boat, another high-quality source, is available in many stores.

homemade hot sauce

This is a riff on a classic spicy Louisiana pepper sauce, and a simple at-home fermentation project, if you're new to the technique. You ferment chiles in a basic saltwater brine, then add vinegar and season the mixture with the same brine you fermented the chiles in. You can adjust the viscosity of the finished product by adding more or less brine; I tend to go heavy, both to achieve a thin texture and to retain more of that fermented flavor I love. I like to use Fresno chiles for their vibrant red color.

makes about 1 quart

1 quart distilled water

2½ tablespoons kosher salt

3 cups sliced Fresno chiles or red jalapeños

¼ cup distilled white vinegar

In a medium saucepan, combine the water and salt and bring to a boil. Immediately remove from the heat and let cool to room temperature.

Place the chiles in a clean container and pour 3 cups of the brine over them. Pour the remaining 1 cup of brine into a resealable plastic bag. Place the resealable bag on top of the chiles to weigh them down and keep them submerged. Cover the container with a clean kitchen towel and secure it around the rim with a rubber band. Place in a cool, dark area (like a pantry or cupboard) for at least 4 days or up to 2 weeks. The longer it sits, the more fermented and funky the flavor will be. The brine will become cloudy and give off a funky, peppery aroma.

Once the chiles are fermented, drain off the brine and set aside. Place the chiles in a blender, add the vinegar, and blend into a thick, pasty puree. Stir in the reserved brine in ¼ cup increments to thin the sauce out—it should still have some body, but look liquidy, like a store-bought hot sauce. You will only need about 3 cups of the brine. Strain the sauce to remove any solids and store in a clean container with a tight-fitting lid.

The hot sauce will keep in the refrigerator for up to 6 months.

aioli

Mayonnaise was always mysterious to me when I was growing up, but I never questioned the omnipresent jar in the back of our refrigerator. Later, when I learned how to make it, I realized it's something that opens up your whole repertoire—an endlessly adaptable back-pocket recipe that's great on its own or as the base for countless other dressings and dips. Sure, you can use store-bought mayo, but putting in the little bit of extra effort to make your own (which takes just 15 minutes) really takes your food to another level.

Basic aioli is great with the Shrimp and Okra Fritters on page 98, or, of course, on any sandwich. But there are a million other ways to use it: Try adding lemon zest and black pepper and serving it with boiled shrimp; adding chopped capers and olives to go with fried zucchini; mixing half aioli and half Dijon for crab or lobster; or folding with equal parts room-temperature cream cheese and a few tablespoons of half-and-half for the world's best potato chip dip.

When you're making an egg yolk–based emulsification in a food processor or blender, make sure you don't add too much oil at once, or the mixture will thicken too much and lose its ability to blend smoothly. Once the emulsification starts forming (you'll know because the mixture will have a pale, creamy look), slow the speed of the food processor or blender and drizzle the oil in more slowly, so you can still see a little whirlpool whirling around. When that whirlpool closes up, stop and check for viscosity. It's worth practicing the technique for making it a few times, until you've got it down. This is a foundational recipe I lean on throughout the book.

makes about 2 cups

2 egg yolks

Juice of ½ lemon

1 teaspoon Dijon mustard

1 clove garlic, finely chopped

2 cups canola oil

Kosher salt

Freshly cracked white pepper

NOTE

You can also make aioli (and variations, such as the Buttermilk Dressing on page 66 and the Caesar Dressing on page 71) by hand, using a mixing bowl and a whisk. If you do, you can use a good-quality extra-virgin olive oil. I call for canola or 80/20 blended oils (see page 30) in this recipe and the others like it because extra-virgin can turn bitter when blended in a high-speed food processor or blender. For more on emulsifying, see page 35.

In the bowl of a food processor, combine the egg yolks, lemon juice, Dijon, and garlic and process on high speed.

When the mixture becomes frothy and pale, slowly and steadily begin drizzling in the oil (with the processor still running) to form an emulsion. When the emulsion looks pale and creamy, you can drizzle in the oil more quickly. If it looks like it's separating (you will see oil beading up on the walls of the bowl), stop adding the oil and let the processor run until the mixture becomes creamy again. The aioli is done when it has the consistency of mayonnaise (you can make a thicker aioli by adding and emulsifying another 1 to 2 tablespoons oil, or a thinner aioli by drizzling in a spoonful of ice water). Season the mixture with salt and white pepper and transfer the aioli to a container with a tight-fitting lid.

Store, covered, in the refrigerator for up to 3 days.

buttermilk dressing

Raw egg yolk emulsions are the base of many sauces in this book. The process is the same for making mayonnaise, Aioli (page 65), or any kind of viscous cold sauce. It's really just a multipurpose tool. The possibilities are endless once you have it down: Add chopped parsley, cornichons, and capers to make tartar sauce; add smoked paprika and saffron to make rouille for bouillabaisse; or puree parsley leaves into the egg mixture and suddenly you have Green Goddess Dressing (facing page).

makes about 2½ cups

1 egg yolk

1½ teaspoons Dijon mustard

2 tablespoons freshly squeezed lemon juice

1½ teaspoons white wine vinegar

1½ cups canola or 80/20 blended oil (see page 30)

¾ cup buttermilk

Kosher salt

Freshly cracked black pepper

1 tablespoon chopped dill fronds

1 tablespoon finely chopped chives

In the bowl of a food processor, combine the egg yolk, Dijon, lemon juice, and vinegar and process on high speed. When the mixture becomes frothy and pale, slowly and steadily begin drizzling in the oil (with the processor still running) to form an emulsion. When the emulsion looks pale and creamy, drizzle in the oil more quickly. If it looks like it's separating (you will see oil beading up on the walls of the bowl), stop and let the machine run until the mixture becomes creamy again.

The goal for this recipe is to overemulsify this sauce: keep adding oil until it's very thick, like pudding. Then, with the food processor on low speed, slowly stream in the buttermilk to thin the sauce to the consistency of dressing. Season with salt and pepper while the machine runs. Transfer the dressing to a container with a tight-fitting lid and then fold in the dill and chives.

Store, covered, in the refrigerator for up to 3 days.

green goddess dressing

This is an adaptation of a classic French sauce verte, which is basically a creamy, herby green mayo. I use sauce verte for everything from shellfish to crudités, as a salad dressing, as a spread for sandwiches that beats the socks off of mayo, and even mixed with bread crumbs and slathered on top of the herb-crusted fish on page 231. The basic recipe is endlessly adaptable and keeps well in the refrigerator, so feel free to experiment with different herbs or more or less lemon, vinegar, or Dijon, as you see fit.

In a food processor, combine the parsley, chives, thyme, tarragon, salt, and oil. Process on high speed for 1 to 2 minutes, until totally smooth, well blended, and bright green. Let rest for 10 minutes. Set a fine-mesh strainer over a measuring cup or bowl, strain out the solids, and set the herb-infused oil aside. Wash and dry the food processor bowl and blade.

In the same food processor bowl, combine the egg yolks, Dijon, lemon juice, and vinegar, and season with white pepper. Blend until frothy and, with the processor still running, slowly drizzle in the herb-infused oil to form an emulsion. When the emulsion looks pale and creamy, drizzle in the oil more quickly. If it looks like it's separating (you will see oil beading up on the walls of the bowl), stop and let the processor run until the mixture becomes creamy again.

Transfer the mixture to a bowl and fold in the crème fraîche until the mixture is uniformly light green and creamy. Season with salt. Spoon the dressing into a container with a tight-fitting lid.

Store, covered, in the refrigerator for up to 3 days.

makes 2 to 3 cups

¼ cup flat-leaf parsley leaves

1 tablespoon coarsely chopped chives

1 teaspoon thyme leaves

¼ cup tarragon leaves

Pinch of kosher salt, plus more as needed

2 cups vegetable oil

2 egg yolks

1 tablespoon Dijon mustard

Juice of 1 lemon

1 teaspoon white wine vinegar

Freshly cracked white pepper

¼ cup crème fraîche (see page 363)

tarragon emulsion

This is another sauce that's related to the Green Goddess Dressing on page 67. I use it more as a sauce for shellfish, which pairs particularly well with tarragon.

makes 2 to 3 cups

¼ cup tarragon leaves

¼ cup flat-leaf parsley leaves

Pinch of kosher salt

2 cups vegetable oil

2 egg yolks

1 tablespoon Dijon mustard

Juice of 1 lemon

1 teaspoon white wine vinegar

Freshly cracked white pepper

In a food processor or blender, combine the tarragon, parsley, salt, and oil. Process on high speed for 2 minutes, or until totally smooth, combined, and bright green. Let rest for 10 minutes. Strain out the solids and set aside the herb-infused oil. Wash the food processor bowl and blade.

In the same food processor bowl, combine the egg yolks, Dijon, lemon juice, and vinegar and season with white pepper. Blend until frothy. With the food processor still running, slowly drizzle in the herb-infused oil to form an emulsion. When the emulsion looks pale and creamy, you can begin to drizzle the oil more quickly. If it looks like it's separating (you will see oil beading up on the walls of the bowl), stop and let the processor run until the mixture becomes creamy again. The finished dressing should be a lovely pale green. Transfer the dressing to a container with a tight-fitting lid and adjust the seasoning.

Store, covered, in the refrigerator for up to 3 days.

caesar dressing

Making this classic dressing is similar to making aioli. It's great, naturally, on salad, though you can also use it as a spread for a sandwich or even in lieu of the White BBQ Sauce for the chicken wings on page 250.

makes about 3 cups

2 anchovies

2 egg yolks

1 clove garlic, coarsely chopped

1 tablespoon Worcestershire sauce

1½ tablespoons freshly squeezed lemon juice

½ cup white wine vinegar

1 tablespoon Dijon mustard

½ teaspoon kosher salt

2 cups 80/20 blended oil (see page 30)

Combine the anchovies, egg yolks, garlic, Worcestershire, lemon juice, vinegar, Dijon, and salt in a blender and pulse. When the mixture becomes frothy and pale, with the blender running, slowly drizzle in the oil, making sure the dressing stays emulsified. Once the emulsification starts forming (you'll know because it will have a pale, creamy look), slow the speed of the blender and drizzle the oil in more slowly; you should still see a little whirlpool whirring around. When it closes up, stop and check for viscosity. The finished dressing should be smooth and creamy. Transfer the dressing to a container with a tight-fitting lid.

Store, covered, in the refrigerator for up to 3 days.

rémoulade

Rémoulade is traditional in old-school restaurants in New Orleans, and every place with history here has a version of shrimp rémoulade or boiled beef with rémoulade. It's essentially a very classic cold egg yolk emulsion, similar to mayo. Often the traditional New Orleans ones have ketchup in them and a pronounced flavor of celery seed and celery.

I like to skip the ketchup and use celery root, which is drier than celery stalks and doesn't water down the sauce. I came up with this recipe one summer while serving shrimp rémoulade. It's very creamy, very acidic, and complements any fish or shellfish (especially if they're chilled), as well as rare roast beef and the turkey pastrami on page 270.

makes about 1 quart

1½ teaspoons Worcestershire sauce

½ teaspoon ground cayenne pepper

1 teaspoon sweet paprika

1 teaspoon celery seeds

2 tablespoons red wine vinegar

¾ cup freshly squeezed lemon juice, plus more as needed

½ cup finely grated celery root

2 cloves garlic

1 cup coarsely chopped green onions, white parts only

1½ teaspoons Tabasco sauce

2 tablespoons whole-grain mustard

1 tablespoon prepared horseradish

¼ cup coarsely chopped flat-leaf parsley leaves

4 egg yolks (see Note)

3¼ cups vegetable oil

Kosher salt

In the bowl of a food processor, combine the Worcestershire, cayenne, paprika, celery seeds, vinegar, lemon juice, celery root, garlic, green onions, Tabasco, mustard, horseradish, parsley, and egg yolks. Process on high speed until all the ingredients are chunky, like salsa. With the machine running on medium speed, slowly stream in all of the oil. The sauce should look creamy, but still noticeably chunky—like a creamy relish. Season with salt and additional lemon juice. Transfer the rémoulade to a container with a tight-fitting lid.

Store, covered, in the refrigerator for up to 3 days.

NOTE
If you have aioli (see page 65) in your refrigerator, you can use 2 cups of it in this recipe. Blend all the ingredients as instructed, omitting the eggs and oil, and then pulse in the aioli until you have the texture described.

appetizers

Appetizers are one of my favorite things to make and eat. I love the role they play in a meal, setting the tone for what's to come.

Given that an appetizer comes before a main, it's important when planning a meal to try to keep it cohesive. Most of the appetizers in this chapter pair well with most of the fish and meat dishes, though it is worth keeping the idea of balance in mind. If you're having rich braised lamb shanks (see page 292) for dinner, balance that out with a lighter, brighter app, like Marinated Octopus (page 100).

Some of the recipes in this chapter are strictly finger food (for example, the Louisiana-Style Pickled Quail Eggs on page 84), but some of them can easily be scaled up to work as mains. And many of them work well as make-ahead items, like the shrimp salad on page 97 and Country Pork Pâté (page 103), which are nice to have around as a snack for family or guests who stop by. Many of these can be served family-style, or as a plated course, or both (for example, the ricotta dumplings on page 141). That's the great thing about appetizers—they're endlessly versatile.

Techniquewise, this chapter runs the gamut, including culturing, pickling, pan-frying, and even basic charcuterie. Some of the techniques introduced in this chapter are repeated elsewhere in the book. The process for breading and frying the green tomatoes on page 78, for example, is used to cook the Rabbit Schnitzel on page 276. Play around in this chapter, and cook whatever appeals to you. Part of the pleasure of eating appetizers is in trying lots of small things, and that holds true for cooking them as well.

pan-fried green tomatoes with burrata and country ham

In Louisiana, we love to serve fried green tomatoes with a creamy aioli or rémoulade-style dressing, while in other parts of the South, they're often eaten with pimento cheese. Basically, any rich, creamy, or cheesy accompaniment will do. Then there's the classic Italian mozzarella and tomato salad, and this dish is the irresistible combination of both of them.

The burrata in this recipe serves as the creamy cheesy component. I didn't want to lose the saltiness of the classic Southern version, hence the addition of country ham, which is salt-cured and dry-aged. (You can substitute prosciutto or Serrano ham if you can't find good country ham.) I love the juxtaposition of hot and cold ingredients here—the contrast is what makes it irresistible.

makes 6 to 8 servings

2 cups all-purpose flour

1 tablespoon plus 1 teaspoon kosher salt

4 eggs

1 cup whole milk

4 cups panko bread crumbs, finely ground in a food processor

4 green tomatoes, cored and sliced ¼ inch thick

1 to 2 cups peanut oil

1 pound burrata

8 to 10 very thin slices country ham (or prosciutto or Serrano ham)

Extra-virgin olive oil for drizzling

Freshly cracked black pepper

Fleur de sel

½ cup oregano leaves

In a flat-bottomed dish, stir together the flour and salt. In a mixing bowl, combine the eggs and milk and whisk to blend well. Transfer this egg wash to another flat-bottomed dish. Place the panko in a third one. Put the green tomatoes in a bowl.

Arrange the dishes in order from left to right: green tomatoes, flour, egg wash, and panko. Line a baking sheet with parchment paper and place it at the end of the line. Line a separate baking sheet with paper towels.

When breading the tomatoes, using one hand for the wet steps and one hand for the dry steps will result in a much tidier breading process and keep your hands from also becoming breaded. One tomato slice at a time, with your right hand, place the tomato into the flour and toss it to thoroughly coat on both sides. With your right hand, drop the slice gently into the egg wash. With your left hand, flip and swirl the tomato to coat. Still using your left hand, remove the tomato slice and gently place it in the panko. Use your right hand again to flip and coat with the panko. Remove the slice with your right hand and place it on the parchment-lined baking sheet. Repeat with the remaining tomatoes and breading.

Fill a large cast-iron or other heavy-bottomed skillet with ½ inch of peanut oil and bring to 350°F on a deep-fry thermometer over medium-high heat. (If your thermometer doesn't register in oil at that depth, test the temperature by sprinkling in a few bread crumbs—if

CONTINUED

pan-fried green tomatoes with burrata and country ham, continued

they fry immediately, your oil is ready.) Working in batches to avoid overcrowding, gently place as many tomato slices in the oil as will fit in a single layer and fry until golden brown and crispy, flipping once, frying for 1½ to 2 minutes per side. Repeat with all of the slices, replenishing with fresh oil as necessary and bringing the temperature back up to 350°F before continuing. Transfer the fried tomatoes to the paper towel–lined baking sheet.

On a large serving platter, arrange the tomatoes, ¼ cup–size scoops of burrata, and the sliced ham. Drizzle the platter with olive oil and sprinkle with cracked pepper, fleur de sel, and the oregano.

The fried green tomatoes are best eaten immediately or within 2 hours and do not hold up to storage.

pan-seared goat cheese dumplings with herb pistou

Here, we get that delicious fried cheese flavor without having to deal with the whole dredging, breading, and frying process. Think of this as a lighter, more cheese-driven version of fried cheese. You can eat these as finger food, running them through the Herb Pistou and popping them in your mouth, or with a fork and knife. Just make sure the pistou is done before you start on the cheese, as the latter comes together quickly.

makes 16 to 18 dumplings

12 ounces soft, creamy, tangy goat cheese (such as Miticrema, a Spanish fromage blanc), at room temperature

1 egg

1½ tablespoons kosher salt

Freshly cracked black pepper

¾ cup semolina flour

2 tablespoons extra-virgin olive oil

1 cup Herb Pistou (page 57)

Fleur de sel

NOTE

Semolina flour is made from coarse-ground durum wheat, a hard variety of spring wheat used for making pasta.

Put the cheese in a large mixing bowl and set aside.

In a separate bowl, whip the egg until uniform in consistency. Season with 1½ teaspoons of the kosher salt and some pepper.

Gently fold the egg into the goat cheese—be careful not to beat the egg into the goat cheese, which will stiffen it up. Gently fold the flour into the egg and cheese mixture, just until combined. Overmixing will trigger gluten development and make your filling less tender.

Using your hands, gently form the mixture into one big ball. Cover in plastic wrap and chill in the refrigerator for about 20 minutes.

While the cheese chills, bring a large pot of water with the remaining 1 tablespoon kosher salt to a gentle boil. Line a baking sheet with parchment paper. Prepare an ice bath with 2 quarts of water and 2 quarts of ice (see page 35). Line a separate baking sheet with paper towels.

Form the cheese mixture into 1-ounce portions, about the size of a Ping-Pong ball, and place on the parchment-lined baking sheet.

Place half of the dumplings in the boiling water and cook until they float, 3 to 5 minutes. Using a slotted spoon, transfer them to the ice water bath for 20 to 30 seconds to stop them from cooking. Transfer to the paper towel–lined baking sheet and pat dry. Repeat with the remaining dumplings.

Heat the oil in a well-seasoned cast-iron skillet or a nonstick pan over high heat until shimmering. Working in batches to avoid overcrowding, cook 6 to 8 dumplings at a time. As they warm in the skillet, the dumplings will soften slightly and flatten, resembling sea scallops.

Sear the dumplings (increasing the heat slightly if necessary), flipping once, until they are a rich golden brown on both sides, about 3 minutes on the first side and 2 minutes on the second. Don't press down on the cheese with a spatula while it cooks.

Spoon the pistou on a serving plate. Arrange the dumplings on top of the pistou, sprinkle with fleur de sel, and serve immediately.

louisiana-style pickled quail eggs

When I go duck hunting in South Central Louisiana, I like to stop at a Cajun meat market named the Best Stop in a little town called Scott. That shop makes some of the best pickled quail eggs I've ever had, in just a simple hot sauce–vinegar brine. I usually buy multiple jars to snack on, and at least one of them is always gone by the time I get back to New Orleans two hours later. When we opened Balise, our restaurant in the Central Business District, I knew I wanted to pay homage to the Best Stop's pickled eggs and serve them with raw oysters; hence this recipe.

makes 24 eggs

24 quail eggs (see Note)

2 cups Homemade Hot Sauce (page 62) or store-bought (preferably Texas Pete's or Crystal)

1 cup distilled white vinegar

Juice of ½ lemon

1 teaspoon kosher salt

Freshly cracked black pepper

NOTE

Quail eggs are available from many Asian grocers. If you're making the two dozen eggs called for, follow the recipe as written, because peeling twenty-four boiled quail eggs isn't that big of a deal. But if you're doubling or tripling it for a crowd and have an extra day to plan, I have a trick: submerge the whole boiled egg, shell and all, in white wine vinegar overnight. The shells will totally dissolve; all you have to do is peel off the loose skin, rinse off the eggs, and drop them into the pickling liquid. Try it sometime—it's crazy how well it works.

To sterilize a glass jar, submerge it in boiling water for 10 minutes. Remove with tongs and set upright on a baking sheet to cool before using.

Bring a medium pot of water to a boil over high heat. Prepare an ice water bath in a large bowl (see page 35). Gently lower the eggs into the pot and boil for 6 minutes. Transfer the eggs directly to the ice water bath to cool for 30 to 60 seconds.

When the eggs are cool enough to handle, peel and rinse to remove any shell fragments. Place the eggs in a sterile quart-size jar with a lid (see Note). In a glass measuring cup, combine the hot sauce, vinegar, lemon juice, salt, and a few grinds of pepper, stirring well to dissolve the salt. Pour the mixture over the eggs. Cover and place in the refrigerator for 24 hours to cure.

Serve the eggs whole as finger food. They will keep, covered, in the refrigerator for up to 2 weeks.

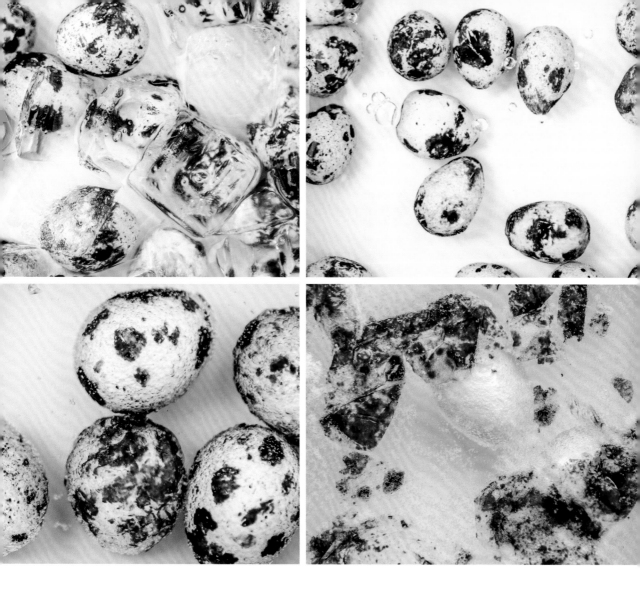

cornbread pancakes with american paddlefish caviar

I love the idea of taking that classic caviar-and-blini combo and applying it to humble cornbread and American paddlefish roe.

Caviar has always been considered a luxury product, but in the past decade or so, access to caviar has changed dramatically, and there are now high-quality, domestically produced paddlefish options at a reasonable price. I like the product from a company called Cajun Caviar, but if you don't want to order it online, look for American paddlefish roe from the South or Midwest, preferably from December through February, when the eggs are harvested. Caviar freezes well; you may find it in the freezer case throughout the year.

The rustic cornbread pancakes here are meant to resemble blini, so it's best to make them in a nonstick or well-seasoned cast-iron pan, using just a little bit of oil. I like to make them silver dollar–size, so people can eat them with their fingers.

makes 32 bite-size pancakes

1 cup fine-ground yellow cornmeal

1 cup all-purpose flour

1½ teaspoons baking powder

½ cup sugar

1 teaspoon kosher salt

1½ cups whole milk

¼ cup unsalted butter, melted

2 eggs

1 teaspoon vegetable oil

½ cup crème fraîche (see page 363)

4 ounces American paddlefish caviar

In a large mixing bowl, combine the cornmeal, flour, baking powder, sugar, and salt and lightly mix. In a separate bowl, combine the milk, butter, and eggs and gently whisk to blend. Pour the wet ingredients into the dry and stir to combine. Let rest for at least 10 minutes or up to 2 hours.

Heat a large nonstick skillet over medium heat. Add the vegetable oil, swirl it around the pan, and then gently wipe out any excess with a paper towel and discard. This will give you a slick surface, so the pancakes don't stick, without any residual greasiness.

Spoon 2 tablespoons of batter per pancake into the hot skillet, cooking four or five at a time. Cook the pancakes on the first side for about 3 minutes, until they're slightly puffed and have little popped bubbles dotting the surface. Gently flip each pancake and cook on the second side for 1 to 1½ minutes, until golden brown.

Serve the cornbread pancakes in a little bowl or basket. Serve the crème fraîche in a small bowl with a small spoon. Keep the caviar in its original container over ice, with a mother-of-pearl spoon, if you feel fancy. Some authorities say that caviar's flavor is affected by metal spoons (and if you want to avoid this you could always use plastic), but remember that most caviar comes in a metal container. Use each pancake as the vehicle for a small spoonful of crème fraîche and a dollop of caviar.

This dish is best made and eaten the same day. The caviar will keep, in its jar on ice, in the refrigerator for 2 to 3 days.

blue crab beignets

Many years ago, I was combing through cookbooks, looking for a garnish for a Cajun court bouillon, or Louisiana-style braised fish stew. I came across a recipe for salt cod fritters in Thomas Keller's *Bouchon*, and I thought the same method would work if I filled the fritters with a creamy crab mixture. So I changed a few things in the batter, swapped the brandade for mascarpone, and traded cod for local blue crab.

Needless to say, these didn't remain a garnish for long. They were such a hit, I had to start serving them at La Petite Grocery as an appetizer, and they are still, to this day, the most popular item on the menu. And what's not to love? It's essentially a cheesy crab doughnut. There would be a riot if I ever removed these from the menu, but if you can't make it to the restaurant, here's how to make them at home. This is one of the more technical recipes in the book, so don't be discouraged if your first few beignets are a little misshapen. The batter can be tricky to work with because it's so loose, but practice a few times and you'll soon nail it.

makes 8 to 12 beignets

FILLING

½ small shallot, finely chopped

6 ounces fresh blue crabmeat, picked over for shells

⅓ cup mascarpone

1 tablespoon finely chopped chives

Pinch of kosher salt

BATTER

1 cup all-purpose flour

⅓ cup cornstarch

1 tablespoon baking powder

½ teaspoon kosher salt, plus more as needed

1 cup amber lager

Vegetable oil for frying (about 1 quart)

Kosher salt

NOTE

You can also use this batter to make sweet beignets. Simply skip the filling and dust the fried beignets with powdered sugar.

To make the filling: Combine the shallot, crabmeat, mascarpone, chives, and salt in a mixing bowl. Gently fold to combine. The mixture will be tacky and creamy. Set aside. The crab mixture can be made up to 4 hours ahead and stored, covered, in the refrigerator.

To make the batter: Whisk together the flour, cornstarch, baking powder, and salt in a large mixing bowl. Gradually whisk in the beer, and continue whisking just until blended (the batter will be thick).

When ready to fry, pour the oil to a depth of at least 3 inches into a Dutch oven or large saucepan fitted with a clip-on deep-fry thermometer. Heat the oil over medium-high heat until it reads 375°F. Line a plate with paper towels.

Measure 1 heaping tablespoon of the crab mixture, roll it into a loose ball, and drop it into the bowl of batter. Spoon batter over the crab mixture to coat it evenly. Lift the crab from the batter with the spoon, trying to collect as much batter on the spoon as possible, along with the filling. This will help to form a nice "shell" while frying. Gently slide or carefully drop the beignet into the oil from just above the surface.

CONTINUED

blue crab beignets, continued

Working in batches to avoid crowding, add a few more beignets to the pot and fry, turning occasionally, until crisp and deep golden brown, about 5 minutes. The beignets probably won't stick to the pot, but if one does, don't try to pop it off immediately. Leave it alone until it releases naturally or it pops off easily. It will separate when it's well cooked; if you try to remove it before it is, you'll rip a hole in the beignet and everything will leak out and dirty your cooking oil.

Using a slotted spoon, transfer the beignets to the paper towels to drain and season with salt. Repeat with remaining crab balls, letting the oil return to 375°F before cooking each new batch. Serve hot.

crawfish pierogi

I grew up eating the pierogi my mom made. Like any good Polish mom, she always made way too many, so we'd eat them day and night. She made "bread crumbs" for pierogi by basically burning and scraping toast over them—if those crumbs were missing, they would be loudly missed.

I like all kinds of fillings, but for me, pierogi are really about that crispy, buttery outer shell. When I became a chef, I thought that shell would make the perfect vessel for almost any filling, hence this recipe, which pays tribute to a classic while also bending the rules a bit. And, of course, I've kept the bread crumbs.

makes 16 to 20 pierogi

PIEROGI DOUGH

2 cups all-purpose flour

½ teaspoon kosher salt

2 eggs

⅓ cup water

CRAWFISH FILLING

3 tablespoons unsalted butter

2 cups very thinly sliced shiitake mushrooms

½ cup very thinly sliced shallots

Kosher salt

1 pound crawfish meat (see Note)

2 cups soft, creamy, tangy cheese, such as farmer's cheese, or a mixture of equal parts goat cheese and mascarpone, at room temperature

1 tablespoon freshly squeezed lemon juice

¼ cup thinly sliced chives

1 egg

2 tablespoons water

All-purpose flour for dusting

Extra-virgin olive oil for coating the pierogi before storing (optional)

2 slices white sandwich bread

To make the dough: In the bowl of a food processor, combine the flour and salt. Turn the machine on and while it's running, add the eggs, one at a time, through the chute. Turn off the processor and pulse to cut the eggs into the dough until combined, about 10 seconds. Slowly stream in the water, while pulsing, until the water is incorporated, about 5 seconds. You should have a smooth, seized-up ball of dough.

Gather the dough with your hands and turn out onto a clean floured work surface. Firmly knead for 7 to 10 minutes, until smooth and no longer sticky. It should feel dense, but have a very smooth, supple texture. Wrap in plastic and set aside to rest at room temperature for at least 30 minutes or up to 2 hours.

To make the filling: In a large sauté pan over medium-high heat, melt the butter. Add the mushrooms and cook, stirring occasionally, until softened, about 5 minutes. Add the shallots, season with a pinch of salt, and cook, stirring occasionally, until the shallots are translucent, about 2 minutes. Transfer the mushroom-shallot mixture to a large mixing bowl. Add the crawfish, cheese, lemon juice, and chives and fold with a rubber spatula until just incorporated. Spread the mixture out in an even layer on a baking sheet and chill in the refrigerator until completely cool.

Bring a large pot of salted water to a boil.

Gather the dough and scoop into 1-ounce pieces. There should be sixteen to twenty altogether. In a small bowl, whisk the egg and water to make an egg wash. Dust a baking sheet with flour.

CONTINUED

¾ cup unsalted butter

8 to 10 sage leaves, torn in half

Juice of 1 lemon

Pinch of kosher salt

Freshly cracked black pepper

½ cup crème fraîche (see page 363)

1 teaspoon thinly sliced chives

NOTE

You can order crawfish meat online year-round, though their season here in Louisiana runs from late winter through early July, then starts again right around Thanksgiving.

Working on a floured surface, with your hands, roll each piece of dough into a ball (it should be golf ball–size). Use a rolling pin to roll out each ball into a disk about 2½ inches in diameter and about ⅛ inch thick.

Put about 2½ tablespoons of filling on each disk. Brush the egg wash around half the edge of each disk and fold in half, like a taco, sealing the edge by pressing with your fingertips. Place on the prepared baking sheet.

Working in batches if necessary to avoid crowding, add the pierogi to the boiling water and cook until they float, 5 to 7 minutes.

From this point, the blanched pierogi can be drained, patted dry, and finished immediately. Or shock in an ice water bath (see page 35), to stop the cooking, and store in the refrigerator for up to 24 hours with a light coating of olive oil to prevent sticking.

Toast the bread until just shy of burnt. You may need to repeat the toasting process a few times to achieve the correct brittle texture and nearly black color. Set aside to cool.

In a large cast-iron skillet or nonstick pan over medium-high heat, melt 1 tablespoon of the butter. Working in batches to avoid crowding, add the pierogi in one layer.

Sear the pierogi, undisturbed, until golden brown on the bottom, decreasing the heat slightly if they brown too quickly, 2½ to 3 minutes. Flip and cook for 30 seconds on the other side and then transfer to a serving platter. Repeat until all the pierogi are cooked, adding a fresh tablespoon of butter between batches.

In the same pan the pierogi were cooked in, over medium heat, melt the remaining butter and add the sage. Fry until the leaves are crispy, 3½ to 5 minutes. Slide the pan off the heat, add the lemon juice to the butter sauce, and season with the salt and pepper. Using the blade of a butter knife, scrape as much of the almost-scorched toast into the butter sauce as possible.

Spoon the butter sauce all over the pierogi. In a serving bowl, stir together the crème fraîche and chives and serve alongside the pierogi.

shrimp salad with preserved lemon and arbequina olives

Shrimp salad is a staple in our region, and this is my take on what grandmothers everywhere used to make for 4-H Club meetings. I like to keep shrimp the star—so instead of adding a bunch of mayo, pickles, and paprika, mine is flavored with preserved lemon, tarragon, black pepper, and a few Arbequina olives for brininess. This is a major crowd-pleaser, and it comes together very quickly.

It's also worth noting that apart from the shrimp and aioli-lemon combo, this recipe is very open to reinterpretation: if you don't have tarragon and shallots, use parsley and red onion, or play around with other soft herbs, like chervil and chives. It's endlessly flexible, so experiment once you have the basics down.

Bring the water to a boil in a large pot over high heat. (Although we're only cooking 2 pounds of shrimp, I like to use a lot of water to ensure that it maintains an even temperature when the shrimp are added. Avoiding temperature fluctuation during cooking, along with the rapid chill at the end, leads to a better texture in the final dish.) Add the halved lemons, bay leaves, and peppercorns. Decrease the heat and simmer for 10 minutes, then increase the heat again and return to a boil.

Add the shrimp and give the pot a big stir. Cook the shrimp for 3 minutes, then transfer to a bowl and ladle about a cup of liquid from the pot over the shrimp. Cover the shrimp with ice to rapidly cool for about 10 minutes, then drain the shrimp and place in the refrigerator to chill.

In a separate bowl, combine the aioli, shallot, chopped parsley, chopped tarragon, preserved lemon, lemon juice, salt, cracked black pepper, and chopped olives. Fold the mixture together, then add the shrimp and fold again.

Let the shrimp salad rest in the refrigerator for at least 20 minutes or up to 1 day (the longer the better).

Nestle about ½ cup of shrimp salad into each lettuce cup. Garnish with the parsley leaves, preserved lemon strips, and pitted olives and serve.

serves 8 to 10

2 gallons water

3 lemons, halved

2 dried bay leaves

2 tablespoons black peppercorns

2 pounds wild shrimp, shelled and deveined (21/25 count)

¾ cup Aioli (page 65)

1 shallot, minced

½ cup chopped flat-leaf parsley leaves, plus 20 leaves

1 tablespoon chopped tarragon leaves

2 tablespoons finely chopped Preserved Lemon Peel (page 342), plus 12 very thinly sliced strips

2 tablespoons freshly squeezed lemon juice

1 teaspoon kosher salt

Freshly cracked black pepper

1 cup Arbequina or Nicoise olives, pitted and finely chopped, plus ¼ cup pitted olives for garnish

2 heads Bibb lettuce, outer leaves removed and inner leaves separated

shrimp and okra fritters

I have a penchant for dipping things in batter and frying them. I really like this recipe, because the fresh shrimp perfume every bite with their sweet, briny aroma while still letting the other ingredients shine. This is classic finger food, best eaten on the porch on a nice summer day.

Okra is a polarizing ingredient, and while I've come to appreciate its slimy quality in certain recipes, it will minimize the crispiness of the fritter if it goes right into the batter. Here, I give it a quick dry roast in high heat, which draws out the moisture and subdues much of the slime. If you're not convinced and don't want to try it, you can use another vegetable here, such as zucchini, summer squash, roasted peppers, or eggplant. That's the beauty of this recipe—the batter is a blank canvas.

makes 15 to 20 fritters

8 ounces okra, sliced ½ inch thick

2 tablespoons extra-virgin olive oil

1 cup all-purpose flour

1 teaspoon baking powder

1 teaspoon kosher salt, plus more as needed

½ cup plus 2 tablespoons whole milk

1 egg

8 ounces wild shrimp, chopped into ½-inch pieces (see Note)

¼ cup thinly sliced green onions, white and green parts

About 1 quart peanut oil

1 cup Aioli (page 65)

NOTE
If you're lucky enough to have access to the tiny local shrimp that are sometimes available near the Gulf in the summer, use them instead, and don't bother chopping them.

Preheat the oven to 425°F. Line a baking sheet with parchment paper. Line a plate with paper towels.

In a mixing bowl, toss together the okra and olive oil. Spread out the okra on the prepared baking sheet and cook until visibly roasted and fairly dry, 15 to 20 minutes. Set aside to cool to room temperature.

In a clean mixing bowl, combine the flour, baking powder, and salt. Add the milk and egg and whisk to form a sticky, shaggy batter with no bits of dried flour remaining. Let the batter rest for 30 minutes. Fold in the shrimp, baked okra, and green onions.

When ready to fry, pour the oil to a depth of 1½ inches in a large heavy-bottomed pot fitted with a clip-on deep-fry thermometer. Heat the oil over medium-high heat until it reads 375°F.

Working in batches to avoid crowding, gently drop the fritters, each about the size of a Ping-Pong ball, into the oil from just above the surface, being careful to avoid splashing. Fry until golden brown on the bottom, about 2½ minutes, then use a clean spoon to gently flip each fritter and cook on the other side for 1½ to 2 minutes. Repeat until you've used up all the batter, letting the oil return to 375°F between batches and replenishing with fresh oil if necessary.

Transfer the fritters to the paper towels to drain and then transfer to a serving platter. Sprinkle with a little salt and serve immediately with the aioli for dipping.

marinated octopus

It took a while for me to have a good octopus experience—my early ones revolved around the flabby, chewy versions on offer at my local sushi bar in California. But in New Orleans, we don't stand for mediocre seafood, and I knew there had to be a way to unlock octopus's rich, briny potential.

After a lot of trial and error, I honed a process that makes a very tender, juicy octopus. It involves briefly cooking the octopus, then building an ice bath using the poaching liquid, and allowing the octopus to reabsorb some of the cooking liquid as it cools. With this process, you can stop cooking the octopus at the perfect point of doneness. That's why I prefer to serve the octopus chilled in this bright, acidic vinaigrette, as opposed to grilling it. (You can grill it after poaching and chilling; just brush it with a little olive oil and you're good to go.)

I actually prefer to shop for frozen whole octopus, ideally from Spain or Portugal, as the "fresh" ones on display at seafood counters are often prefrozen and defrosted. Fishmongers and Mediterranean markets are good places to look.

makes 4 to 6 servings

OCTOPUS

1 (2- to 4-pound) octopus

2 lemons, halved

4 dried bay leaves

1 sprig rosemary

4 cloves garlic, mashed (see page 37)

3 tablespoons kosher salt

MARINADE

¼ cup white wine vinegar

¼ cup freshly squeezed orange juice

2 tablespoons freshly squeezed lemon juice

1 tablespoon freshly squeezed lime juice

2 shallots, sliced into rings

1 clove garlic, minced

¾ cup extra-virgin olive oil

2 oranges, supremed (see page 36)

1 lemon

1 lime

¼ cup chopped flat-leaf parsley leaves

¼ cup chopped chives

2 tablespoons chopped tarragon leaves

½ cup shaved radishes (shaved with a mandoline)

½ cup shaved fennel (shaved with a mandoline), plus a handful of tops

To cook the octopus: Place the octopus in a large pot and wash repeatedly with cold water until the water is free of ink. Rinse the pot and return the octopus to it. Add the lemon halves, bay leaves, rosemary, garlic, and salt. Cover with cold water and bring to a boil over high heat. Remove from the heat, cover the pot, and let the octopus soak for 30 minutes. (If you're worried about overcooking, you can take out the meat a little early and slice off a piece to test.)

Transfer the octopus to a large mixing bowl and ladle about 1 cup poaching liquid from the pot over it. Cover with ice to rapidly cool the octopus for about 20 minutes. Discard the remaining poaching liquid.

Transfer the chilled octopus to a cutting board and detach the tentacles at the base, where they meet the head. With a paring knife, remove the flabby membrane from the tentacles, and cut the tentacles into rounds about ¼ inch thick.

To make the marinade: In a large mixing bowl, combine the vinegar, citrus juices, shallots, garlic, and oil and stir together. Place the octopus in the marinade, cover tightly with plastic wrap, and refrigerate until very cold. At this point, the octopus will keep in the refrigerator for up to 2 days.

Transfer the octopus and marinade to a serving bowl and add the citrus supremes, herbs, radishes, and fennel and fold to combine. Serve cold, garnished with the fennel tops.

country pork pâté

This is one of the best and simplest entry-level charcuterie projects to try at home. Yes, it takes a few days, but most of that time is spent waiting, not cooking. I really enjoy watching the transformation of pork shoulder into a country-style pâté—it's a process where you see a big change from beginning to end.

Another thing I love about a country pâté like this is its versatility. You can go high and serve it on a special occasion with fancy pickles and fruit jam; put it on a sandwich or cracker for a midday snack; or even turn it into sausage for a breakfast sandwich. I have a few suggestions here, but really, the possibilities here are endless. This pâté takes 2 to 3 days to make, so plan ahead.

A day or two before you plan to make the pâté, cut the pork shoulder into 1-inch cubes and place in a resealable bag with the tarragon and thyme. Pour the brandy over the meat and seal the bag, squeezing out any air. Refrigerate for 24 to 48 hours. If you're using preground meat, omit this step.

Lightly brush a 1¼-quart terrine mold with vegetable oil. Place a large piece of plastic wrap over it and gently line the mold, making sure to get all of the air bubbles out and allowing some plastic to hang over the sides. Set aside.

Combine the peppercorns, cloves, nutmeg, ginger, allspice, and juniper berries in a clean spice grinder and grind until fine. Set aside.

Pour out the brandy and make sure the marinated meat mixture is very cold—it should register 30°F on an instant-read thermometer. (Place in the freezer for 1 hour if need be.)

Grind the meat and herbs through a meat grinder with a coarse plate, and season with the kosher salt and pepper. Or, if using preground meat, mix together the meat, herbs, kosher salt, and pepper in a mixing bowl.

Working quickly to keep the mixture as cold as possible, add the ground spices and pink curing salt to the meat. Make a small patty with your hands; this will be a tester to check for seasoning. Heat a small skillet over medium-high heat and add the patty. Sear on one side, then flip and cook on the other side, 2 to 3 minutes in total. Taste for seasoning. The patty should taste strongly seasoned or even borderline overseasoned

makes 1 (1¼-quart) terrine

2¾ pounds pork shoulder or ground pork (see Note)

2 tablespoons chopped tarragon leaves

2 tablespoons thyme leaves

½ cup brandy

1 tablespoon vegetable oil, plus more for brushing

2 teaspoons black peppercorns

1 teaspoon whole cloves

1 teaspoon ground nutmeg

½ teaspoon ground ginger

½ teaspoon ground allspice

3 juniper berries

1 tablespoon plus 1 teaspoon kosher salt

1 teaspoon freshly cracked black pepper

¼ teaspoon pink curing salt (see Note)

1 cup half-sour pickles (see page 351)

¼ cup Violet Mustard (page 347)

¼ cup Strawberry-Tarragon Jam (page 357)

Crusty bread for serving

CONTINUED

country pork pâté, continued

continued

NOTE

If you don't have a 1¼-inch terrine mold, you may use a loaf pan instead.

The temperature and grind of the pork is important to the success of this dish. It's preferable to freeze and grind your own meat, but if that's not in the cards, ask your butcher to freeze and loosely grind the pork for you. When the fat is too warm, you end up with what I call unintentional smear—the fat melts into grease, leaving you with a mealy, unemulsified pâté, instead of the ideal mixture of meat and evenly dispersed chunks of white fat.

Pink curing salt, aka Prague powder #1 or TCM (tinted curing mix), is available at butchers and online.

when eaten hot—this is okay, because the pâté will be served chilled or room temperature, and cold temperatures mute salty flavors.

Adjust the ground pork mixture for seasoning, and spoon it into the plastic-lined mold, pressing firmly to force out air bubbles. Fold the plastic wrap over the meat and smooth over with your hand, completely sealing the pâté. Put the lid on the terrine mold or cover with foil.

Preheat the oven to 375°F.

Place the terrine in a roasting pan and add enough water to come half-way up the sides. Bake until the internal temperature reaches 155°F on an instant-read thermometer, about 1 hour. Start checking the temperature after 45 minutes, as the pâté rises in temperature quickly after it hits about 120°F.

Remove the terrine mold from the roasting pan, dump the water out of the pan, and refill it with ice and cold water. Put the terrine mold back in the ice bath to shock it and prevent overcooking; let cool in the ice water for 1 hour.

Outline the bottom of the terrine mold on a piece of cardboard, cut it out, and wrap it in foil. Place on top of the pâté, and weigh the cardboard down with heavy cans. Refrigerate overnight.

Uncover the pâté and tug on the plastic wrap a little to loosen the meat. Unmold the pâté onto a plate or cutting board, and clean off the pâté as necessary with a flat-edged knife, trimming off aspic and fat from the edges.

With a sharp knife, halve the pâté crosswise, then slice each half into eight slices. Serve on the fanciest platter you have, with little bowls of the pickles, mustard, jam and crusty bread on the side. Spread a bit of each ingredient on a piece of bread and enjoy it all together.

biscuit and pâté brunch sandwiches

This is ideal for using leftover pâté the morning after your fancy French platter. It's equally delicious with sliced American cheese or a super-nice foreign import—use whatever you have.

makes 4 servings

4 Buttermilk Biscuits
(page 372)

1 tablespoon extra-virgin
olive oil

4 slices Country Pork Pâté
(page 103)

4 slices cheese

1 tablespoon unsalted butter

4 eggs

¼ cup Strawberry-Tarragon
Jam (page 357)

Preheat the oven to 350°F. Line a baking sheet with parchment paper. Split the biscuits in half and place on the prepared baking sheet.

In a sauté pan over medium-high, heat the oil until shimmering. Add the pâté and sear until golden brown and crispy, about 2 minutes per side. Set a piece on the bottom half of each biscuit and top with a slice of cheese.

Give the pan a quick wipe and add butter and melt in the pan over medium-high heat. Crack the eggs into the pan and cook until the whites are set, about 2 minutes, then flip and cook on the other side for 1 minute more. Remove from the heat and place an egg on top of each slice of cheese. Place the baking sheet in the oven to slightly melt the cheese, 45 seconds to 1½ minutes. Close the biscuits with the tops to make sandwiches. Transfer to a serving platter and press gently on the biscuit tops to break the yolks. Serve with the jam on the side.

steak tartare with dill, horseradish, and fried quinoa

Steak tartare seems to be experiencing a bit of a renaissance lately, but when I took over La Petite Grocery thirteen years ago, it was dying off. I've always loved a good tartare, and I wanted to bring it back, with a bit of a twist. The flavor profile here almost resembles a Scandinavian smoked fish dish—with the creamy dressing, dill, and horseradish. That's why, if I'm not up for making the fried quinoa, I serve it with toasted rye bread.

The fried quinoa has a backstory: Superchef Ashley Christensen, in Raleigh, North Carolina, learned the technique from me when we worked an event together years ago. She adapted it and published it in her cookbook *Poole's*, and now I'm borrowing (stealing) it back. The stuff is addictive. You'll eat it all the time if you have it around, which you can do because it keeps well for weeks. Once marinated and fried, the grain holds the flavor of the vinaigrette and stays super-crunchy, even after it's folded into the beef tartare. I use fried quinoa whenever I want the crunch that a crouton or cracker provides, such as in a Caesar salad, a vegetable soup, or tuna salad. This subrecipe makes about 2 cups, which gives you enough to garnish the tartare and save some for other uses.

makes 6 to 8 servings

FRIED QUINOA

¼ cup red wine vinegar

1½ teaspoons freshly squeezed lemon juice

1 tablespoon Dijon mustard

1½ teaspoons cane syrup (see Note) or honey

2 tablespoons plus 2 teaspoons kosher salt

¾ cup extra-virgin olive oil or olive pomace oil

Freshly cracked black pepper

2 quarts water

1 cup red quinoa

1½ cups vegetable oil

1 pound beef tenderloin

¼ cup minced shallots

¼ cup capers, rinsed, dried, and chopped

½ cup chopped flat-leaf parsley leaves

½ cup Dijon mustard

½ cup extra-virgin olive oil

¼ cup freshly squeezed lemon juice, plus more as needed

2 tablespoons kosher salt, plus more as needed

Freshly cracked black pepper

1 small knob horseradish, grated with a Microplane

½ cup dill fronds

½ cup Buttermilk Dressing (page 66)

To make the fried quinoa: In a mixing bowl, combine the vinegar, lemon juice, Dijon, cane syrup, and the 2 teaspoons salt. Whisk to combine, then slowly stream in the olive oil, whisking constantly to emulsify (see page 35). Grind some black pepper over the top and set the vinaigrette aside.

Bring the water and remaining 2 tablespoons of salt to a boil. Add the quinoa, decrease the heat to medium, and cook until the grains are tender and have doubled in size, about 20 minutes. Drain the quinoa and add directly to the vinaigrette. Stir to coat the quinoa well. Spread out the quinoa in a single layer on a baking sheet to cool evenly and avoid clumping. Place the baking sheet in the refrigerator and chill completely, 4 to 6 hours.

Line a baking sheet with paper towels. Fill a large heavy-bottomed sauté pan fitted with a clip-on thermometer with about 1 inch of the vegetable oil and heat over medium-high heat until the oil reaches 375°F. Drain off the vinaigrette from the quinoa and toss. Working in batches to avoid crowding, sprinkle the quinoa in an even layer over the bottom of the pan and cook, stirring as it fries, until very crisp, about 2 minutes. Using a fine-mesh strainer, transfer the quinoa to the paper towels to drain.

Set aside to cool. The quinoa will keep, in an airtight container in the refrigerator, for up to 4 weeks.

With a sharp knife, slice the beef about ¼ inch thick. Cut those slices into batons, and cut the batons into ¼-inch cubes. If necessary, chop a few more times with the knife to even out the cubes.

Fill a mixing bowl with ice cubes, then nest another mixing bowl in the ice. In the top bowl, combine the beef, shallots, capers, parsley, Dijon, extra-virgin olive oil, lemon juice, and salt. Mix thoroughly to combine and taste for seasoning, adjusting with a little more lemon juice or salt if needed. Fold in the fried quinoa.

Arrange the tartare on a platter. Garnish with a few cranks of pepper, and the horseradish and dill fronds; drizzle with the buttermilk dressing. Serve immediately.

NOTE
Cane syrup, a Southern ingredient, is thick, sweet, and molasses-like and adds a distinctive malty richness to the Fried Quinoa.

side dishes

CASAMENTO'S RESTAURANT

OYSTERS

LUNCH
TUES - SAT 11:00AM

DINNER
THUR-FRI-SAT 5:30PM - 9:00PM

RESTAURANT

I am of the opinion that you should be as proud of your side dishes as you are of any main courses. I gave them their own chapter—instead of making them subrecipes in main dish recipes—to underscore how the mighty side dish deserves its place among everything else in this book. What I like about sides is their mix-and-match, plug-and-play utility. I also wanted to give you the chance to focus on the techniques involved in these recipes, so you can get comfortable making one or a few of these and applying your own creative touches and preferences as you build meals. Serving several sides with a main gets more flavors and textures on the table than one dish with a bunch of components, which get lost in the hodgepodge.

The recipes in this chapter showcase the main ingredient in each dish. There's a lot of vegetable cookery here—you'll learn how to properly pan-roast vegetables, braise greens, and take a single vegetable, like a potato, in two wildly different directions (super-fancy French style in the Pommes Anna-ish on page 134, and super–down home grandma-style in the Classic Potato Salad on page 138). It's not all vegetables, though—this chapter contains the coveted La Petite grits recipe (see page 133), which is modeled after the world's most buttery movie theater popcorn.

Many of these recipes involve simple techniques to cook single ingredients to the best of their potential. But these recipes are also key to understanding how to use those same ingredients in other ways. For example, I might take the braised collards on page 120 and pair them with Sticky Chicken (page 252) and serve it over Foolproof Rice (page 369). I often think about how best to combine individual components into something greater than the sum of its parts. I hope that as you cook your way through this chapter, you start to think the same way.

pan-roasted mushrooms with shallots, lemon, and thyme

When I was contemplating which sides to put in this book, I asked my wife, Mia, for advice, and she reminded me that this is one of her all-time favorites. Who am I to argue? This is a foolproof method for pan-roasting many types of mushrooms, flavored with a combination of aromatics and herbs that have stood the test of time. This goes well with nearly everything in the Meat chapter, but feel free to get creative. We use this method pretty much any time we need a cooked mushroom, whether it's being served as a stand-alone side dish, folded into risotto or eggs, or tossed in a vegetable or grain salad.

makes 4 servings

3 tablespoons extra-virgin olive oil

4 cups cleaned and halved cremini mushrooms

1 teaspoon kosher salt, plus more as needed

Freshly cracked black pepper

3 tablespoons unsalted butter

2 tablespoons minced shallots

1 tablespoon thyme leaves, plus 1 sprig

2 teaspoons freshly squeezed lemon juice, plus more as needed

In a large heavy-bottomed sauté pan over medium-high heat, add the oil and heat until shimmering. Spread out the mushrooms in one layer, working in batches if necessary. It's important not to crowd the pan, because the mushrooms will release liquid as they cook, and if they're too close together, the liquid won't evaporate and you'll end up with mushy, flabby 'shrooms. Sear the mushrooms until golden and slightly caramelized, flipping once, 3 to 5 minutes per side.

Stir in the salt, pepper, butter, shallots, and thyme leaves. Decrease the heat to medium-low and cook, stirring occasionally, until the ingredients are melded and the mushrooms are slightly glossy, 8 to 10 minutes. In the last minute of cooking, add the lemon juice, then taste for seasoning and add more lemon juice or salt if necessary.

Transfer the mushrooms to a serving platter, and garnish with the thyme sprig. Store leftovers in an airtight container in the refrigerator for up to 3 days. Reheat gently over low heat.

roasted broccoli

This is a way to make roasted broccoli more exciting. Searing it in a hot, heavy pan over high heat gives the edges a beautifully roasted and charred exterior, while the interior remains crisp-tender but totally cooked through. Don't fuss with broccoli too much once it hits the pan; let it caramelize on one side before turning it over, to get a perfect sear. The bagna cauda lends a buttery umami flavor from the anchovies, garlic, and brown butter, making this a great side for any grilled or roasted meat, or even a simple pasta dish.

In a large heavy-bottomed sauté pan over high heat, add the oil and heat until shimmering. Add the broccoli and decrease the heat to medium-high. If the broccoli looks dry, add the 1 teaspoon oil. Sear the broccoli and let it caramelize on one side, undisturbed, 2 to 3 minutes. Turn and repeat on the other side.

Season the broccoli with the salt and stir in the bagna cauda to evenly coat. Decrease the heat to medium-low and squeeze in the juice from about a quarter of the lemon. Cook for 1½ minutes, then stir in the parsley and remove from the heat.

Transfer to a serving platter, garnish with the chile flakes, and serve the remaining lemon wedges on the side. The broccoli will keep in the refrigerator, tightly sealed, for up to 3 days. Reheat in a 300°F oven.

makes 4 to 6 servings

2 tablespoons extra-virgin olive oil, plus 1 teaspoon as needed

1 head broccoli, separated into florets, stems reserved for another use (such as the Broccoli Caesar on page 165)

½ teaspoon kosher salt

¼ cup Bagna Cauda (page 60)

1 lemon, cut into wedges

1 tablespoon finely chopped flat-leaf parsley leaves

1 teaspoon dried red chile flakes, ideally piment d'Espelette or Korean gochugaru (see page 32)

roasted cauliflower steaks with toasted almonds and brown butter

You see sauce almondine (or amandine) on many menus in New Orleans, almost always served on fish. It's a classic (just ask anyone who's been to Galatoire's), but for this vegetarian take, I use thick cauliflower steaks. Cauliflower is one of those vegetables that can be the star of a plate. This dish comes together quickly and with minimal ingredients, but it's important to keep an eye on each component as it cooks, because a few seconds is all it takes to burn the cauliflower as it sears or the butter as it toasts.

makes 4 to 6 servings

1 head cauliflower

½ cup extra-virgin olive oil

Kosher salt

¼ cup unsalted butter

½ cup sliced blanched almonds

2 tablespoons minced shallots

¼ cup chopped flat-leaf parsley leaves

2 tablespoons freshly squeezed lemon juice

Freshly cracked black pepper

Preheat the oven to 375°F.

Trim and discard the outer leaves off the cauliflower. Turn the cauliflower stem-side up and cut in half through the center of the stem. Trim off the outer florets so that you are left with two "steaks," each 1½ to 2 inches thick. (Reserve the florets for another use, such as the Lobster Chowder with Cauliflower Puree on page 188.)

Place a rack on a baking sheet. In a large sauté pan over high heat, add the oil and heat until shimmering. Working one at a time, brown the cauliflower steaks. Place a steak in the hot oil, decrease the heat to medium-low, and cook until golden brown and caramelized on the edges, 7 to 10 minutes per side. Watch carefully, as the cauliflower can burn easily; adjust the heat if necessary. Drain and discard the oil in the pan.

Transfer the cauliflower to the prepared baking sheet, and repeat with the other steak. Place the baking sheet, with the cauliflower steaks, on the oven rack (for an even flow of heat all around) and roast for 5 to 7 minutes, until golden. Remove from the oven and season lightly with salt.

In the sauté pan in which you browned the cauliflower, melt the butter over medium-high heat, add the almonds, and swirl butter and almonds around in the pan. With a wooden spoon or a spatula, fold the almonds and butter together. The butter will start to foam and the almonds will begin to toast. Continue stirring until the butter is golden brown and aromatic and the almonds are toasted, about 5 minutes, paying close attention to avoid burning.

Add the shallots and fry stirring, for about 30 seconds. Stir in the parsley and lemon juice, which will help stop the browning of the butter. Season with salt and pepper.

To serve, transfer the cauliflower to a platter and spoon the almond mixture over it. The cauliflower will keep in the refrigerator, tightly sealed, for up to 3 days. Reheat in 350°F oven.

roasted turnips and their greens with bacon vinaigrette

Turnip greens get tossed out all too often. Here's a great way to use the whole vegetable—by cooking down the greens and dressing them with a nice, acidic bacon vinaigrette, a nod to the classic combination of braised greens and smoked pork. The turnips themselves get their due, too, dry-roasting in a hot oven until they become tight and caramelized, and the flesh inside turns soft and fluffy. If you can, try getting local turnips just after a cold snap, when the roots convert their starches to sugars and taste extra-sweet.

makes 4 to 6 servings

1 bunch turnips, with greens (about 6 turnips)

2 tablespoons extra-virgin olive oil

1 tablespoon minced chives

Kosher salt

Freshly cracked black pepper

¼ cup Bacon Vinaigrette (page 59)

Preheat the oven to 425°F.

Cut off the turnip greens and rinse well, removing any large stems. Pat the greens with paper towels and chop into 1-inch pieces. Set aside.

Peel the turnips. If they are the size of golf balls, cut in half; if they are larger, cut into quarters.

Heat the oil in a roasting pan on the stove top over high heat until rippling. Carefully add the turnips, cut-side down, and cook until golden brown, about 2 minutes. Turn over the turnips and roast in the oven until fork-tender, about 10 minutes.

Remove from the oven and let cool for 3 to 5 minutes. Add the greens and chives to the pan and stir so they wilt slightly. Season with salt and pepper.

Transfer to a serving platter. Drizzle with the vinaigrette, scooping up an extra spoonful or two of the bacon lardons from the dressing to use as a garnish. The turnips will keep in the refrigerator, tightly sealed, for up to 3 days. Reheat in a 300°F oven.

braised collards with chopped ham hocks

makes 6 to 8 servings

1 tablespoon canola oil

1 pound smoked ham hocks

2 cups small-diced onions

1 tablespoon finely chopped garlic

1 cup beer, such as ale

2 quarts chicken stock (see page 49) or water

1¼ pounds collard greens, well washed and coarsely chopped

1½ tablespoons apple cider vinegar

Greens in general (collards, mustards, turnips, etcetera) are a staple of Southern cooking, so it's only natural that as a Southern transplant, I learned how to cook them. Tough greens like these are traditionally slow-cooked in a very porky, smoky, flavorful broth called potlikker to mellow their bitter flavor and soften their fibrous texture and are served in that broth with the whole ham bone or hock intact. There's no occasion necessary—greens are just always on the table.

My variation is to chop up the cooked hock into fine pieces, and spread it across the greens, which enhances the flavor and gives the dish an unexpectedly rich, meaty texture. And it ensures everyone gets a few bites of meat, as opposed to fighting over a whole bone. While I use collards in this recipe, the same technique can be applied to cooking mustard greens, turnip greens, kale, cabbage, beet tops, Swiss chard, and any other tough green you come across.

In a large sauté pan over medium-high heat, add the oil and heat until shimmering. Add the ham hocks and sear as evenly as possible on all sides, 7 to 9 minutes.

Transfer the hocks to a plate and set aside. Add the onions to the pan. Decrease the heat to medium and cook, stirring often, until the onions are golden brown, 5 to 7 minutes. Add the garlic and continue cooking until the onions are evenly browned and super-soft, 10 to 12 minutes total. Add the beer and reduce until almost completely evaporated, about 20 minutes. Add the stock or water and one-fourth of the greens. Return the hocks to the pan, nestling them in the greens, so they steam. Let the greens wilt enough to make room in the pan for another one-fourth, 5 to 7 minutes. Add the next batch of greens and repeat until all of the greens are in the pot.

Decrease the heat to a low simmer, partially cover the pan, and cook until you're able to easily pull the meat off the ham hocks, about 1 hour. Again, transfer the hocks to a plate and set aside to cool while you continue simmering the greens. When the hocks are cool enough to handle, pull off all of the meat, fat, and skin, and discard the bones. Coarsely chop the pork into small pieces and return them to the pan. Stir and simmer the greens for another 15 minutes. Just before serving, stir in the vinegar.

Serve the greens and pork with a few spoonfuls of the flavorful potlikker. Store leftovers, covered, in the refrigerator for up to 3 days. Reheat gently over low heat.

butter beans and rice

This recipe goes way back—it's one of the first things I ever learned to cook. When I was growing up, my dad made butter beans (aka lima beans) and rice, but his version was a pan of sausage with two cans of butter beans dumped on top, simmered together, and mashed up into a creamy, beany mess. That was a nostalgic dish for him, and when he taught me how to make it, it became a nostalgic dish for me too, though over the years I've adapted it, using a more sound technique.

Sometimes I simmer the beans with stock and Parmesan cheese rinds for an Italian flavor. Other times, I add sausage at the end, or whatever pork product my dad shows up with from Cajun country when he comes over for dinner. It's a versatile recipe; use what you like and have on hand.

Although this is a rustic dish, it's cooked carefully to maximize flavor from simple ingredients. On that note, use chicken stock if you have it, but water is totally fine instead; there's so much pork in here that it almost makes its own stock while cooking.

About 12 hours in advance, put the beans in a large bowl, cover with 3 to 4 inches of water, and soak for 10 to 12 hours. Drain and rinse. Limas have a thick skin, which gets papery and loose when soaked. Pick over the beans, and discard any loose skins that have separated from them.

In a large heavy-bottomed pot or Dutch oven, add the oil and heat over high heat until shimmering. Add the diced pork. As it starts to cook (it may sputter and splatter a bit, so use a screen if you have one), decrease the heat to medium-high and sear the meat, stirring occasionally, until the pork is golden on all sides and slightly crispy, about 10 minutes. As you cook, if you see any brown bits (fond) collecting on the bottom of the pot, scrape them off with your spoon and stir them back into the mixture to release their flavor.

Add the bacon or other cured pork product and cook, using the liquid it releases to scrape up any fond on the bottom of the pan, until the fat is mostly rendered and the meat is chewy, but not crisp, 8 to 10 minutes. With a slotted spoon or spider, remove the meat from the pot and set aside in a bowl.

Return the pot with the remaining fat to the stove, increase the heat to high, and immediately add the onions, bell pepper, poblano pepper,

CONTINUED

makes 4 to 6 servings

¾ cup large dried butter beans (aka lima beans) or dried red beans

1 tablespoon extra-virgin olive oil

1 pound boneless pork shoulder, medium diced

8 ounces bacon, guanciale, pancetta, or salt pork (slightly chilled in the freezer for easier dicing; see page 375), small diced

1½ cups small-diced onions

¾ cup small-diced green bell pepper

½ cup small-diced poblano pepper

1 tablespoon minced garlic

1½ quarts chicken stock (see page 49) or water

3 dried bay leaves

1 sprig rosemary

1 tablespoon thyme leaves

Kosher salt

Freshly cracked black pepper

1 tablespoon plus 2 teaspoons oregano leaves

½ cup chopped flat-leaf parsley leaves

2 to 3 cups hot freshly cooked white rice (see page 369)

Homemade Hot Sauce (page 62) or store-bought sauce (preferably Texas Pete's or Crystal)

and garlic. Cook, stirring frequently to avoid scorching, scraping up any fond on the bottom and sides of the pan, about 2 minutes. Decrease the heat to medium-high and continue cooking until the onions are soft and translucent and the peppers are wilted and shriveled, 8 to 10 minutes.

Return the pork to the pot and stir to combine. Add the beans to the pot, stir to combine, and pour in the chicken stock. The mixture should look loose and soupy at this point. Increase the heat to high, bring the mixture to a boil, and then decrease the heat to low. Add the bay leaves, rosemary, and thyme and cover the pot. Cook for 45 minutes, then remove and discard the rosemary. Continue cooking, covered, stirring occasionally, until the pork shoulder is falling-apart tender and the beans are creamy and breaking apart, 2½ to 3 hours. The ideal texture is more of a thick, starchy pork and bean gravy than a liquidy sauce or soup. Remove the bay leaves.

Season with salt and pepper—the amount of salt you add very much depends on the type of cured pork you used, which can change the salt level of the finished dish dramatically.

When ready to serve, stir in the oregano and parsley. Put the hot rice in a serving bowl, ladle the beans over the rice, and serve with hot sauce on the table. Store any leftovers, covered, in the refrigerator for up to 3 days. Reheat gently over low heat.

field peas in tomato gravy

My version of this classic was created to accompany a roasted pork dish at an outdoor event I cooked at years ago. They wanted me to make two dishes, so I decided to make a roasted pork shoulder with this gravy, but I also wanted the gravy to work as a stand-alone option for vegetarians (I used vegetable stock). This recipe nailed it. The dark roux gives that rich, quintessentially South Louisiana flavor, combined with that nice, hearty summertime field pea and tomato combination. You can serve this over rice, with meat, or just eat a bowl on its own, like stew. It's rich, yes, but also feels fresh because of the vegetables, so there's balance.

You can use any type of field pea here: black-eyed peas, crowder peas, purple hull peas, pinkeyes, or lima beans. If using frozen peas, rinse them under warm water to remove any freezer ice and to help them come up to temperature quickly.

Following the instructions on page 46, make a dark roux with the flour and peanut oil in a large sauté pan.

Add the onions and increase the heat to high. The roux will seize up a little, which is okay—stir it and allow the onions to cook, stirring often, for about 5 minutes. Add the bell pepper, celery, and garlic. Cook, stirring, for 1 to 2 minutes, so the vegetables break down a bit.

Add the stock or water and stir to dissolve the roux, 1 to 2 minutes. Stir in the tomato puree and ½ cup water. Add the field peas, 1 tablespoon of the thyme, the salt, and 5 grinds of black pepper and let the mixture come to a boil. Decrease the heat to low, cover the pot, and cook the peas at just below a simmer until they are completely tender, the sauce has thickened up a little, and the vegetables are very soft, about 1½ hours.

Taste and add more salt. Remove from the heat and stir in the parsley, green onions, and lemon juice. Stir and taste for seasoning again.

Transfer to a serving dish and garnish with the remaining 1 teaspoon of thyme. If you like, serve with rice. The peas will keep in the refrigerator, tightly covered, for up to 5 days. Reheat gently over low heat.

makes 6 to 8 servings

1 cup all-purpose flour

⅔ cup peanut oil

2 cups small-diced onions

1 cup small-diced red bell pepper

½ cup small-diced celery

2 tablespoons chopped garlic

2 cups chicken stock (see page 49), vegetable stock, or water, at room temperature

2 cups tomato puree

½ cup water

1½ pounds fresh or frozen field peas

1 tablespoon plus 1 teaspoon thyme leaves

2 teaspoons kosher salt, plus more as needed

Black peppercorns

¼ cup chopped flat-leaf parsley leaves

½ cup thinly sliced green onions, white and green parts

Juice of ½ lemon

3 to 4 cups hot, freshly cooked white rice (see page 369; optional)

lentil ragout

I'm a huge fan of lentils, which I fell in love with while working at Peristyle in the early 2000s. This is a beautiful ragout to enjoy hot, but you can also cool the lentils and use them a million ways—toss them into a salad or a sandwich wrap, or transform into a dip. They can do anything.

This recipe is a play on a classic French ragout in which lentils are cooked in a quick stew with root vegetables and stock and finished with a swirl of butter. It has a rich, hearty, almost earthy flavor with the root vegetables and thyme. You may swap out the vegetable components—try shiitake mushrooms or chopped kale in lieu of carrots or beets—this is more about technique and process than the specific ingredients, so let your preferences be your guide.

makes 6 to 8 servings

2 cups peeled, small-diced carrots

2 tablespoons extra-virgin olive oil

Kosher salt

2 cups peeled and small-diced red beets

1 quart water

1½ cups black lentils

2 dried bay leaves

¼ cup minced shallots

1 clove garlic, finely chopped

1 tablespoon thyme leaves

1 cup chicken stock (see page 49)

¼ cup unsalted butter

½ cup chopped flat-leaf parsley leaves

Freshly cracked black pepper

1 lemon wedge

NOTE

If at all possible, use home-made stock here—this is a recipe that truly benefits from the collagen in the real thing, which provides a better, stickier texture. At the restaurant, we make this dish with ½ cup of chicken stock and ½ cup of beef demi-glace (see page 50), which you should feel free to try if you have them on hand.

Preheat the oven to 375°F. Line a baking sheet with parchment paper.

In a mixing bowl, toss the carrots with 1½ teaspoons of the oil and a pinch of salt, making sure they're coated evenly. Arrange the carrots in one layer on one side of the baking sheet.

In the same bowl, toss the beets with another 1½ teaspoons of oil and a pinch of salt and spread out on the other half of the baking sheet. Roast until the vegetables are slightly soft and shriveled (but not mushy) and the edges are beginning to crisp, 35 to 45 minutes. Set aside to cool.

While the vegetables are roasting, cook the lentils. In a medium pot, bring the water to a boil over high heat. Add the lentils, bay leaves, and ½ teaspoon of salt. Let the mixture come to a boil, then decrease the heat to medium-low. Simmer for 20 minutes, and check for doneness—the lentils should be tender and slightly creamy, but not mushy. They should have a little bit of pop, but no chalkiness or raw flavor.

Remove the pot from the heat and drain the lentils through a fine-mesh strainer, discarding the cooking liquid and bay leaves. Rinse the lentils under cold water until the water runs clear, which also helps cool the lentils. Set aside.

Rinse and dry the cooking pot and place it over medium heat. Add the remaining 1 tablespoon of oil, and when shimmering, add the shallots and garlic and cook until tender and just barely light gold, 5 to 7 minutes. Stir in the thyme and let cook until it releases its aromas, about 1 minute.

Add the chicken stock to the pot, and increase the heat to bring to a boil. Reduce the volume of the liquid by half, 15 to 20 minutes.

Decrease the heat to medium-low and add the lentils, carrots, and beets to the pot. Gently stir together to allow everything to warm up, then decrease the heat to low and gently stir in the butter. Once the butter has melted, fold in the parsley.

Season with salt and pepper and a squeeze of lemon. The lentils will keep in the refrigerator, tightly covered, for up to 5 days. Reheat gently over low heat.

pearled barley with preserved lemon and dill

Barley is one of those foods that most people have eaten in a cereal or soup, but not as a stand-alone grain. It has a lovely, mildly nutty flavor that works well with brighter ones, and a slight chewiness that registers more as meaty than undercooked. In this application, I treat it as I would treat farro or freekeh in a grain salad, by cooking it, chilling it, and giving it a bright, acidic marinade to hang out in. Serve this as a side to a light fish or chicken dish, or alongside a heartier braised meat when it's chilly out—barley is versatile that way.

makes 4 servings

2 quarts water

1 cup pearled barley
(see Note)

⅓ cup Herb Pistou (page 57)

2 tablespoons finely chopped
Preserved Lemon Peel
(page 342)

1 lemon wedge

Kosher salt

Freshly cracked black pepper

2 tablespoons dill fronds

NOTE
Pearled barley is barley
that has been processed to
remove its hull and bran,
making it softer and faster to
cook; it is the most common
type of barley sold in grocery
stores. It's important to use a
high ratio of water to barley
so that the starch from the
barley can disperse into the
water; otherwise you'll end
up with starchy barley.

In a medium pot, bring the water to a boil. Add the barley and decrease the heat to medium-low. Simmer the barley until tender, but with a slight chewiness, 30 to 35 minutes (start tasting after 30 minutes, checking every minute thereafter to get to your desired texture).

Drain the barley and rinse with cold water. Spread out in a single layer on a baking sheet and set aside to cool to room temperature, about 30 minutes. At this point, the barley can be stored, covered, for up to 1 day in the refrigerator.

Place the barley in a large mixing bowl and stir in the pistou to combine. Fold in the preserved lemon. Squeeze the lemon wedge over the barley, season with salt and pepper, and stir to mix well. Taste and add more salt or pepper as needed.

Transfer the barley to a serving bowl and garnish with the dill. Store leftovers in the refrigerator for up to 3 days. Reheat gently over low heat.

buttered grits

The goal is to make these insanely rich grits taste like movie theater popcorn—salty, buttery, corny, and completely delicious. There's an almost (*almost*) outrageous amount of butter in these—don't eat them every day, even though you'll definitely want to. My sister, who used to hate grits, once said, "I don't know what the difference is, but these grits have made me a believer." I have yet to tell her why they're so good.

I can't help but notice the similarities between polenta and grits, so I treat them similarly: Bring the liquid to just under a boil, slowly whisk in the grits, then decrease the heat and stir frequently and for a long time, until they're perfectly creamy and tender. A lot of the success here has to do with getting the heat level just right—if the temperature is too high, the grits will be stiff, and if it's too low, they'll be wet. Just play around a little bit with the heat and keep a few tablespoons of extra milk (or water) on hand to adjust the texture so the grits stay creamy the entire time that they cook. If the grits seem too thin, just let them cook a little more. You really can't overcook grits.

makes 6 to 8 servings

1 quart water, plus more as needed

1 quart whole milk, plus more as needed

1½ cups medium-grind grits

¾ cup unsalted butter, cubed

1 tablespoon kosher salt, plus more as needed

In a medium pot, bring the water and milk to just under a boil, then slowly whisk in the grits and continue whisking, making sure there are no lumps, until the mixture comes up to temperature.

Decrease the heat to low, switch to a wooden spoon, and cook, stirring frequently, until the grits are creamy and tender. If you're lucky enough to be using very freshly stone-ground grits, this might only take 45 minutes, but if you're using store-bought grits that may have been sitting on the shelf for longer, it might take up to 1½ hours. Around the 45-minute mark, start tasting in 5-minute increments until the grits are to the consistency of your liking. Each time you stir the mixture, dislodge any grits that are beginning to thicken on the side or bottom of the pot to prevent them from overcooking into hard chunks. Adjust the consistency with a few tablespoons of water or milk if necessary.

Slowly stir in the butter and add the salt. Taste and stir in more salt as needed. Transfer to a shallow serving plate and serve hot. The grits can be held over very low heat for up to 2 hours before serving. Leftovers keep, refrigerated, for up 2 days. Reheat in a 300°F oven.

pommes anna-ish

I've been cooking these potatoes since the start of my career, because they're so good—I'm absolutely in love with them. When executed correctly, it's like having crispy golden brown potato chips on the outside and soft, smooth confit potatoes inside. The potatoes slowly cook and soften up in tons of butter, which solidifies when cooled, allowing you to cut the potatoes into any shape you like before giving them a final crisp in the oven.

This is based on a classic French dish, but a very tricked-out version— usually pommes Anna are done from start to finish in one pan and served right away. My stop-and-start method is helpful because it gives you a chance to assess what stage of cooking the potatoes are at and finish them accordingly, as opposed to the more watchful and vexing traditional process. Serve these any time you want potatoes alongside a piece of meat or fish, or even with fried eggs for breakfast.

makes 6 to 8 servings

4 russet potatoes

3 cloves garlic, mashed (see page 37)

2 sprigs thyme, plus 1 tablespoon leaves

¾ cup plus 3 tablespoons unsalted butter

1 tablespoon kosher salt

1½ teaspoons freshly cracked white pepper

1 tablespoon fleur de sel

Preheat the oven to 350°F.

Peel the potatoes and place them in a bowl filled with cold water as you go. You can let the potatoes sit in the water as you complete the next steps.

In a small pot, combine the garlic, thyme sprigs, and ¾ cup of the butter. Melt the butter over low heat, then set aside and let the garlic and thyme sprigs steep for 10 minutes.

Using a pastry brush, apply an even layer of melted butter to a 9-inch round cake pan. Line the pan with a sheet of parchment paper large enough to hang over the edge of the pan slightly, using the butter as an adhesive. The paper will help you unmold the cooked potatoes.

Working with one potato at a time, slice the potatoes into $1/16$-inch-thick rounds on a mandoline. Arrange the potatoes in a spiral in the pan, working from the outside in and overlapping the edges. When you have finished a layer, brush the potatoes with the garlic butter and sprinkle with the kosher salt and white pepper. Repeat until all of the potatoes are layered, in six to eight layers. If there's any butter left, pour it over the top of the potatoes.

Place another piece of parchment paper over the potatoes, pressing it gently against their surface, and bake until bubbling with hot butter and completely tender when poked with a skewer, about 1½ hours.

CONTINUED

Place a plate that is slightly smaller than the size of the pan the potatoes are in on top of the parchment. You don't need to weigh the plate down—the idea here is just to keep the top layer of the potatoes from curling up as they cool. Chill in the refrigerator until completely cool, at least 4 hours or up to overnight.

Once cool, remove the plate, and, using the bottom parchment paper, lift the potato "cake" onto a cutting board. Carefully peel off the top piece of parchment. (If it seems difficult to get the potatoes out of the pan in one piece, place the pan in a 400°F oven for 30 seconds to loosen up the solidified butter.) Cut the potatoes into wedges. At this point, the wedges can be stored, covered, in the refrigerator for up to 3 days.

Preheat the oven to 400°F.

Place two large cast-iron or nonstick skillets over medium-high heat, and melt the remaining 3 tablespoons butter, 1½ tablespoons in each skillet.

Arrange three wedges of potato in each pan and place the pans in the oven until golden brown and crispy on top, about 10 minutes. Remove the pan, gently flip the potatoes, and repeat on the second side. Remove from the oven and place on a rack to rest. Sprinkle with the fleur de sel and thyme leaves and serve warm.

classic potato salad

I have a real fondness for potato salad, which has one of those instantly recognizable, nostalgia-inducing flavors for so many. In South Louisiana, it's popular to put a scoop of potato salad in your gumbo, but at La Petite Grocery, I've surprised a few people by serving it alongside sweetbreads, fried oysters, caviar ... the list goes on. I firmly believe potato salad is the perfect accompaniment to all that and more.

My goal is to keep it simple. I want potato salad to taste like Grandma's version. I respect the classic form, even if I like to play around with what to serve it with. So this recipe is pretty bare-bones, with a simple herbaceous, creamy dressing. You can add hard-boiled eggs or crunchy things, like celery or pickles, if you really want, but at its core, this is what I think potato salad should be.

Dress the potatoes gently, without beating them up, which would make them starchy and gloopy—that's the secret to a perfect home-made potato salad and cafeteria potato salad. I like to just coat the potatoes and then let them sit in the refrigerator to soak up some of that creamy dressing. This way, they're still delicate and fluffy when you bite into them.

makes 8 servings

6 medium Yukon gold potatoes, peeled and cut into large dice

2 tablespoons minced shallots

2 tablespoons finely chopped tarragon

2 tablespoons minced chives

¼ cup finely chopped flat-leaf parsley

½ cup Aioli (page 65) or mayonnaise

2 tablespoons Dijon mustard

1½ teaspoons apple cider vinegar

1 small lemon

1 tablespoon kosher salt

Freshly cracked black pepper

Chervil leaves or additional parsley leaves for garnish

Place the potatoes in a large pot and cover with about 2 inches of water. Bring the water to a boil, then decrease the heat to medium-high, and boil until the potatoes are fully cooked and tender, about 15 minutes. They should mash when pressed gently with a spoon. Drain and then transfer to a baking sheet. Spread out in a single layer and set aside to cool completely to room temperature, about 1 hour.

Stir together the shallots, tarragon, chives, parsley, aioli, Dijon, and vinegar in a large mixing bowl. Using a Microplane, add three strokes of lemon zest. Halve the lemon, squeeze out 2 tablespoons of lemon juice, and add to the mixture. Add the salt and 5 grinds of black pepper. Add the potatoes to the mixing bowl and gently fold to evenly coat with the dressing.

Cover the mixing bowl with plastic wrap and store in the refrigerator for at least 4 hours or up to overnight. To serve, transfer to a platter and garnish with the chervil or parsley leaves and a few more shavings of lemon zest. The salad will keep in the refrigerator, tightly covered, for up to 4 days.

ricotta dumplings with parmesan and nutmeg

Light and luxurious all at once, these pillow-soft dumplings are an elegant, ethereal stand-alone appetizer or side. The first time a guest eats one, she is usually mystified—how did you get that texture? It's like biting into a warm, cheesy cloud. I focus on getting the best ricotta I can, and keep the rest of the dish simple, with just a little Parmesan for sharpness and nutmeg for aroma.

Bring a large pot of water to a boil and add the ¼ cup salt.

In a large mixing bowl, combine the drained ricotta, egg yolks, and remaining 1 teaspoon of salt. Fold together with a rubber spatula until blended. Sprinkle the flour over the ricotta mixture and, using your fingers, very gently incorporate, pressing lightly to avoid activating the gluten in the flour, which will make the cooked dumplings less tender. When properly mixed, the dough should feel like fresh ricotta—light, wet, and fluffy.

Make a tester dumpling by taking a pinch of the dough and forming it into a small, tubular dumpling about 1 inch long (like a Tater Tot) in the palm of your hand. Drop into the boiling water and cook until it floats. The goal is for the dumpling to hold together as it cooks and then is removed, while also achieving an extremely soft and pillowy texture, like airy cheese. If it doesn't hold together, there isn't enough flour in the dough; add more flour, 1 tablespoon at a time, and repeat the test until you have the right texture. It's important to add the flour in small increments, as too much flour leads to gummy dumplings. Ideally, you will nail the texture on the first or second test.

Once you've gotten the right texture, working on a well-floured surface, pat down the dumpling dough into a square about 1 inch thick. Cut the dough into 1-inch-wide strips about 5 inches long, and sprinkle some more flour on top.

Using your palms, very gently roll each strip into a 6-inch-long rope. Cut each rope into 1-inch-long pieces, which should resemble marshmallows. You should have about 20 dumplings. Gently move the dumplings from the work surface onto a rimless surface, like a floured cutting board, so you can easily scoot them off into the cooking water. (This helps them keep their shape when you transfer them to the pot—the less they're jostled,

makes 4 servings

¼ cup plus 1 teaspoon kosher salt

2 cups whole-milk ricotta, drained (see Note)

2 egg yolks

1 cup all-purpose flour, plus more as needed

5 tablespoons unsalted butter, melted

Freshly cracked white pepper

2 teaspoons freshly squeezed lemon juice

1 whole nutmeg

1 (2- to 3-ounce) chunk Parmesan (see Note)

NOTE
Avoid mass-produced ricottas for this dish, and seek out a low-moisture, thicker-curd version (sheep's milk, if possible) from a quality source. I like to press and drain even the best ricotta in a cheesecloth-lined colander or thin linen towel for a few hours to further reduce the moisture. The less water in the cheese, the less flour you have to use as a binder, making for a softer, more pillowy dumpling. The same holds true for the Parmesan; buy the highest-quality version you can find, preferably Parmigiano-Reggiano.

CONTINUED

the better.) At this point, the dumplings can be cooked immediately or refrigerated overnight (but not frozen) and cooked the next day.

Working in batches to avoid overcrowding, cook the dumplings in the boiling water until they float, about 3 minutes. Using a wire-mesh strainer, transfer the dumplings to a shallow bowl or serving platter, placing them in a single layer. Reserve ¼ cup of the cooking water to sauce the dumplings. (You use the cooking water, rather than fresh water, because the residual starch in the water from blanching the dumplings will help the sauce emulsify, and it has the added benefit of already being seasoned.)

In a mixing bowl, add the pasta-cooking water and the butter and stir to combine. Season with the remaining 1 teaspoon of salt, a few grinds of white pepper, and the lemon juice and stir again. Spoon the butter sauce evenly over the dumplings.

Using the smallest holes on a box grater, grate the nutmeg ten times over the dumplings, dusting the surface evenly. Grate the Parmesan over the dumplings and serve immediately.

hazelnut spaetzle with butternut squash and maple syrup

New Orleans is a brunch city—or, as I like to call it, second breakfast. At one time, restaurants in the French Quarter served a "late night" meal to butchers ending their shifts around 11 AM. Perfectly situated between breakfast and lunch for most people, the butcher's nightcap usually involved a mixture of sweet and savory components, just like this dish. Make it for breakfast, lunch, or at the end of a long overnight shift—there are no rules here.

Making spaetzle might seem complicated, but it's really closer to making pancakes than to rolling out noodles. One of my favorite accidental kitchen inventions was frying spaetzle in butter, which tasted like the ends of burnt pancakes. So I decided to fold in roasted butternut squash, and pour maple syrup on top of the whole thing.

In addition to a second breakfast, spaetzle can be served as a side for any fall or wintery dish, like the Rabbit Schnitzel on page 276 or Duck Confit on page 269.

makes 4 to 6 servings

2 cups medium-diced peeled butternut squash

2 tablespoons extra-virgin olive oil

1 teaspoon kosher salt

Freshly cracked black pepper

HAZELNUT SPAETZLE

½ cup buttermilk

3 eggs, beaten until frothy

2 cups all-purpose flour

Pinch of kosher salt, plus more as needed

Pinch of grated nutmeg

1½ cups chopped roasted hazelnuts (see Note)

¼ cup vegetable oil

1 tablespoon thyme leaves

3 tablespoons maple syrup

Flaky sea salt

Preheat the oven to 425°F. Line a baking sheet with parchment paper.

In a mixing bowl, toss the squash with the olive oil, salt, and a few cranks of pepper. Spread out on the prepared baking sheet in a single layer and roast until the squash is lightly browned around the edges and tender, 20 to 25 minutes. Set aside.

While the squash roasts, make the spaetzle: In a mixing bowl, combine the buttermilk and eggs and whisk vigorously until completely blended and liquidy (there should be no egg chunks floating around).

In a separate bowl, whisk together the flour, salt, and nutmeg. Whisk the egg-buttermilk mixture into the flour mixture. It should have the texture of a thick pancake batter. Fold in 1 cup of the chopped hazelnuts.

Tie one piece of kitchen twine across a large pot from handle to handle— it should look like a tightrope above the surface of the water. Fill the pot with water, salt well, and bring to a boil.

Place the spaetzle batter into a disposable pastry bag and cut the tip to about the diameter of a pencil. Twist the top of the bag and secure with a rubber band.

CONTINUED

hazelnut spaetzle with butternut squash and maple syrup, continued

NOTE
Roasted hazelnuts are commonly available, but you can easily toast raw hazelnuts, which will taste just as good: Spread the nuts in one even layer on a baking sheet. Toast in the oven at 325°F, checking and gently shaking after 7 minutes. They will start to release their oils and get very aromatic and change color. Remove after 10 to 12 minutes and rest until cool enough to handle before chopping.

Squeeze 1½-inch pieces of spaetzle into the boiling water, using the twine to cut the rope of batter that comes out of the bag cleanly for each piece. Working in batches if necessary to avoid crowding the pan, cook until the spaetzle float, about 2 minutes. Using a slotted spoon, transfer to a colander to drain and toss with 2 tablespoons of the vegetable oil to prevent sticking as they cool.

In a large cast-iron or nonstick skillet, heat the remaining 2 tablespoons of vegetable oil over high heat until shimmering. Add the spaetzle in a single layer and cook on one side until puffy and golden brown, 1 to 1½ minutes. Stir to turn over the spaetzle, and cook on the other side for 1 minute more.

Remove the pan from the heat and gently stir in the squash. Transfer the spaetzle to a serving bowl, sprinkle with the thyme, maple syrup, the remaining ½ cup of hazelnuts, and flaky sea salt. Serve immediately.

CONTINUED

black pepper mac-and-cheese with cornbread-crumb topping

This is an unholy but deeply delicious cross between cacio e pepe, pasta Alfredo, and mac-and-cheese, made Southern and slightly sweet with the addition of cornbread crumbs. My technique for making the crumbs is a little different from making regular cornbread: the batter is the same but I intentionally bake it in a thin layer so the crumbs will be crispy. They are also delicious sprinkled into soups and salads, and on top of stewed or braised meats. For the pasta, I sometimes use broken-up pieces of bucatini, but this dish is just as good with classic elbow macaroni.

makes 6 servings

1 recipe Cornbread (page 371), baked and cooled for 30 minutes

1½ cups macaroni or other small dried pasta

3 cups heavy cream

1½ cups grated pecorino cheese

1 tablespoon freshly cracked black pepper

½ teaspoon fleur de sel

1 sprig thyme, leaves picked from the stem

Preheat the oven to 225°F. Line a baking sheet with parchment paper.

Remove the cornbread from the pan, in hunks. Either by hand or by pulsing in a food processor, crumble the cornbread into pieces about the size of quinoa. Spread out the crumbs in an even layer on the prepared baking sheet, and bake until dry and crunchy, about 1½ hours.

Bring a large pot of salted water to a boil. Add the macaroni and cook for 2 minutes less than package instructions suggest, so it's slightly al dente. Drain the pasta and set aside to cool.

Preheat the broiler.

Pour the cream into a large saucepan over medium-high heat and bring to a full boil. Keep an eye on the pan—if the cream looks like it may boil over, simply remove the pan from the heat for 10 seconds, or until the cream level settles back down, and return the pan to the burner.

Once the cream reaches a boil, decrease the heat to medium and reduce the liquid for 6 to 8 minutes, until the bubbles have changed from frothy and foamy to dense and slightly viscous. Remove the pan from the heat and whisk in the pecorino and pepper.

Fold the cooked pasta into the cream mixture until it's well coated.

Spoon the pasta mixture into a 2-quart baking dish or soufflé dish and sprinkle 1½ cups of the cornbread crumbs over the top. (Reserve any leftover crumbs for another use. Store in an airtight container at room temperature for up to 3 days. Place the mac-and-cheese under the broiler for 1 to 2 minutes, until the top is golden brown and toasted, but not scorched.)

Garnish with the fleur de sel and thyme leaves. Serve immediately, straight out of the cooking vessel. Store leftovers, covered, in the refrigerator for up to 3 days. Reheat in a 300°F oven.

savory bread pudding

You don't see as many savory bread puddings as you do sweet ones, and that's a shame, because it's a fantastic way to use up old bread, which I always seem to have around. The combination of the aromatics here and the custardy texture make this a worthwhile starch in lieu of a rice or pasta dish. It's particularly awesome when served with meat dishes that have a lot of gravy or sauce, like braised short ribs (see page 293), Sticky Chicken (page 252), or even brisket and kale stew (see page 205). It functions like a Yorkshire pudding, soaking up all of the savory juices. Sometimes I even smother it with the demi-glace on page 50, or a variation of a red wine and mushroom gravy or chicken velouté, a rich white sauce made with chicken stock and roux. But this bread pudding is flavorful enough to stand as its own side, with or without toppings.

makes 8 servings

2 tablespoons unsalted butter

2 cups heavy cream

2 cups whole milk

3 eggs

12 cups day-old crusty bread, torn into rough 1-inch cubes

1 teaspoon chopped garlic

1 tablespoon minced shallot

2 teaspoons thyme leaves

2 teaspoons kosher salt

Freshly cracked black pepper

Coat the inside of a 9 x 13-inch casserole dish with the butter. In a large mixing bowl, combine the cream, milk, and eggs, whisking to combine until smooth and lump free. Add the bread, garlic, shallot, thyme, salt, and a few grinds of pepper.

Using clean hands, work this mixture together until evenly combined and the bread is saturated with the cream and eggs; give the bread a few squeezes to help it develop a spongelike feel and soak up the creamy coating.

Transfer the bread mixture to the prepared casserole dish and place in the refrigerator to soak for a minimum of 1 hour or up to 2 hours. This soak will help the bread pudding get that custardy, creamy, pudding texture while it bakes.

Preheat the oven to 350°F.

Remove the dish from the refrigerator and cover with foil. Bake for 1 hour, then remove the foil and bake for another 30 minutes, or until the pudding is golden brown around the edges, but the center is still slightly jiggly and custardlike.

Serve hot. Store leftovers, covered, in the refrigerator for up to 3 days. Reheat in 300°F oven.

salads

I'll admit that New Orleans food, with its roux, sauces, and shellfish, can veer toward heavy if you don't balance it out with some green. Fortunately, we're surrounded by incredible produce here, which makes for ample salad-eating opportunities. I like to enjoy salads based on how I feel—sometimes I want a crunchy, lettuce-based side salad with a classic Green Goddess Dressing (page 67), and sometimes I want a spinach salad that's loaded with smoked bacon and cheese (see page 159) as an entree. This chapter contains recipes for both—and a lot more in between.

Although there's certainly a place in my kitchen for a simple green salad, I generally like to make salads that are a little more interesting. A lot of them don't even contain lettuce. I might, for example, decide to char my cucumbers before mixing them with mint and chile vinegar (see page 160), or use broccoli stems in lieu of romaine leaves in a not-so-classic Caesar (see page 165). I like that element of surprise, and salads offer so many opportunities to play around with colors, textures, techniques, and ingredients.

Given that salads revolve around vegetables, they're a good way to get in touch with seasonality—the celery root and apple recipe on page 168, for example, is definitely a dish for fall, when both of those ingredients are at their peak, whereas the Mediterranean-leaning summer squash salad with crushed-olive vinaigrette on page 164 is, as its name implies, best when local summer squash are ripe.

I can't talk about salads without talking about dressings, of course. The dressing makes the salad, and enhances our understanding about the flavor balance of fat, acid, and salt. Creamy Green Goddess Dressing pairs well with delicate butter lettuce but isn't necessarily the ideal choice for juicy cucumbers, which can stand up to a sharper, more acidic vinaigrette. But most vegetables, given that they don't have a lot of fat or acid, act nicely as a vehicle for acidic vinaigrettes, which you can use to brighten a vegetable and coax out its best flavor.

Salads also showcase technique. Mastering the cold egg yolk emulsions introduced in the Stocks, Sauces & Dressings chapter is key to perfecting creamy dressings, such as the Tarragon Emulsion (page 70) and the Caesar Dressing (page 71). I'll also show you how to make a classic vinaigrette with vinegar and oil, emulsifying those two to form a looser, more acidic dressing. There's a salad for every mood and every season in this chapter.

butter lettuce with green goddess dressing, toasted almonds, and shaved radishes

makes 4 to 6 servings

¼ cup sliced almonds

2 heads Bibb lettuce

¾ cup Green Goddess
Dressing (page 67)

1 teaspoon kosher salt

Freshly cracked black pepper

3 radishes, very thinly sliced

2 tablespoons dill fronds

2 tablespoon chives, cut into
½-inch batons

2 tablespoons torn
mint leaves

2 tablespoons extra-virgin
olive oil

Sometimes you just want a leafy green salad that's not too fussy. This is that salad. But simple doesn't mean boring—this has a punch of flavor from the dressing, and a ton of crunch and succulence from the Bibb lettuce. The result is so satisfying that we keep this salad on our menu at La Petite at all times.

Preheat the oven to 325°F. Spread out the almonds in an even layer on a baking sheet and toast until fragrant and golden brown, checking after 5 minutes and toasting for up to 10 minutes. Set aside to cool.

Peel off and discard the outer leaves of the Bibb lettuce (the ones that look overly floppy and extra green). Start removing the more tender interior leaves (the ones that are yellowish green and feel more firm) and place them in a colander. Rinse under cold water and dry with clean kitchen towels. Alternatively, if you have a salad spinner, this is the time to use it, working in batches and cranking for 10 seconds or so, allowing the spin to slow until it stops on its own each time.

In a large mixing bowl, combine the lettuce and the dressing, gently tossing to evenly coat the leaves. Sprinkle with the salt from 12 inches above to ensure even seasoning, and give one more gentle toss.

Transfer to a serving bowl and grind a generous amount of black pepper over the top.

Add the radishes and sprinkle in the toasted almonds. Add the dill, chives, and mint; drizzle with the oil; and serve immediately.

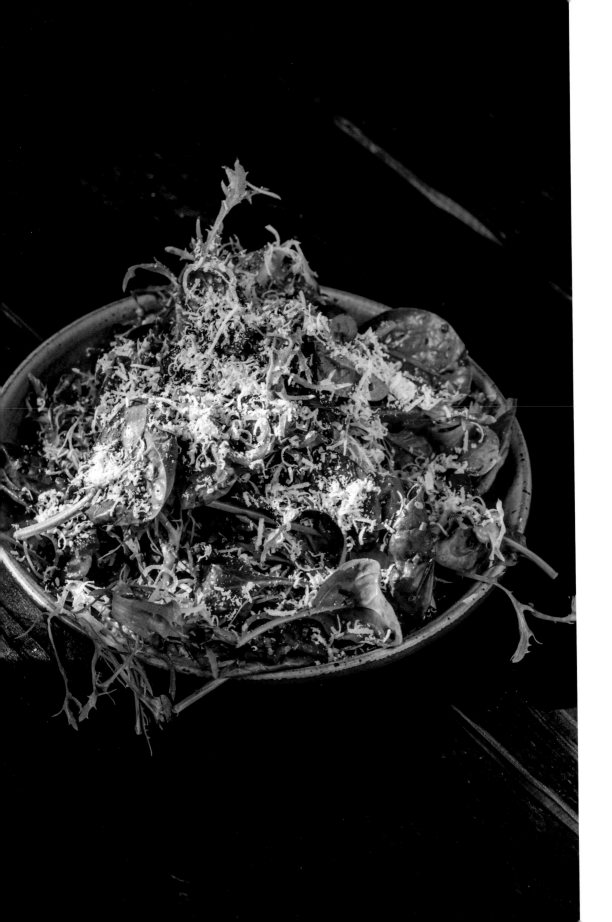

warm spinach and frisée salad with pickled shallots, bacon, and ricotta salata

This is the kind of recipe to turn to when you want to eat a salad for a main course. The frisée is slightly bitter and crunchy, and the spinach wilts a bit beneath the warm vinaigrette, making for a hearty riff on a classic Lyonnaise salad. While the traditional version usually involves a fried egg, I like to use ricotta salata instead. It adds a similarly soft, milky note that helps cut through some of the strong, pungent flavors in the bowl (hello, pork fat and bitter greens).

Remove the outer leaves of the frisée, discarding any brown or damaged parts. Keep the tender inner leaves (the ones that are yellowish white). Remove the bases of the heads and separate the leaves. Give the leaves a good wash to remove any sand or dirt. Wash the spinach as well and dry in a spinner or with clean kitchen towels. Place the greens and shallots in a large bowl and set aside.

Cut the bacon or pancetta into ¼-inch lardons. Line a plate with paper towels. Add the bacon to a sauté pan over medium-high heat. Cook until the bacon releases its fat (it should bubble and look slightly foamy) and begins to fry, about 7 minutes. When the lardons are brown and crispy, use a slotted spoon to transfer them to the paper towels and discard the fat from the pan, leaving the residual coating of bacon fat in the pan. Decrease the heat to medium and add the vinaigrette to the pan to deglaze, using a wooden spoon to loosen the flavorful bits stuck on the bottom of the pan (the fond) and release them into the sauce.

Add the bacon and vinaigrette to the bowl with the greens. Add the chives. Toss together and taste. Season with the salt if necessary. Transfer the salad to a serving bowl and garnish with the ricotta salata and a few grinds of pepper.

makes 6 to 8 servings

2 heads frisée

1 cup baby spinach leaves

2 tablespoons Pickled Shallots (page 352)

2 slices bacon or pancetta (see page 375)

3 tablespoons Brown Butter Vinaigrette (page 55)

1 tablespoon chopped chives

¼ to ½ teaspoon kosher salt (optional, depending on the saltiness of the bacon)

¼ cup grated ricotta salata

Freshly cracked black pepper

charred cucumber-mint salad with pickled shallot, cane vinegar, and piment d'espelette

makes 4 to 6 servings

2 cucumbers, at room temperature

2 tablespoons Pickled Shallots (page 352)

10 torn mint leaves

¼ cup cane vinegar (see Note)

1 tablespoon extra-virgin olive oil

1½ teaspoons piment d'Espelette (see page 32)

1½ teaspoons fleur de sel

NOTE

I like using cane vinegar, which is made from fermented sugarcane syrup and has a mellow, malty flavor. You can order it online, or substitute any other vinegar that's slightly acidic and not too sweet, such as malt, apple cider, white wine, or Banyuls vinegar.

Most everyone in the South with a garden has cucumbers in the summer, and most everyone in the South has a childhood memory of eating them dressed simply with vinegar, salt, and pepper. It's a classic picnic dish that I like to give a slightly more interesting flavor profile.

Here you get the experience of a charred vegetable in an ice-cold salad, with a strong spike of vinegar, aromatic red pepper, and the sharp contrast of pickled shallots. Mixed with the cool melon flavor of the cucumber itself, it's an incredibly refreshing summertime salad.

Preheat your grill to its hottest setting, or heat a cast-iron grill pan over high heat until screaming hot if cooking indoors. (If your grill doesn't get very hot, use the pan—you will need searing heat for this.) Place the cucumbers on the heat and char the skin all over, cooking them as quickly as possible to avoid liquefying their insides, ideally no longer than 3 minutes. Refrigerate the cucumbers until completely chilled, about 45 minutes.

Slice one cucumber into thin rounds. Cut the other into chunks by halving and quartering it lengthwise, and then cutting those quarters crosswise into ½-inch pieces. Transfer the cucumber rounds and chunks to a mixing bowl and toss evenly with the pickled shallots and half of the mint leaves.

Transfer the cucumbers to a serving platter with a low rim to collect the juices and vinegar. Spoon the vinegar directly over the cucumbers and scatter the remaining mint leaves over the top. Drizzle with the oil and season with the piment d'Espelette and fleur de sel. Serve immediately.

shaved summer squash salad with fresh herbs and crushed-olive vinaigrette

This is my antidote to mushy cooked summer squash, which is what can happen when it sits. Instead of cooking the squash, I shave it raw and toss with the vinaigrette. The finished product is crunchy, fresh-tasting squash, livened up with fresh herbs and the brininess of the crushed olives and vinegar—perfect for those long, late-summer nights.

makes 6 to 8 servings

3 summer squashes, such as zucchini, crooked neck, or straight neck

6 pattypan squashes (if unavailable, use 2 additional summer squashes)

1 teaspoon kosher salt

2 tablespoons freshly squeezed lemon juice

2 tablespoons extra-virgin olive oil

Freshly cracked black pepper

1 tablespoon snipped chives

½ cup Crushed-Olive Vinaigrette (page 58)

24 oregano leaves

6 to 10 basil leaves

Using a knife or a mandoline, slice the summer squashes into thin coins about $\frac{1}{16}$ inch thick. Cut the pattypan squashes into quarters or sixths, depending on their size, for variety of texture.

Place all the squash in a mixing bowl and season with the salt. Set aside for about 5 minutes—as it sits, the salt will start to pull water out of the squash, making the texture of the vegetable slightly more pliable, and therefore easier to make into a salad.

Add the lemon juice, oil, and 2 grinds of pepper to the bowl. Add the chives and gently toss to incorporate. Place the squash salad on a large platter and spoon the vinaigrette over the top. Tear the oregano and basil by hand and distribute evenly over the dish. Finish with a last grind of pepper and serve immediately.

broccoli caesar with torn croutons and piave vecchio

Broccoli appears to be making a bit of a comeback after years of being considered uncool or "untasty," and I'm glad it's finally getting the respect it deserves. This salad features partially cooked and then cooled broccoli in its crunchy form, as opposed to blanched or steamed, though you could make it using fully raw, roasted, or grilled florets. However cooked, broccoli has long been a vehicle for sauce (think cheesy broccoli casserole, or mayo-based salads), so recruiting broccoli to masquerade as the lettuce in a Caesar isn't much of a stretch. It's also a nice way to use the stems, which are often tossed, but here provide a nice, clean crunch.

makes 6 to 8 servings

3 quarts water

Kosher salt

2 bunches broccoli

½ cup Caesar Dressing (page 71)

1 cup Torn Croutons (page 370)

Freshly cracked black pepper

1 tablespoon extra-virgin olive oil

1 tablespoon oregano leaves

3 ounces Piave Vecchio or Parmesan cheese

Set up a bed of clean kitchen towels on your counter. Set up a salted ice water bath (see page 35) near your stove, using 1 tablespoon of salt. In a large pot, bring the water to a boil with 1 tablespoon of salt.

Cut off the large stems of the broccoli and set aside. Break the tops into bite-size florets, add them to the boiling water, and cook for 1½ minutes. Transfer with a slotted spoon to the ice bath to stop the cooking.

While the broccoli florets cool, peel the stems and trim off any blemishes. Slice the stems into thin coins and place in a large mixing bowl. Drain the broccoli florets in a colander, dry with a clean kitchen towel, and add to the bowl with stems. Add 2 teaspoons of salt and the dressing and toss to combine, working the dressing in a little bit without breaking up the broccoli too much. Add the croutons and toss together once more.

Transfer the salad to a serving platter and grind the pepper over the top. Drizzle with the oil and sprinkle with the oregano leaves. Use a Microplane to finely shave a big, fluffy pillow of cheese over the top just before serving.

chilled beet salad with tarragon emulsion

Beets are a well-known match for cool, creamy things such as goat cheese, crème fraîche, and sour cream (as you often see in Eastern European cooking). This is my version of the classic combo, taking the French flavor of tarragon and aioli and turning it into the condiment. Served cold, this is a refreshing take on a time-tested combination.

When it comes to the beets themselves, feel free to use any type you'd like, though yellow beets are less messy than red. Roasting them this way makes peeling a cinch; if the skins don't come off easily, the beets likely weren't roasted long enough, so veer toward over-cooking if you're not sure where the skins stand.

makes 6 servings

3 large yellow or red beets

½ cup Tarragon Emulsion (page 70)

1 teaspoon kosher salt

¼ cup Pickled Shallots (page 352)

2 tablespoons tarragon leaves

2 tablespoons snipped chives

Extra-virgin olive oil for drizzling

Freshly cracked black pepper

Preheat the oven to 400°F.

Trim off the tops and bottoms of the beets. (Reserve the greens for another use, such as braising them with ham hocks—see page 120—or cooking them in a little butter with shallots.)

Place the beets in a shallow pan. Add ½ inch of water and cover with foil. Roast until tender when poked with a skewer, about 1 hour. Remove and chill completely in the refrigerator.

Peel the beets by working the chilled skins off with your thumbs (you may want to use gloves to avoid dyeing your hands red if using red beets). Cut the beets into bite-size wedges.

In a large bowl, fold the beets and the emulsion together. Add the salt and fold again. Place the beets on a serving platter and garnish with the pickled shallots, tarragon, and chives. Drizzle with oil, grind fresh black pepper over the top, and serve. Store leftover salad in the refrigerator, covered, for up to 2 days.

celery root and apple salad with blue cheese, toasted walnuts, and fresh herbs

makes 4 servings

WHITE WINE VINAIGRETTE

½ cup white wine vinegar

¼ cup Dijon mustard

2 teaspoons sugar

1½ cups vegetable oil

Kosher salt

Freshly cracked black pepper

½ cup walnut halves

1 small celery root, peeled and cut into matchsticks

2 Gala apples, cored, seeded, and thinly sliced

2 teaspoons thyme leaves

2 teaspoons finely chopped flat-leaf parsley leaves

1 teaspoon finely chopped tarragon leaves

1 teaspoon finely chopped chives

2 ounces crumbled blue cheese

Kosher salt

Freshly cracked black pepper

This was one of the first salads I put on the menu at La Petite Grocery when I took over in 2007, and it makes a repeat appearance every fall, when the weather cools off a little and apples come into season. It's a delightfully crunchy, acidic, slawlike salad with toasty nuts and sharp blue cheese, that leans toward a classic Waldorf.

I like to use a mandoline for speed-slicing at the restaurant, but a sharp chef's knife suffices when making it at home. Just be sure the celery root is well peeled and sliced uniformly thin so you get the flavor but not the woodiness of raw celery root. And don't skip the tarragon—that's what really sets things off here, with its sweet, licorice-y flavor that goes so well with apples and blue cheese.

The vinaigrette is fairly straightforward. You can use it on other salads, and also modify it by adding fresh herbs and spices. That said, I particularly like it here because the acidity in the white wine vinegar balances the tartness of the apples, and allows their sweet, fruity flavor to shine through.

To make the vinaigrette: In a small bowl, whisk together the vinegar, Dijon, and sugar. Whisk in the oil. Taste and season with salt and pepper. The vinaigrette will keep, tightly covered, in the refrigerator for up to 3 days.

Preheat the oven to 325°F.

Spread out the walnuts in an even layer on a baking sheet and toast until fragrant and golden brown, checking after 5 minutes and cooking for up to 10 minutes. Set aside to cool, about 10 minutes.

In a large bowl, combine the celery root, apples, thyme, parsley, tarragon, chives, cheese, and walnuts. Dress the salad generously with the vinaigrette, toss gently, and taste. Season with salt and pepper and serve immediately.

poached shrimp and green bean salad with buttermilk dressing

My method for poaching shrimp is a little different than most, but it ensures that they won't be dry or overcooked, which is a terrible thing to do to shrimp, especially the super-fresh ones from the Gulf that we get here in New Orleans. The poaching liquid is an aromatic broth with light, subtle flavors, which are enhanced by the acidity of the white wine vinegar. Poaching the shrimp in that liquid very briefly helps tighten them up as they cool, giving each one that perfect curled shape and a tender, silky texture.

To poach the shrimp: Fill a large stockpot with water and add the vinegar, bay leaves, garlic, salt, peppercorns, and lemon zest and juice. Bring to a boil over high heat. Add the shrimp and remove from the heat. Let the shrimp sit in the poaching liquid until they just start to turn white, but don't look completely cooked through, 1 to 1½ minutes.

Using a wire skimmer, transfer the shrimp to a large platter in a single layer. Place the platter in the refrigerator until the shrimp are chilled through, about 2 hours. As they cool, the residual heat will continue to "cook" the shrimp slightly, and they will solidify.

Arrange a bed of clean kitchen towels on your counter. Set up a salted ice water bath (see page 35) near your stove, adding 1 tablespoon of salt. The salted ice water bath ensures your green beans will stay well seasoned through every step. (Shocking them—or stopping the residual heat from further cooking them—in plain ice water would wash off the seasoning they get during blanching.)

Bring a large pot of salted water to a boil. Add the green beans and blanch for 2 minutes. They should still have a raw-vegetable crunch and be very bright green in color. Using the wire skimmer, transfer the beans to the ice water bath and shock them for 1 minute, then move them to the kitchen towels to drain. I like keeping the green beans whole, but if desired, you may cut them into 1½-inch pieces so they're bite-size.

In a large mixing bowl, gently toss the shrimp, green beans, and dressing and arrange on a serving platter. Taste and add salt if needed. Scatter the pickled shallots around the salad and garnish with the dill and chives.

makes 4 to 6 servings

POACHED SHRIMP

¾ cup white wine vinegar

4 dried bay leaves

4 cloves garlic, mashed (see page 37)

1 teaspoon kosher salt

1 teaspoon black peppercorns

Zest and juice of 2 lemons (remove the zest in strips), plus juice of 2 additional lemons

1½ pounds (12-count) wild shrimp, shelled, deveined, and split in half lengthwise

Kosher salt (optional)

1 pound green beans, trimmed

½ cup Buttermilk Dressing (page 66)

¼ cup Pickled Shallots (page 352)

½ cup chopped dill fronds

½ cup chopped chives (¼-inch pieces)

blue crab and tomato salad with artichoke-yogurt dressing

This is a cool, refreshing, juicy salad that makes the most out of the crown jewels of a New Orleans summer—tomato, cucumber, and crab—which are all at their peak at the same time. I love providing a creamy element in the dressing without relying on a heavy egg-based emulsification. Use high-quality, live-culture yogurt here to get the best results. The yogurt is the vehicle for bringing the artichokes into the salad and really captures their flavor. The resulting dressing is almost like an artichoke dip, but a whole lot fresher and cleaner.

makes 6 servings

ARTICHOKE-YOGURT DRESSING

1 gallon water

1 tablespoon kosher salt, plus more as needed

4 large artichokes

1 cup plain full-fat Greek yogurt

2 tablespoons freshly squeezed lemon juice

Freshly cracked black pepper

8 ounces fresh blue crabmeat, lump or jumbo lump, picked over for shells

1 pound ripe tomatoes, preferably heirloom (see Note)

1 cucumber, thinly sliced into rounds

Kosher salt

Freshly cracked black pepper

2 tablespoons extra-virgin olive oil

¼ cup coarsely chopped dill fronds

¼ cup torn basil leaves

2 tablespoons mint leaves

NOTE

Buy the tomatoes that look best at the market—you can use a mix of cherries and heirlooms. They don't need to be uniform, but they should taste perfectly ripe.

To make the dressing, start by cooking the artichokes: In large stockpot, combine the water with the salt and bring to a boil over high heat. Peel off the outer leaves of each artichoke. Cut ½ inch off the bottom of the stem, and about 1 inch off the top of the artichoke. Place the artichokes in the pot, decrease the heat to medium, and cook at a low boil until very soft and almost falling apart, about 1½ hours. Transfer to a platter and set aside until cool enough to handle, about 15 minutes.

Once cool, remove the artichoke leaves. Using a spoon, scrape the meat off the inner leaves. (Feel free to snack on the outer leaves while you work.) Clean the fibrous parts from the heart and stems. Chop the hearts very finely, almost into a puree (you should have 1½ to 2 cups).

In a medium mixing bowl, mix the mashed artichoke with the yogurt to fully combine. Fold in the lemon juice and season with salt and pepper. Cover and chill in the refrigerator for at least 30 minutes or up to 1 day.

When ready to serve, fold the crabmeat into the dressing. Cut the tomatoes into irregular bite-size pieces.

Spoon the artichoke-crab mixture onto a serving platter in an even layer. Randomly place the tomatoes across the top and intersperse the cucumbers. Season with salt and pepper, drizzle with the oil, and top with the dill, basil, and mint. Serve immediately.

soups & stews

I've always been a big soup person; I love making it and eating it in equal measure. For many years, while working in professional kitchens, I made soup every single day, and I always took pride in it, so soups have a special place in my heart. They aren't just a way to recycle leftover vegetable and meat scraps—they should be treated with great respect.

Soups can showcase the most refined cooking techniques, or they can go rough and rustic. Both directions are equally valuable; this wide variety is what draws me to them.

The recipes in this chapter demonstrate the diversity of style, flavor, texture, and technique in the soup universe. New Orleans loves its soup—most famously, gumbo, but also Creole tomato soup, oyster-Brie soup, crab-artichoke soup, and more. It has always amused me that in this swampy, humid city, these rich, heavy soups are so popular, but that's just how we do it here. When I'm cooking at home, I usually take a lighter approach, swapping pureed vegetables for roux and cutting back on cream. The lobster chowder on page 188, for example, is thickened with blitzed cauliflower instead of cream, though it's just as rich and velvety as the traditional version.

Of course, there are some heartier recipes here. The gumbo on page 201 is made with duck and andouille; its success ultimately relies on mastering the roux technique on page 46. The Chicken and Black-Eyed Pea Soup (page 198) is chunky and brothy (pure comfort food in the style of my mom's cooking), while the Pumpkin and Shellfish Bisque with Pumpkin Seed Pistou (page 195) might be served as a first course at a fancy fine-dining restaurant. One of the things I love about soup is its power to transform even the humblest ingredients. The parsnip soup on page 184, made from a lowly root vegetable, is one of the most decadent recipes in this book.

Soups are a particularly easy place to get creative and tweak recipes according to your personal style and preferences. Many of the ones offered here are about the technique more than the specific ingredients. The lobster chowder recipe, for example, is really about learning to use cauliflower in lieu of dairy, which you could easily employ in another creamy soup. The Chicken and Black-Eyed Pea Soup is, at its core, about simmering country ham, legumes, and herbs together to make a comforting broth, into which you can add all kinds of vegetables and meat. Try new things here—soups are forgiving and flexible like that.

caramelized onion soup with smoked bacon and blue cheese

This is my version of French onion soup. The ingredients are mostly the same, but I puree the soup and pass it through a strainer to make a silky-smooth broth, garnished with bacon and cheese. It's rich, luscious, velvety, and very comforting, especially in the winter (which lasts about six nights a year here in New Orleans, but that's beside the point).

It's important to take the time to caramelize the onions right. It's not a quick job, and it takes a whole lot of raw onions to make not a lot of caramelized onions, but it's worth it. I like to make a large quantity and keep leftovers in my refrigerator, to have on hand. For this reason, I recommend cooking the onions in oil rather than butter, which resolidifies in the refrigerator and leaves you with a big, cold brick of onions. With oil you get beautifully jammy, soft onions you can scoop out as needed.

Finally, if possible, get yourself a hunk of slab bacon (check out Benton's Smoky Mountain Country Hams or Col. Bill Newsom's Kentucky hams), which you can cut into pieces that are big enough to render and cook up chewy, as opposed to the thin presliced stuff, which cooks up very crispy.

makes 6 servings

½ cup plus 1 tablespoon canola oil

6 large yellow onions, thinly sliced

5 cloves garlic

1 sprig thyme

2 quarts chicken stock (see page 49)

4 or 5 slices white bread, crusts cut off and discarded, bread torn into bite-size chunks to make 2½ cups

About 5 strips thick-cut bacon, cut crosswise into matchsticks about ¼ inch thick to make ½ cup

Kosher salt

Freshly cracked black pepper

1½ ounces high-quality blue cheese, crumbled (see Note)

NOTE

You may substitute goat cheese or the traditional grated Gruyère for blue cheese, if desired.

Heat 1 tablespoon of the oil in a large heavy-bottomed pot over high heat until rippling. Add the onions, stir to coat, then decrease the heat to medium-low and cook, stirring frequently, until the onions are a golden caramel color, about 1 hour.

Meanwhile, place the garlic in a small saucepan and cover with the remaining ½ cup of oil. Cook over low heat until lightly toasted and softened, about 40 minutes.

Add the thyme sprig to the onions, then add the chicken stock. Strain the garlic cloves and add them to the pot. Bring to a boil, then decrease the heat and simmer for 20 minutes. Remove from the heat. Add the bread to the pot and let stand for 10 minutes, or until the bread has become soft and saturated with liquid.

While the bread soaks, cook the bacon. Line a plate with paper towels. Heat a small sauté pan over medium heat. Add the bacon and cook

CONTINUED

caramelized onion soup with smoked bacon and blue cheese, continued

slowly, stirring, so it releases its fat, until crispy and dark red in color, about 10 minutes. Drain on paper towels and set aside.

Working in batches, starting on low speed and working up to high, puree the soup in a blender until completely smooth. Pass the mixture through a fine-mesh strainer.

Season the soup with salt and pepper and adjust the consistency by adding water, if needed, 1 tablespoon at a time. Ladle into individual bowls, garnish with the bacon and blue cheese, and serve. Store leftover soup, without the garnishes, in an airtight container in the refrigerator for up to 3 days.

winter greens and vegetable soup

Sometimes you hit cooking ruts in the winter, when fresh produce feels so far away. But there's still a lot you can work with, like greens and root vegetables—the perfect combination for winter doldrums.

Here the sweet, earthy flavor of the root vegetables plays off the rough, fibrous greens; both are enlivened by the bright, herbaceous pistou added at the very end. I use chicken stock here because I like the flavor of roasted bones, but you can make this just as rich and delicious with vegetable stock, or even water.

Use as much pistou as you like. It keeps well, and if you have extra, it's fantastic on anything savory that needs a kick of herbs, such as roasted meats or vegetables, or even as a dip for crusty bread.

makes 6 to 8 servings

1 tablespoon extra-virgin olive oil

½ cup small-diced onion

⅓ cup small-diced celery

⅓ cup small-diced fennel bulb, stalks and fronds reserved

2 cloves garlic, finely chopped

½ bunch lacinato kale, stems removed, washed, and chopped into 1-inch pieces

½ bunch Swiss chard, chopped into 1-inch pieces

½ cup dry white wine

1½ quarts chicken stock (see page 49) or vegetable stock or water

⅓ cup medium-diced peeled carrots

⅓ cup medium-diced peeled parsnip

⅓ cup medium-diced peeled celery root

Juice of 1 lemon

1 tablespoon kosher salt

Freshly cracked black pepper

½ cup finely chopped flat-leaf parsley leaves

¼ cup finely chopped chives

3 tablespoons finely chopped tarragon leaves

6 tablespoons Herb Pistou (page 57)

Heat the oil in a large pot over high heat until shimmering. Add the onion and cook, stirring occasionally, until tender, about 5 minutes. Add the celery, fennel, and garlic and cook, stirring often, until they are all softened and any liquid they've released has evaporated, 7 to 9 minutes.

Add the kale, chard, and wine. Cook for 2 minutes, to steam and wilt the greens. Add the stock or water. Add the carrots, parsnips, and celery root and bring to a boil, then decrease the heat to a low simmer and cook uncovered, stirring occasionally, until the greens and vegetables are tender, 45 minutes to 1 hour.

Just before serving, stir in the lemon juice, salt, a few grinds of pepper, the parsley, chives, and tarragon. Divide evenly among bowls, garnish each bowl with about 1 tablespoon of the pistou, and serve. Store leftovers in an airtight container in the refrigerator for up to 3 days.

brown butter–parsnip soup with pecorino and sage

makes 4 to 6 servings

1 cup unsalted butter

2 cups diced peeled parsnips

2 shallots, diced

1 teaspoon chopped fresh rosemary leaves

10 sage leaves

1 quart chicken stock
(see page 49)

1 cup heavy cream

1 teaspoon kosher salt

1 teaspoon freshly cracked white pepper

¼ cup vegetable oil

3-ounce wedge pecorino

I've always been a big fan of pureed soups, especially ones that involve emulsifying brown butter into vegetables, which delivers a new level of richness and flavor. This is a rather decadent soup, bolstered with a dark-roasted broth and pecorino for a hit of sharp, funky flavor. It's not a classic, per se, but it is luxurious, with an old-school French vibe. I have been known to shave black truffles or incorporate little pieces of seared foie gras into it, although that's by no means required.

Sage is a classic foil for nutty brown butter, and in this soup it also balances the sweet root vegetable flavor of the roasted parsnips. As elegant as this soup is, my favorite thing about it is that it's made from humble, all-too-often forgotten parsnips, which are inexpensive and available just about everywhere.

Preheat the oven to 400°F.

In a medium saucepan, melt the butter over medium heat, and continue to cook until the water has evaporated and only the butterfat and solids are left, 3 to 5 minutes. Allow the butter to toast until golden brown and nutty in aroma, another 2 to 3 minutes, stirring with a spatula to prevent the milk solids from sticking to the bottom of the pan. Remove from the heat.

Place the parsnips in a mixing bowl and toss with 1 tablespoon of the brown butter. Line a baking sheet with parchment paper. Spread out the parsnips on the prepared baking sheet. Roast until light gold around the edges, 30 to 35 minutes. Remove from the oven and let cool.

In a medium pot, heat ¼ cup of the brown butter over high heat. Add the shallots, stirring often to sweat (soften and release their aroma without browning) until translucent and tender, about 3 minutes. Add the rosemary and 3 of the sage leaves, and cook, stirring, for 30 seconds. Add the roasted parsnips and the chicken stock, bring the mixture to a boil, then decrease the heat to medium-low and simmer for 30 minutes, stirring occasionally. Remove from the heat and add the cream, salt, white pepper, and the remaining brown butter.

Working in batches if necessary, transfer the parsnip mixture to a blender and puree until silky and smooth, 1½ to 2 minutes. Transfer the blended mixture to a stockpot over low heat, cover, and keep warm while you fry the sage.

Line a plate with a paper towel. In a nonstick pan, heat the oil over medium-high heat until shimmering. Add the remaining 7 sage leaves and fry for 30 seconds, then remove with a slotted spoon to the paper towel and set aside.

When ready to serve, ladle the soup into bowls and shave the pecorino over the top. Crumble the sage leaves over the cheese and serve. Store leftovers in an airtight container in the refrigerator for up to 5 days.

chilled corn and coconut soup with basil and blue crab

Here in New Orleans, corn and crab bisque is on the menu of every grand-dame restaurant, along with gumbo and turtle soup. At La Petite Grocery, we've always been interested in tweaking heritage dishes (for example, the Blue Crab Beignets, page 88), and this is no exception. I make a super-simple corncob stock right in the pot, then lace it with coconut for richness, lime juice for brightness, and fish sauce for a slightly Southeast Asian flavor profile, a nod to our Vietnamese population. There's something wonderful about the combination of corn and coconut—the sweetness of the former somehow elevates the latter into a bigger flavor.

The blue crab salad is optional, but delicious if you have access to fresh crab, which happens to be in season at the same time as nearly everything else that goes in the pot. Spicy chiles and fish sauce are other welcome additions to the soup, which can be served warm or chilled.

Cut the corncobs in half. Stand one upright on its end and slice down to cut off the kernels, rotating the cob until all the kernels are removed. Transfer the kernels to a bowl, and set aside the cob. Repeat with the remaining corn. Place the cobs in a stockpot, cover with the water, and bring to a boil over high heat. Cover the stockpot with a lid, remove from the heat, and set aside to let the corncobs steep for 45 minutes.

With a slotted spoon, remove the cobs from the pot and discard. Stir the corn kernels into the stock. Bring to a boil over high heat, then decrease the heat to medium-low and simmer for 15 minutes. Remove from the heat and stir in the coconut milk, jalapeño, and basil.

Working in batches of about 2 cups at a time, puree the mixture in a blender until very smooth and velvety, 1½ to 2 minutes per batch, and transfer the pureed soup to a serving vessel.

Juice 2 of the limes and stir the juice into the soup, followed by 1½ tablespoons of salt, and the fish sauce. Place in the refrigerator and chill for at least 3 hours or, ideally, overnight. (You will notice the soup thickens up after chilling.) If you prefer to serve it warm, skip the chilling step.

When ready to serve, toss the crabmeat with the oil, basil, and a pinch of salt. Juice the remaining lime and add to the crabmeat; lightly toss to combine.

Ladle the soup into bowls and top with a spoonful of crab salad. Store leftover soup, without the crab topping, in an airtight container in the refrigerator for up to 2 days.

makes 6 servings

6 ears corn, husked and cleaned of silk

1½ quarts water

1 cup unsweetened coconut milk

½ jalapeño, or more or less depending on your spice tolerance

5 large basil leaves

3 limes

Kosher salt

2 tablespoons fish sauce (preferably Three Crabs or Red Boat; see page 28)

8 ounces fresh blue crabmeat, lump or jumbo lump, picked over for shells

3 tablespoons extra-virgin olive oil

1 bunch basil, leaves pulled from stems

NOTE

If you're serving the soup chilled, it's best to make it a day in advance to give the flavors time to meld.

lobster chowder with cauliflower puree

This is a way to combine the texture and creaminess of a classic chowder with a decadent seafood, such as lobster, but without the dairy or gluten that's usually included. There's no roux and no cream in here—I use cauliflower puree for creaminess plus rich nuggets of lobster meat, handfuls of fresh herbs, and spikes of citrus in the broth. It's a neat trick that works for many other "creamy" soups as well.

makes 10 to 12 servings

3 (1½-pound) live lobsters

5 to 6 strips thick-cut smoked bacon, cut into matchsticks about ⅛ inch thick to make 1 cup

6 cups cauliflower florets (from a 2- to 3-pound head)

3 quarts shellfish stock (see page 48)

1 leek, white part small-diced, and green part reserved

1 sprig parsley plus ¼ cup chopped flat-leaf parsley leaves

3 sprigs thyme plus 1 tablespoon thyme leaves

2 dried bay leaves

1 cup very finely diced shallots

½ cup small-diced peeled carrots

½ cup small-diced celery

¼ cup chopped tarragon leaves

¼ cup freshly squeezed lemon juice

1 tablespoon kosher salt

½ teaspoon freshly cracked white pepper

2 tablespoons minced chives

Extra-virgin olive oil for drizzling

First, cook the lobsters. This step can be done up to 12 hours in advance. Prepare an ice water bath in a large pot—it should be mostly ice with just enough water to loosen the ice (see page 35).

Bring a large stockpot full of water to a boil and submerge the lobsters. Cover the pot, turn off the heat, and leave the lobsters in the hot water for 5 minutes. Using tongs, transfer the lobsters to the ice water bath. Let them cool for about 20 minutes.

Remove the lobsters from the ice water bath and lightly dry them off with a clean kitchen towel. Next, remove the tails by twisting them and pulling gently away from the body. You might want to use a few towels to protect your hands from the jagged shells.

Remove the claws and the large front legs. Use sharp kitchen scissors to cut through the tails, and a small mallet to break the claw shells so you can pull out all the meat, being careful to remove all of the shell fragments. Set the meat aside in a small bowl. Slit the tail down the middle and discard any vein that might be present. Cut the tail meat into large but bite-size morsels and add to the bowl. Store the meat in the refrigerator, and if you like, save the shells to make shellfish stock.

Line a plate with paper towels. In a large heavy-bottomed pot over medium-high heat, cook the bacon, stirring often, until darkened and crisp, 5 to 7 minutes. You'll be able to tell when it's ready because the fat will have cooked out of the bacon, or rendered, leaving a shimmery, highly flavorful liquid grease in the pan.

Using a slotted spoon, transfer the bacon to the paper towels to drain. In the same pot, lightly cook the cauliflower in the leftover bacon fat for 2 minutes, stirring, to remove its raw taste from the puree.

CONTINUED

lobster chowder with cauliflower puree, continued

Add the stock to the pot and increase the heat to bring the liquid a boil. Decrease the heat to medium and cook until the cauliflower is completely tender, about 20 minutes.

Turn off the heat, and using an immersion blender, blend the liquid and cauliflower in the pot until smooth and emulsified. This can take up to 10 minutes. Or use a regular countertop blender, and pulse on low speed to avoid building up steam, which can cause a dramatic soup explosion that requires extensive clean up (and could burn you). The goal is to achieve a velvety texture reminiscent of a creamed soup. Fortunately, the type of starch in the cauliflower allows you to blend the heck out of it without having to worry about developing the gummy or sticky texture you might get with potatoes.

Return the blended soup to the cooking pot. Tuck the sprigs of parsley and thyme and the bay leaves inside the reserved leek greens and tie with twine to make a modified bouquet garni and set aside.

Add the shallots, white part of the leek, carrots, and celery to the pot and stir into the soup. Add the bouquet garni and simmer on low heat for 10 minutes. Stir in the reserved lobster meat, chopped parsley, thyme leaves, and tarragon leaves and warm for 2 minutes.

Remove from the heat and season with the lemon juice, salt, and white pepper. Ladle into bowls. Garnish with a few pieces of crispy bacon, a little pinch of chives, and a drizzle of olive oil and serve. Store leftover chowder, without the bacon garnish, in an airtight container in the refrigerator for up to 1 day.

shellfish stew with collard greens and potlikker

This is a one-pot stew to shake up your weeknight dinner routine, and it doubles easily to feed a crowd on a Sunday afternoon. It's as much about the potlikker as it is about the shellfish—the latter obviously shines, but that classic Southern broth, rich with pork and greens, picks up the essence of the shellfish to create something magical. This stew is a bold, big-flavored dish, but there's very little fat in it, so it doesn't sit heavy on the belly. It will be quite briny, so it's best to season it at the end to avoid oversalting. Serve it with biscuits and try to eat it all in one day, as the shellfish doesn't keep well.

makes 6 to 8 servings

5 strips high-quality smoked bacon, cut into matchsticks

1½ cups small-diced yellow onion

5 cloves garlic, thinly sliced

5 cups coarsely chopped collard green leaves (1-inch squares; see Note)

2 non-IPA beers (I like an amber lager—nothing too hoppy)

1 quart shellfish stock (see page 48)

12 littleneck clams

1 pound wild shrimp, cleaned and deveined (16/20 count)

12 oysters, shucked (see pages 212 and 213) and shells discarded

8 ounces fresh blue crabmeat, lump or jumbo lump

½ cup finely chopped flat-leaf parsley leaves

½ cup finely chopped chives

¼ cup freshly squeezed lemon juice

Kosher salt

Freshly cracked black pepper

Buttermilk Biscuits (page 372) for serving (optional)

In a large heavy-bottomed pot over medium-high heat, cook the bacon, stirring often, until the fat renders and the meat crisps up, 7 to 10 minutes.

Add the onion and garlic to the pot, stirring often to sweat (soften and release their aroma without browning), until the onions are translucent, about 5 minutes. Add the collard greens and beer. Cook to slightly steam and wilt the greens, 7 to 9 minutes. Once they're wilted and cooking in the liquid, decrease the heat to low and cook, stirring occasionally, until the greens are quite tender and there's no bitter flavor, about 1 hour.

Add the stock to the pot and bring to a boil over high heat. Decrease the heat to medium-high and add the clams. Cover and cook until they open slightly, 5 to 10 minutes depending on how stubborn the clams are feeling. Discard any that refuse to open. Add the shrimp and cook, uncovered, for 1 minute. Add the oysters and cook for 1 minute, or until their edges barely curl up. Add the crab and cook until hot, about 1 minute. Remove from the heat.

Add the parsley, chives, and lemon juice. Taste and season with salt and a few grinds of pepper. Serve with the biscuits.

NOTE
I like to cut the greens into small squares so they fit easily on a spoon.

pumpkin and shellfish bisque
with pumpkin seed pistou

Fall in New Orleans means the peak of white shrimp season, and the beginning of squash and gourd time. I like to take advantage of their overlap by making this sweet, nutty soup. I use the starchiness of pumpkins to create a silky texture, the shrimp to accentuate the sweetness of the pumpkin, and the herbaceous pistou to tie it all together.

Speaking of the pistou, this particular version is a great example of the versatility of the master recipe (see page 57). Here I've simply varied the base by adding a couple of ingredients (pumpkin seeds, oregano) to help it fit the flavor of this soup. This recipe will make extra pistou, which keeps for a few days and is excellent on grilled meats, roasted vegetables, and pasta.

To make the pistou: In a small saucepan, heat the vegetable oil over medium heat. Add the pumpkin seeds and gently toast, stirring and flipping often, until slightly puffed and aromatic, 7 to 10 minutes. Set aside to briefly cool.

Combine the garlic, parsley, oregano, salt, lemon juice, and chile flakes in a blender. Add the slightly cooled seeds and half of the olive oil or 80/20 oil. Begin to puree the mixture on medium speed, slowly pouring in the remaining olive oil or 80/20 oil until you have a slightly smooth yet still textured puree, 20 to 30 seconds.

Scrape the pistou out of the blender and into a container with a tight-fitting lid. The pistou can be made up to 2 days in advance and stored in the refrigerator; bring to room temperature and stir before using.

To make the bisque: Heat the vegetable oil in a medium stockpot over high heat and immediately add the onion, stirring often to sweat (soften and release its aroma without browning) until translucent and tender, about 5 minutes. Add the pumpkin and stock, bring to a boil, then decrease the heat to medium-low. Add the thyme and simmer until the pumpkin is falling-apart tender, about 30 minutes. Remove the pot from the heat, remove the bundle of thyme, and stir in the cream.

CONTINUED

makes 4 to 6 servings

PUMPKIN SEED PISTOU

1 tablespoon vegetable oil

½ cup raw shelled pumpkin seeds (pepitas)

1 clove garlic

1 cup coarsely chopped flat-leaf parsley

1 tablespoon oregano leaves

1½ teaspoons kosher salt

Juice of ½ lemon

Pinch of dried red chile flakes

½ cup extra-virgin olive oil or 80/20 blended oil (see page 30)

BISQUE

2 tablespoons vegetable oil

1 cup small-diced onion

3 cups diced peeled pumpkin or other autumn squash

1 quart shellfish stock (see page 48)

3 sprigs thyme, tied with kitchen twine

1 cup heavy cream

¼ cup unsalted butter, quartered

2 tablespoons freshly squeezed lemon juice

1 tablespoon kosher salt

1 teaspoon freshly cracked white pepper

pumpkin and shellfish bisque with pumpkin seed pistou, continued

Working in batches, puree the soup in a blender. Add one-quarter of the soup and 1 tablespoon of the butter to the blender and blend on medium speed until silky-smooth, 1½ to 2 minutes. Transfer the puree to a clean pot large enough to hold all the soup and repeat with the remaining soup and butter.

Season the soup with the lemon juice, salt, and white pepper. Ladle into bowls, top each bowl with a spoonful of pistou, and serve. Store leftover soup, without the pistou, in an airtight container in the refrigerator for up to 3 days.

chicken and black-eyed pea soup

Black-eyed peas are a staple of the Deep South, including Louisiana. The addition of ham gives this soup that quintessential porky flavor you look for in a black-eyed pea dish. Make a big batch of this and freeze the leftovers, as it holds up well when thawed and reheated on chilly winter nights.

Fresh black-eyed peas are the ultimate Southern summer treat, though they can be tough to find. Use them if you're lucky enough to have them, but the far more common flash-frozen field peas are just as good, as they are frozen at their peak to maintain freshness.

makes 10 servings

1 (3- to 4-pound) chicken

3 sprigs thyme, tied with kitchen twine

2 dried bay leaves

¼ cup extra-virgin olive oil

½ cup diced country ham, unsmoked bacon, or pancetta (see page 375)

3 cups small-diced onions

5 cloves garlic, finely chopped

1 cup small-diced carrots

1 cup small-diced celery

2 cups (½ pound) fresh or frozen black-eyed peas or soaked dried black-eyed peas

1 cup finely chopped flat-leaf parsley leaves

¼ cup finely chopped thyme leaves

2 tablespoons finely chopped tarragon leaves

1 tablespoon kosher salt

1½ teaspoons to 1 tablespoon dried red chile flakes, ideally piment d'Espelette or Korean gochugaru (see page 32)

Juice of 1 or 2 lemons

NOTE
Dried peas are also fine here. If using dried, soak them in about 1½ quarts of water overnight before proceeding.

In a large heavy-bottomed pot, place the chicken, breast-side up, and cover with water. It's important here to use a pot that fits the chicken snugly—the ideal chicken to water ratio is in favor of the chicken, so the water obtains the most flavor. Too much water, and you'll end up with a bland broth that barely tastes like chicken.

Add the tied thyme and the bay leaves to the pot and place over medium heat until small bubbles and steam form, but don't let it come to a boil (adjust the heat if necessary). Poach the chicken until just cooked through, about 1 hour. Remove from the heat and let the chicken rest for 1 hour in the poaching liquid.

Remove the chicken and set aside until cool enough to handle. Strain the broth into a clean vessel and set aside; wash and dry the poaching pot.

Heat the oil in the clean pot over high heat until shimmering. Add the ham, bacon, or pancetta and cook, stirring, until the fat has rendered and the meat is golden brown, 7 to 10 minutes. Decrease the heat to medium, add the onions, and cook, stirring occasionally, until soft and translucent, about 5 minutes. Add the garlic and cook until the aroma is undeniable, 2 to 3 minutes. Add the carrots and celery and cook until slightly tender, about 5 minutes. Add the poaching broth and the black-eyed peas to the pot and bring to a boil.

With your fingers, pull the chicken meat from the bone (feel free to snack) and set aside. Once the broth has come to a boil, decrease the heat to medium-low and simmer, skimming off the foam that rises to the top as necessary, until the vegetables are tender and the peas are very soft, about 30 minutes.

Just before serving, stir in the parsley, thyme, tarragon, salt, chile flakes, and pulled chicken. Brighten the soup with fresh lemon juice to taste and then serve. Store leftover soup in an airtight container in the refrigerator for up to 5 days.

duck and andouille gumbo

Gumbo is the quintessential Louisiana dish; it's practically a religion here. Everyone makes it a little differently, but everyone makes it— and has very strong opinions on the right way to do it. I learned to make gumbo from my uncle, who learned it from my grandma. But I waited a long time before putting it on the La Petite menu, because it's such a personal thing.

Gumbo has gone through so many creative interpretations that once you understand the essentials, it really just comes down to making it however you want to make it. I use duck because I like to go duck hunting, but if you prefer chicken, that works, too. These days, I'm not so concerned with making a super-traditional gumbo—I'd rather throw in some poblano peppers and greens, and if you want to call it blasphemy, that's fine with me. I think it's delicious.

A few things to note about the cooking technique: The success of a great gumbo lies in the roux (which in this case is a flavoring agent, more than a thickening one). This recipe can be easily doubled to feed a crowd (and freezes well); make it in advance if possible, since it always tastes better the second day. It's traditional to serve gumbo with rice, though my favorite accompaniment is a super-simple potato salad with mustard, mayonnaise, and vinegar (see page 138)—that's a classic southwestern Louisiana way to eat it.

Preheat the oven to 400°F.

Place the duck legs on a baking sheet and season on both sides with the salt and pepper. Roast, undisturbed, until the skin is golden brown and crispy, about 1 hour.

While the duck roasts, make a dark roux with the flour and oil (see page 46 for step-by-step instructions).

Add the onion, celery, poblanos, and garlic directly to the pot with the hot roux. This will cause a volatile, steamy reaction. Stir the vegetables frequently to sweat (soften and release their aroma without browning) and blend into the roux, until visibly wilted and cooked through, 10 to 20 minutes. The roux will thicken and get slightly darker.

CONTINUED

makes 6 to 8 servings

4 duck legs

1 tablespoon kosher salt, plus more as needed

1½ teaspoons freshly cracked black pepper, plus more as needed

1 cup all-purpose flour

⅔ cup peanut oil

1 cup small-diced onion

½ cup small-diced celery

¾ cup small-diced poblano peppers

1 tablespoon minced garlic

2 quarts chicken stock (see page 49)

1 bunch mustard greens or other hearty greens, trimmed and cut into ribbons (about 4 cups)

4 cups okra, cut into ½-inch rounds

1 pound andouille sausage, cut into ½-inch rounds

2 tablespoons Worcestershire sauce

1 tablespoon hot pepper vinegar, such as brine from pickled jalapeños (see page 353) or other pickled peppers

1 tablespoon coarsely chopped thyme leaves

1 cup coarsely chopped flat-leaf parsley leaves

1 cup thinly sliced green onion, white and green parts

Add the stock to the pot, gradually while whisking out any lumps of roux. Simmer for 20 minutes, stirring with a flat-edged spoon to make sure nothing is sticking to the bottom.

Add the greens, okra, andouille, and the whole roasted duck legs to the pot. Stir in the Worcestershire, vinegar, thyme, and parsley. Simmer until the duck meat is falling off the bones, about 1 hour. Remove the legs from the pot and set aside until cool enough to handle. Pick all of the meat off the bones and stir it back into the pot. Discard the bones.

Add the green onion and season with salt and black pepper. Waiting to season until the andouille has cooked is important because the sausage releases a bit of its seasoning as it cooks.

Remove from the heat and let the gumbo rest for 20 minutes before serving. Or, ideally, cool to room temperature, refrigerate overnight, and gently reheat the next day to give the flavors more time to meld. Store leftover gumbo in an airtight container in the refrigerator for up to 5 days.

brisket and kale stew with oven-dried tomatoes and horseradish

Think of this as a rendition of a pot roast or classic beef stew, with the addition of hearty greens, plus some acid from the oven-dried tomatoes and a kick from the fresh horseradish. The recipe builds on others in the book (the tomatoes and beef stock), and is a nice example of how basic building blocks add up to something rich and complex.

I like using brisket here, which you don't see that often in a stew, as opposed to the more traditional chuck. Brisket is a little fattier, giving the finished dish a softer, more unctuous feel than you'd get with stew meat and a ton of rich, beefy flavor. Keep an eye on the meat as it simmers, and skim often as the fat rises to the surface to ensure a clear, clean-tasting broth.

Heat the oil in a large pot over high heat until shimmering. Working in batches if necessary to avoid crowding, add the brisket pieces and decrease the heat to medium-high. Sear until evenly browned on both sides, about 5 minutes per side. Remove the brisket from the pot and set aside.

Add the onion, carrots, celery, and garlic to the pot and cook until the vegetables are tender and any liquid they release evaporates, about 10 minutes. At this point, the vegetables will start to caramelize on the bottom of the pan. Encourage more caramelization by scraping up any bits on the bottom of the pot (the fond) with a spoon or spatula. Once a nice fond has formed on the bottom of the pot, about 15 minutes, add the red wine and scrape the bottom until all of the stuck bits are free.

Continue cooking until the wine has almost evaporated, about 10 minutes, then add the stock and season with salt and pepper. Nestle the brisket pieces back in the pot and add the rosemary and thyme. Bring to a boil, then decrease the heat to medium-low, cover, and simmer, skimming as necessary, until the brisket is fork-tender, 2 to 3 hours.

Remove the pot from the heat and rest the stew for 30 minutes. Remove the brisket from the pot and arrange in a large bowl or high-sided serving platter. Return the pot with the cooking liquid to the stove over medium heat. Add the kale and simmer for 5 minutes.

When ready to serve, spoon the kale and broth over the brisket and garnish with the tomatoes. Using a Microplane, shave horseradish over the top. Spoon into shallow bowls and serve. Store leftovers tightly covered in the refrigerator for up to 5 days.

makes 6 to 8 servings

¼ cup vegetable oil

3 pounds brisket, trimmed of fat and sinew, cut into 2-inch squares

1 cup small-diced onion

½ cup small-diced peeled carrots

½ cup small-diced celery

8 cloves garlic, thinly sliced

1 cup red wine

2 quarts beef stock (see page 50)

2 tablespoons kosher salt

Freshly cracked black pepper

1 sprig rosemary

5 sprigs thyme, tied together with kitchen twine

1 bunch lacinato kale, stems removed, washed, and chopped into 2-inch pieces

12 Oven-Dried Tomatoes (page 344), at room temperature

1 knob horseradish

seafood

Naturally, when it comes to discussing seafood, I have to brag a little about where I live. New Orleans is ground zero for some of the best seafood on Earth. We have the shrimp, crab, oysters, and crawfish that people usually associate with our city, but that's just the tip of the iceberg. Louisiana juts out into the Gulf of Mexico, so in addition to our prolific inshore fishing, we're close to deep and open blue water, where the abundance of species is just crazy. We catch snapper, grouper, cobia, tuna, amberjack, triggerfish, tripletail, and more in our backyard. That biodiversity is really what makes our region unique.

Many of the recipes in this chapter are my interpretation of classic New Orleans dishes, like my Southeast Asian–style riff on barbecue shrimp on page 218; or the baked oysters smothered in a bacon-Parmesan–collard greens compound butter on page 213. But just because we have the best seafood in the world doesn't mean we won't enjoy things from farther afield—the seared scallops on page 225, borrow from my cold-water neighbors to the north to delicious result.

All of that said, use what's local to you. The techniques matter here more than the specific type of fish; all of these recipes will taste better with whatever is freshest.

Cooking seafood at home can seem a little intimidating, because fish is expensive and you don't want to mess it up. But a lot of these recipes are forgiving—the seared tuna on page 242 will get you accustomed to searing fish, using a firm species that handles well. Once you have that mastered, you can move on to more delicate types, like flounder. As you cook your way across this chapter, you might notice some of the techniques start to repeat themselves. The process for making compound butter for the baked oysters, for example, appears again in the herb-crusted snapper on page 231, albeit with a different shape and flavor profile.

Many of the recipes in this chapter also build on some of the fundamental techniques that are introduced earlier in the book—making a brown butter vinaigrette for the seared scallops, for example, or whipping up a perfectly emulsified aioli to whisk into the steamed clam broth on page 210. Hopefully, you'll be able to see how these skills build on each other, resulting in seafood dishes that not only showcase the fish or shellfish but also taste like more than the sum of their parts.

steamed clams with white wine–aioli broth and fresh vegetables

Clams are inexpensive and delicious, and one of the only bivalves that really hit their peak, flavorwise, in the summer. The Gulf South isn't really known for clamming, but it does happen—we get ours from Cedar Key, Florida, past where the Panhandle curves into the Peninsula, and they are some of the best I've ever had.

This recipe is a low-key riff on bouillabaisse, with the idea of enriching the shellfish broth with aioli and classic aromatics that give it that Provençal flavor profile. The anise flavor from fennel is a traditional pairing with shellfish, and so is light, delicate tarragon. You can use this cooking method for all kinds of shellfish—shrimp, mussels, or even a lobster cut in half. Whatever you do, I suggest serving it with a crusty French bread or buttered baguette to soak up all of the juices.

makes 4 servings

24 littleneck clams

3 cups dry white wine

1½ cups water

1 leek, white part only, sliced into rounds

1 fennel bulb, fronds reserved, bulb thinly sliced

1 carrot, peeled and cut into matchsticks about 2 inches long and ⅛ inch wide

3 cloves garlic, thinly sliced

½ cup Aioli (page 65)

2 tablespoons finely chopped flat-leaf parsley leaves

2 tablespoons minced chives

2 tablespoons finely chopped tarragon leaves

½ lemon

Kosher salt

Freshly cracked black pepper

Crusty bread for serving (optional)

Wash each clam individually under cold running water to remove any sand or particles, and pull off any beard or hair on the outside of the shell.

In a large cocotte (enamel-coated cast-iron pot) or Dutch oven, combine the clams, white wine, and water and bring to a boil over high heat. Add the leek, fennel bulb, carrot, and garlic and cover. Steam for 7 to 10 minutes, until the clams open—it's okay if they don't open all the way. Discard any clams that remain completely closed.

Place the aioli in a mixing bowl. Nestle the bowl into a kitchen towel on the countertop for stability, as you will need both hands for the next step.

Push the clams to the side of the pot, gently ladle out about ½ cup of the hot steaming liquid, and slowly drizzle it into the aioli, while whisking with your other hand, to temper the aioli. This will emulsify into a frothy, milky white sauce. Ladle out another ½ cup steaming liquid and whisk that into the aioli. Pour the aioli mixture over the clams in the pot. Stir in the parsley, chives, and tarragon and squeeze the lemon over the top. Season with salt and pepper and serve immediately, straight from the pot, ladling the clams and liquid into deep bowls. Accompany with crusty bread, if desired.

baked oysters with greens, bacon, and parmesan

This dish is so embedded in my repertoire that I don't even know when I started making it, but my earliest memory of cooking it was around age fourteen, when I made oysters with spinach and bacon from one of Emeril's cookbooks. I've been a baked-oyster fanatic ever since, and I've played around with a million different toppings, though this combination is tough to beat.

Baking oysters, as opposed to frying them, is a good way to retain their raw essence when cooking them. Finally, there's something about roasting oysters when it's cold out that makes them taste better—and it's often cold outside during oyster season. As good as they are raw, nippy weather and roasted oysters go together perfectly.

Preheat the oven to 450°F.

Fill a cast-iron casserole dish halfway with rock salt and place in the oven to come up to temperature. Meanwhile, using an oyster knife, shuck the oysters: Holding an oyster securely, bottom-side down, insert an oyster knife into the pointier end of the oyster, its joint or hinge. Using your wrist, twist and rotate the knife over until you feel the oyster pop open. This step is all about feeling the sweet spot in the joint. If your oyster seems brittle or you break the joint without opening the oyster, move on to the next one, at least until you get the hang of opening oysters. Then you can return to the tougher ones.

Once the oyster is popped, run your knife along its seam to get to the wider end of the oyster, then give it another twist, so it pops open halfway. With the edge of the knife facing you, pull forward, while scraping the inside of the upper oyster shell, releasing the top connector muscle. The shell will then disconnect, leaving you with the oyster on the bottom, aka the half shell. Repeat with the remaining oysters and set aside.

In a large bowl, stir the butter until creamy and add the greens, bacon, garlic, thyme, chives, Parmesan, and lemon juice and fold until incorporated and emulsified. Season with salt and pepper.

Pull the heated casserole out of the oven. Carefully place the oysters on the salt and dollop each with a generous amount of the compound butter. Return the pan to the oven until the butter melts and the edges of the oysters are slightly curled, 4 to 5 minutes (or up to 7 minutes for very large oysters, such as some Gulf varieties).

Serve right out of the hot pan with cocktail forks.

makes 6 servings

3 pounds rock salt (sometimes sold as ice-cream salt)

24 large oysters in the shell, such as Bluepoints or Gulf

½ cup unsalted butter, at room temperature

1 cup cooked greens (chard, spinach, or mustard greens), coarsely chopped

½ cup coarsely chopped cooked bacon

3 cloves garlic, finely chopped

1 tablespoon thyme leaves

¼ cup minced chives

¾ cup grated Parmesan

Juice of 3 lemons

Kosher salt

Freshly cracked black pepper

fried oyster po'boys

There is perhaps no food more quintessentially New Orleans than a po'boy, which can be stuffed with anything from roast beef to fried shellfish to chicken and more. The origin of the sandwich is endlessly debated, but legend has it that striking street-car workers in the 1920s were given sandwiches named for their recipients' circumstances—hence "poor boys." What's not up for debate is that po'boys play a significant role in the fabric of New Orleans food and are available everywhere from corner stores to some of the finest restaurants in town.

Whether you're in a meat (see Roast Beef Po'Boys, page 296) or a seafood kind of mood, your bread choice is important. In New Orleans, we make po'boys on a particular type of French bread that has a cottony interior and a thin, crispy cracker-like crust. If you don't have access to New Orleans-style French loaves, I recommend using a loaf of Texas toast or white bread cut lengthwise, as opposed to a baguette or anything fancy. This is a blue-collar sandwich, after all.

makes 8 to 10 servings

GARLIC BUTTER

3 tablespoons unsalted butter

2 cloves garlic, smashed

FRIED OYSTERS

2 cups all-purpose flour

2 cups cornmeal

¼ cup cornstarch

1 tablespoon kosher salt

1 teaspoon freshly cracked black pepper

48 oysters, shucked from their shells and reserved with juices (see pages 212 and 213)

Peanut oil for frying (about 1 quart)

2 large loaves po'boy bread or French bread

1 cup Rémoulade (page 72)

½ large head iceberg lettuce, shredded

1 cup LPG Burger Pickles (page 350)

2 tablespoons Homemade Hot Sauce (page 62) or store-bought sauce (preferably Crystal), plus more for serving

To make the garlic butter: In a small saucepan over medium heat, melt the butter. Add the garlic and decrease the heat to low. Simmer for about 45 minutes, until the garlic is translucent but not brown and the butter has taken on the garlic flavor. Strain the butter and set aside, discarding the garlic. The garlic butter can be made up to 1 day in advance.

To fry the oysters: In a large bowl, whisk the flour, cornmeal, cornstarch, salt, and pepper to combine. One by one, transfer the oysters into the bowl with the dry ingredients. Gently toss with your fingers to evenly coat the oysters with the dredge.

Line a plate with paper towels. Pour the oil to a depth of at least 2 inches into a large cast-iron or nonstick skillet over medium-high heat. The peanut oil is ready when it shimmers and sizzles when you add a pinch of cornmeal. Working in batches to avoid overcrowding, gently place the oysters in the pan about 1 inch apart to ensure even crispiness.

Fry the oysters on each side until crispy and golden brown, about 1½ minutes per side, then transfer to the paper towels to drain.

Preheat the oven to 400°F. Cut the bread into 8-inch portions (or desired length) and slice horizontally lengthwise. Brush the inside of the bread with the garlic butter and toast in the oven for 4 to 5 minutes, until crispy and just slightly brown.

Brush each side with 2 tablespoons of the rémoulade. Top with the fried oysters, the lettuce, and pickles, then place top half of bread on top. Serve with hot sauce and extra napkins.

seafood boil

Seafood boils are a spring and summer tradition here, our favorite excuse to get together, drink beer, and peel and eat an abundance of fresh seafood. I've scaled this recipe down for indoor home cooking, as opposed to the 50-gallon stockpot I usually bust out in my backyard, but even so, I do encourage you to move the party outside if you can. Lay down some newspaper on a table, pour the goodies across it, and get in there with your fingers. That's what a seafood boil is all about.

There's no shame in using a store-bought crab boil mix, especially if you have a favorite one, but making your own boil mix gives you the freedom to switch up or add spices or aromatics as you see fit. I like the spicy red pepper notes in this one, balanced with the citrus from an orange, and a slightly Caribbean flavor from the allspice to finish.

In a medium mixing bowl, combine the paprika, chile flakes, allspice, celery seed, black pepper, and salt until fully incorporated. Set aside 3 tablespoons of the seasoning in a separate small bowl. In a large stockpot, combine 1 gallon of water with the remaining seasoning.

Add the bay leaves to the pot. Cut the oranges in half, squeeze their juice into the pot, and add the orange halves to the pot. Add the garlic and potatoes and bring the mixture to a boil over high heat. Cook until the potatoes are cooked through and tender, about 15 minutes. Add the corn, thyme, and butter, making sure the pot is still at a boil. Add the shrimp and stir with a wooden spoon. Cook the shrimp for approximately 90 seconds, or until completely cooked through and opaque.

Using a slotted spoon or spider, remove all of the solids from the boiling pot and transfer to a large platter with sloped sides to catch the juice. Discard the boil liquid. Sprinkle the platter with all of the reserved seasoning. Serve immediately, with extra napkins.

makes 6 to 8 servings

¼ cup plus 2 tablespoons sweet Spanish paprika

1 tablespoon Korean dried red chile flakes (gochugaru; see page 32)

¼ teaspoon ground allspice

½ teaspoon celery seed

½ teaspoon freshly ground black pepper

¼ cup kosher salt

3 bay leaves

2 oranges

1 head garlic, sliced in half lengthwise

12 small potatoes, such as red bliss or small Yukon golds

3 ears of corn, cut into thirds

5 sprigs thyme, tied with butcher's twine

½ cup unsalted butter

2 pounds shell-on shrimp (16/20 count)

NOTE

This recipe can be doubled or tripled. You can also substitute the same amount of crawfish or crab for the shrimp. For crawfish, cook in boiling water for 7 minutes, then place in a clean pot with a lid or a backyard cooler to steam for 10 minutes before seasoning with the reserved spice mix. For crab, cook for 10 minutes, steam for 10 minutes, season, and serve.

garlic-chile "bbq" shrimp

In New Orleans, "BBQ" shrimp is a classic dish in which shrimp aren't barbecued at all (hence the quotation marks), but rather pan-roasted and served swimming in a lavish pool of a butter and Worcestershire–based sauce. It's rich, messy, and totally delicious.

My Southeast Asian–inspired treatment is foolproof enough to make everyone feel like a champion cook. All you do is heat shrimp on the stove top with garlic, white wine, and a splash of lemon juice; then sprinkle Korean chile flakes and a load of butter on top to create a rich sauce. Toss it with cilantro at the end, and you're left with a juicy, satisfying main course that comes together in minutes.

makes 4 servings

2 to 3 tablespoons vegetable oil

12 large head-on wild shrimp (10/12 count size), shells left on, deveined (see Note)

3 tablespoons finely chopped garlic

2 tablespoons Korean dried red chile flakes (gochugaru; see page 32)

½ cup dry white wine

½ teaspoon fish sauce (preferably Three Crabs or Red Boat; see page 28)

½ cup unsalted butter, at room temperature

1 tablespoon freshly squeezed lime juice

2 tablespoons chopped cilantro leaves

½ teaspoon kosher salt

French bread for serving

NOTE

When shopping for shrimp, try to buy fresh, not frozen, and head-on if at all possible. The heads impart a rich crustacean flavor.

In a large skillet over high heat, add 2 tablespoons of the oil and heat until shimmering. Add the shrimp and sear for 1 minute. Flip the shrimp and sear for 1 minute on the other side. Remove the shrimp from the pan and set aside on a plate.

In the same skillet over high heat, add the garlic and chile flakes. You should still have enough oil to sweat (soften and release aroma without browning) the garlic in the pan; if not, add the remaining 1 tablespoon. Give the aromatics a few quick stirs, then add the wine and deglaze pan, scraping up the flavorful bits (the fond) stuck on the bottom and stirring them into the liquid. Cook the wine, stirring occasionally, until it has reduced in volume by two-thirds, and then decrease the heat to medium.

Add the fish sauce, stirring briefly, then stir in the butter and continue stirring until it emulsifies smoothly. The idea here is to melt the butter into the sauce without separating the butterfat from the milk solids. Your sauce should look creamy, rather than oily.

Return the shrimp to the pan, decrease the heat to medium-low, and cook for about 3 minutes total, flipping after the first 1½ minutes, until the shrimp are cooked through. Stir in the lime juice, cilantro, and salt.

Divide the shrimp and pan sauce among four bowls and serve with hunks of the French bread for dipping.

shrimp and grits

Shrimp and grits is a classic Low Country dish that fits perfectly in New Orleans, given our access to fresh Gulf shrimp, affinity for grits, and love of brunch. The sweet, snappy shrimp play against the creamy corniness of the grits, and the earthy mushrooms and smoky bacon tie it all together.

Use the Buttered Grits recipe as the base for this recipe—you can make them first and keep warm over low heat. The mushroom gravy is on the lighter side, to balance the ultra-buttery grits, and the star is the shrimp.

In a large heavy-bottomed sauté pan, heat the oil until shimmering. Add the mushrooms in one layer, working in batches if necessary. It's important not to crowd the pan because the mushrooms will release liquid as they cook, and if they're too close together, the liquid won't evaporate and you'll end up with mushy, flabby 'shrooms. Sear the mushrooms until golden and slightly caramelized, flipping once, 3 to 5 minutes per side.

Stir 1 tablespoon of the butter and the salt into the pan and season with pepper. Decrease the heat to medium-low and simmer, stirring occasionally, until all the ingredients are well-incorporated and the mushrooms are slightly glossy, 6 to 8 minutes. Set the mushrooms aside.

Line a plate with paper towels. Heat a medium saucepan pan over medium heat. Add the bacon and slowly cook, so it releases its fat and begins to fry. Stir slowly until crispy and dark red in color, about 10 minutes. Using a slotted spoon, transfer to the plate to drain and set aside. Reserve the fat in a separate container.

In a large sauté pan over medium-high heat, heat ¼ cup of the bacon fat until it shimmers. Add the shrimp and sear on each side for 1½ minutes, or until light golden. The goal here is not to cook the shrimp through, but just to sear the outside. Set the shrimp aside.

Add the shallot and garlic to the pan and sauté very briefly (1 to 2 minutes), until they are just translucent. Add the wine, Worcestershire, and thyme to the pan. Reduce the volume by half, about 3 minutes.

Then, add the mushrooms and shrimp to the pan. Reduce the heat to medium. Add the remaining 2 tablespoons butter cubes, stirring frequently to emulsify, until fully incorporated, 2 to 3 minutes.

Taste for seasoning and adjust as desired. Spoon the grits into serving bowls or onto a platter with sides. Spoon the shrimp, mushrooms, and sauce over the grits. Garnish with the rendered bacon and chives. Serve with the lemon wedges on the side.

makes 4 to 6 servings

2 tablespoons olive oil

2 cups cremini mushrooms, cleaned and halved

3 tablespoons unsalted butter; 2 tablespoons cut into ½-inch cubes and kept cold

1 teaspoon kosher salt, plus more as needed

Freshly cracked black pepper

6 strips thick-cut smoked bacon, cut into ⅛-inch batons

24 to 30 shrimp, cleaned and deveined (16/20 count)

1 tablespoon minced shallot

1 tablespoon minced garlic

1½ cups white wine

½ teaspoon Worcestershire sauce

6 sprigs fresh thyme, picked (about 1 tablespoon)

1 recipe Buttered Grits (page 133)

2 tablespoons thinly cut chives

1 lemon, cut into wedges

crawfish étouffée

Étouffée is French for "smothered," and it's also a classic Cajun dish from this region, almost always served over rice. I like to think of the smothering in two ways—you're either smothering the fish or meat in a gravy-like sauce, or you're smothering the rice itself. I think the French word sometimes throws people for a loop, but the truth is that this is a quick, one-pot stew that can feed a lot of people—nothing to be intimidated by.

As with most things, the success of your étouffée is directly related to the quality of your ingredients. Use domestically harvested Louisiana crawfish (frozen is okay if they're not in season), and practice your roux-making technique to get the perfect velvety texture.

You can order crawfish meat online year-round, though their season here in Louisiana runs from late winter through early July, then starts again right around Thanksgiving.

makes 6 to 8 servings

3 tablespoons unsalted butter

1 tablespoon finely minced garlic

1 cup diced onion

½ cup diced celery

½ cup diced bell pepper

2 quarts Shellfish Stock (page 48)

2 cups Brown Roux (page 45)

3 bay leaves

2 tablespoons paprika

1 tablespoon thyme leaves

3 tablespoons Worchershterstire sauce

3 tablespoons Homemade Hot Sauce (page 62) or store-bought sauce (preferably Texas Pete's or Crystal), plus more for serving

1 pound crawfish tail meat

1½ tablespoons kosher salt

2½ teaspoons freshly cracked black pepper

2 tablespoons chopped flat-leaf parsley

¼ cup thinly sliced green onion

Juice of 2 lemons

1 recipe Foolproof Rice (page 369)

In a large heavy-bottomed pot or Dutch oven over medium-high heat, melt the butter until it has stopped steaming and is almost clear in color. Add the garlic and onion, which should immediately sizzle as they hit the pan. Stir until very lightly browned, 5 to 7 minutes, then add the celery and bell pepper. Stir until the vegetables are wilted and sweat out most of their liquid, about 5 minutes. Add the stock and bring to a boil over high heat.

Place the roux in a medium mixing bowl and whisk in about 3 cups of the hot liquid from the pot (avoid ladling out the vegetables as much as possible), working in 1 cup at a time, until the roux is fully dissolved. If the mixture looks too thick and viscous to pour, thin it with another ladleful of liquid. Add the roux mixture back to the pot and whisk to combine. This two-step process helps make a sauce with a consistent, lump-free texture.

Add the bay leaves, paprika, thyme, Worchestershire, and hot sauce to the pot and simmer over medium-low heat for 30 to 45 minutes, until all of the floury texture from the roux has cooked out and the sauce has a velvety-smooth texture. Skim any foam that forms on the top as the sauce simmers.

Stir in the crawfish meat and simmer for 5 minutes to heat through. Add the salt, pepper, parsley, and green onion. Stir to combine, then add the lemon juice, taste for seasoning, and adjust if needed. Serve over the rice. Store leftover étouffée in an airtight container in the refrigerator for up to 2 days.

seared scallops with garlicky brown butter pan sauce

This is a simple dish that's all about proper technique. True scallop glory comes from perfecting a sear that creates a uniform, crispy, golden brown crust, as opposed to a scallop that's brown around the edges but still gummy inside. You can achieve this by getting dry-packed scallops, then patting them totally dry before seasoning, and making sure the pan and oil are hot enough before cooking them. Once the scallops are in the pan, don't mess with them until they have that perfect crust; once you flip and baste, the basting helps build even more crust.

For the pan sauce, you'll want to whisk the brown butter and the vinegar-mustard mixture thoroughly to combine, but don't worry about perfectly emulsifying the two. This sauce is intentionally served "broken" (when the fat and liquid separate), and the fat itself (in this case, the brown butter) is plenty flavorful on its own. Cold-water shellfish, such as scallops and lobster, have an almost natural nuttiness, and the toasty flavor of brown butter with that rich shellfish flavor is a match made in heaven. I didn't come up with the combination, but I am partial to it, so I just keep revisiting it. I like to serve these scallops with the roasted cauliflower on page 116.

makes 4 to 6 servings

GARLICKY BROWN BUTTER
PAN SAUCE

2 tablespoons sherry vinegar

2 teaspoons Dijon mustard

2 teaspoons honey

Juice of ½ lemon

1½ cups unsalted butter

1 shallot, finely diced

1 clove garlic, mashed
(see page 37)

1 pound dry-packed scallops
(about 12 scallops)

Kosher salt

Freshly cracked black pepper

2 tablespoons vegetable oil

1 tablespoon thyme leaves

1 tablespoon minced chives

1 tablespoon finely chopped
flat-leaf parsley leaves

Freshly squeezed lemon juice

To make the pan sauce: In a mixing bowl, combine the sherry vinegar, Dijon, honey, and lemon juice and stir to combine.

In a medium sauté pan over medium-high heat, melt the butter. The butter will start to brown once the water is cooked out and there is no longer any steam, 3 to 5 minutes. When the butter is lightly toasted around the edges, remove the pan from the heat and let sit for 1 minute to continue the carryover cooking.

Add the shallot and garlic to the pan and stir to soften. Scrape as many little toasted butter bits as possible from the bottom of the pan; these bits hold great flavor. Once the brown butter is slightly cool, whisk it into the bowl with the sherry-Dijon mixture and continue whisking to thoroughly combine.

Dry the scallops with a paper towel and season both sides with salt and pepper. Heat a large heavy-bottomed sauté pan or cast-iron skillet over high heat, add the oil, and heat until shimmering. The scallops should

CONTINUED

sizzle and very noticeably start searing as soon as you add them to the pan.

Let the scallops sear, untouched, for 5 minutes on one side, then flip one to check—it should be crusty, crispy, and a uniformly rich golden brown across the surface. Flip all the scallops and sear the second sides to your desired doneness. I like mine just medium-rare to medium doneness, or just warmed through, about 2 minutes.

Remove the scallops from the pan and drain the oil, but don't rinse the pan. With the pan off the heat, add the sauce to warm it, scraping up any seared bits (the fond) from the bottom of the pan. Add the herbs. Just before serving, taste the sauce and season with salt and pepper, if needed, and add the lemon juice.

pan-seared crab cakes

A lot of crab cakes have the same problem, which I call "overprocessing"—shredded bits of crab in a dense, heavily breaded puck. This recipe is the opposite of that. It's the Platonic ideal of crab cakes: light, sweet, and juicy, with a spotlight on the star of the show, the crab.

You need high-quality fresh crabmeat for this dish, and you don't want to do a whole lot to it, beyond some simple seasoning to enhance its natural flavor. It's important to maintain a gentle touch when handling the crab, whether mixing the ingredients together or flipping the cakes in the pan, so they maintain their distinct lumpy texture. There's no mustard, no egg, and no breading—just a dab of aioli mixed with a handful of bread crumbs so the cakes don't fall apart; minimal alliums; a few herbs; and lemon juice. The oil in the aioli, the bread crumbs, and the crab sear together to form a nice crust around the delicate crab cakes.

To make the tartar sauce: Preheat the broiler.

Coat the jalapeños in the olive oil and place in a cast-iron or other oven-proof skillet. Place the pan under the broiler and broil until the skins blister and char, about 5 minutes. Flip the jalapeños to evenly blister all sides, another 5 minutes. Remove the pan and cover with a lid until the jalapeños are cool, about 25 minutes. Wearing plastic gloves, peel the loosened skin off the jalapeños and remove the seeds and pith from the inside. Finely dice the jalapeños and transfer to a mixing bowl, along with any juices that have collected in the pan.

Add the mustard, lemon juice, parsley, shallot, and aioli or mayonnaise to the jalapeños, and season with salt and black pepper. Fold with a spatula to combine and then refrigerate until ready to use. You will only need about half of the 1½ cups this recipe makes, but you'll find a million other uses for homemade tartar sauce. The tartar sauce will keep in an airtight container in the refrigerator for up to 5 days.

To make the crab cakes: Combine the crab meat, aioli or mayonnaise, parsley, tarragon, chives, and lemon juice in a large mixing bowl and gently fold with a rubber spatula, being careful not to break up the delicate crabmeat (the more defined the crab lumps are, the better the cakes will be). Gently fold in the bread crumbs and season with salt and white pepper. Form the crab mixture into four cakes, place them on a plate, and refrigerate for 30 minutes.

CONTINUED

makes 4 cakes

ROASTED JALAPEÑO TARTAR SAUCE

2 jalapeños

1 teaspoon extra-virgin olive oil

2 tablespoons whole-grain mustard

2 tablespoons freshly squeezed lemon juice

¼ cup finely chopped flat-leaf parsley leaves

3 tablespoons finely diced shallot

1 cup Aioli (page 65) or mayonnaise

Kosher salt

Freshly cracked black pepper

CRAB CAKES

8 ounces fresh blue crabmeat, lump or jumbo lump, picked through for shells

6 tablespoons Aioli (page 65) or mayonnaise

2 tablespoons chopped flat-leaf parsley leaves

1 tablespoon chopped tarragon

1 tablespoon chopped chives

2 tablespoons freshly squeezed lemon juice

¼ cup panko bread crumbs, finely ground in a food processor

Kosher salt

Freshly ground white pepper

pan-seared crab cakes, continued

3 tablespoons vegetable oil

1 lemon, sliced

Line a baking sheet with paper towels. In a large nonstick pan, heat the vegetable oil over high heat until shimmering. Place the crab cakes in the pan, one or two at a time, and sear until golden brown, 4 to 5 minutes per side. Be very gentle, as these cakes are delicate. Using a spatula, transfer the cakes to the paper towels to drain.

Serve piping hot with the lemon slices and a dollop of tartar sauce.

garlic-and-herb-crusted snapper with oven-dried tomatoes and pistou

I learned this technique almost two decades ago and still find myself returning to it today. The idea is to make a compound butter, but utilize it differently than you normally would, by flattening it into sheets and melting it over a fish fillet to form a crispy, buttery crust. It's a technique I've kept in my back pocket for years, because it's an easy and versatile way to elevate any kind of protein. You can get creative with flavors and herbs in the butter, and use any fish or meat—it's very much a plug-and-play recipe, once you have the method down.

That being said, this recipe is all about the fish, and after nailing the compound butter, you'll wind up with a beautiful snapper fillet with a crispy, herbaceous, buttery crust on top. Add a sharp, concentrated tomato flavor and the brightness of the pistou, and you have a lovely dish for someone special. Even though the recipe calls for a lot of butter, most of it runs off during broiling, so the fish still manages to feel light and breezy, like summer in Provence.

Preheat the oven to 225°F.

Place the bread on a wire rack and bake in the oven until totally dry and stiff, but without color, about 45 minutes. Place bread, on its rack, over a baking sheet, and let cool. Using the rack as a grater, rub the bread against the rack to make crumbs. With your hands, rub the crumbs to make them finer, like coarse sand—they don't have to be perfectly uniform, but you don't want big chunks. Set the bread crumbs aside—one 6-inch French loaf will make exactly enough for this recipe, but if you make more or have extra, leftover crumbs will keep well in a resealable bag in the freezer for up to 3 months.

To make the butter: In a mixing bowl, combine the softened butter, parsley, oregano, lemon juice, garlic, salt, and 3 to 5 grinds of pepper. Fold together to combine and taste—the butter should be bright, herbaceous, floral, slightly garlicky, and overall balanced.

Add 1¼ cups of the bread crumbs to the butter, and fold together with a spatula to completely blend.

Cut two 2-foot sheets of parchment paper or wax paper and lay one on a clean work surface. Place the butter on the paper and spread it across

makes 2 servings

1 (6-inch) loaf French bread, halved lengthwise

GARLIC-AND-HERB BUTTER
1 cup unsalted butter, at room temperature

½ cup finely chopped flat-leaf parsley leaves

2 tablespoons chopped oregano leaves

1 tablespoon plus 1½ teaspoons freshly squeezed lemon juice

1 clove garlic, finely chopped

1 teaspoon kosher salt

Freshly cracked black pepper

3 tablespoons extra-virgin olive oil

2 (5- to 7-ounce) snapper fillets

Kosher salt

½ cup Oven-Dried Tomatoes (page 344)

¼ cup Herb Pistou (page 57)

CONTINUED

the middle of the sheet, stopping 3 to 4 inches from the edge on all sides. Cover with the second sheet. Using a rolling pin, roll over the parchment to make an even layer of butter about ¼ inch thick. Place the covered butter in the freezer—you can fold it to fit if necessary—and chill for 30 minutes.

Remove the butter from the freezer, and, leaving it covered in parchment paper, use kitchen scissors to cut the sheet into rectangular pieces the same size as your fish fillets. Transfer the cutouts to a resealable plastic bag and return to the freezer until you have seared the fish (any leftover butter will keep in the freezer indefinitely).

Preheat the broiler. Place a cooling rack on a baking sheet.

Heat the oil in a large sauté pan over medium-high heat until shimmering. Meanwhile, pat the fish dry with a paper towel and season with salt. Gently lay the fish in the pan, flesh-side down, and cook until pale gold, but not crispy, 4 to 6 minutes. Flip the fillets and cook on the other side for 3 minutes. Transfer to the prepared cooling rack.

Remove two pieces of the compound butter from the freezer. Peel off the parchment and lay each one across a fish fillet, giving it a blanket of frozen butter. Place the fillets on the rack on the baking sheet.

Place the baking sheet under the broiler and cook the fillets for 2½ to 3½ minutes. As they cook, much of the butter will melt and baste the fish, leaving behind a crust of toasty, crispy bread crumbs and herbs. The fish is done when the butter is completely melted and the crust is crisp, but not burnt.

To serve, arrange the fish on a platter, scatter the roasted tomatoes around the fillets, and garnish with dollops of the pistou.

cornmeal-crusted trout with buttered grits, fried egg, and hot sauce

This is a total fish-camp breakfast—crispy fried freshly caught trout over beautiful stone-ground grits with a fried egg on top and hot sauce. What more could you want on a cool, misty morning? This is the way God intended trout to be eaten, with a perfectly crusty outside and a soft, steamy texture inside. (I am only half kidding.)

I learned this technique from one of my veteran cooks, who's from down the bayou. He showed me the trick of marinating trout in buttermilk and hot sauce and then shaking it in a bag with cornmeal before frying. I showed this technique to David DiBenedetto, editor in chief of *Garden & Gun*, and he loved it so much, he devoted an entire editor's letter to it. (Thanks, Dave!)

Start the grits first, because they'll take the longest to cook. Everything else will come together quickly, with the runny egg yolk and the hot sauce combining to make a delicious poor man's hollandaise sauce to coat the fish and grits.

makes 4 servings

8 eggs

1 cup buttermilk

3 or 4 dashes Homemade Hot Sauce (page 62) or store-bought sauce (preferably Texas Pete's or Crystal), plus more for serving

5 (3- to 5-ounce) speckled trout, catfish, or drum fillets, skin and pinbones removed

3 cups finely ground cornmeal

2 tablespoons kosher salt, plus more as needed

1½ teaspoons freshly cracked black pepper, plus more as needed

½ cup peanut oil or other oil with a high smoke point

2 to 3 tablespoons unsalted butter

1 recipe Buttered Grits (page 133)

Beat 3 of the eggs in a mixing bowl, then add the buttermilk and hot sauce. Transfer to a resealable plastic bag or lidded container. Add the fish and place in the refrigerator to marinate for 20 minutes.

Place the cornmeal, salt, and pepper in a large paper bag. Clench the top closed and shake to combine. Remove the fish from the marinade and allow the excess marinade to drip off. Add a fillet to the paper bag and shake to coat. Remove the coated fish, set aside on a plate, and repeat with the remaining fillets.

Line a plate with paper towels. Heat the oil in a large cast-iron or nonstick skillet over medium heat until it shimmers, and when you add a tiny pinch of cornmeal it sizzles. Working in batches to avoid overcrowding, gently place the fillets in the pan. The fish will leach some liquid as it cooks, so keep the fillets 1 to 1½ inches apart in order to achieve a crispy, golden crust (as opposed to floppy steamed fish with breading). Fry until crispy and golden brown, about 2 minutes per side. Transfer to the paper towels to drain.

Clean out the pan you fried the fish in, or use a large, clean nonstick skillet for frying the eggs. Heat the pan over medium-high, and when the pan is hot, add the butter and swirl it around to melt quickly. Once

CONTINUED

the butter is melted and bubbling, crack in the remaining 5 eggs, which should immediately start to fry. Cook on the first side until the whites are mostly set but not the yolks, 2 to 3 minutes, and then flip and cook for 1 minute more. Transfer the fried eggs to a plate and season with salt and pepper.

Spoon the grits onto individual plates or a platter, drape the catfish over the grits, and lay the fried eggs on top. Season with a few more dashes of hot sauce and serve.

serrano-wrapped cobia
with salsa verde

Consider this my variation on the Italian dish saltimbocca, and further evidence that most things are better when wrapped in ham. Fish fillets don't usually have the ability to get crispy unless they're fried, but wrapping them in thinly sliced Serrano or dry-aged country ham adds a salty, crispy casing that's extremely satisfying to crack through when you sit down to eat.

Cobia is a pelagic fish, living in the upper level of the water column. Around here, they swim along the grass line offshore, where brown brackish water meets blue water, hunting for baitfish. If you can't get your hands on wild cobia, there's a really nice farm-raised supply on the market from a company called Open Blue, and their fish tastes amazing.

Cobia is white and very firm, with a meaty, lean texture, comparable to tuna or swordfish. When you cut into a whole fish, you get long loins, as opposed to thin, flaky fillets. It has a slightly briny flavor that tastes great with acidic, herbaceous salsa verde, and plays really well with the funky flavors of aged ham. You can serve this as is, or with the summer squash salad on page 164 or the pearled barley on page 130, or both.

makes 4 servings

4 (5-ounce) portions fresh cobia or other firm-fleshed fish, such as tuna

Kosher salt

Freshly cracked black pepper

2 teaspoons grated lemon zest

4 thin slices Serrano ham or country ham

1 tablespoon canola oil

Heaping ½ cup Salsa Verde (page 56)

Preheat the oven to 375°F.

On a clean work surface, place the fish on two paper towels. Lay two more paper towels on top and gently pat to absorb any excess moisture. Discard the towels. Season each piece of fish with a pinch of salt (go easy here to respect the saltiness of the ham), a few grinds of black pepper, and ½ teaspoon of the lemon zest.

Place the ham on the work surface, laying it out vertically. Place one piece of the fish over each slice of ham. One set at a time, starting with the ends closest to you, roll up the fish and ham to form a tight wrap with the ham on the outside.

Heat a large cast-iron or nonstick skillet over high and add the oil. Place the fish in the pan, leaving 1 inch between the pieces, positioning them seam-side down. This will help create an initial seal around the fish.

Decrease the heat to medium-high and continue to sear the fish on the seam side until the ham is crispy and a bright, almost candy-apple red, about 3 minutes. Gently flip and repeat on the other side. Once the ham on the second side reaches the same red color, the fish will be at about medium doneness (about 135°F in the center), which is my preference for cobia or tuna. If you want to cook the fish further, place it on a baking sheet and roast in a 400°F oven for 6 to 8 minutes.

To serve, cut the fish once crosswise to expose a cross-section of the meat and show the contrast between the fish and the ham, and place the two halves on plates or a platter. Top each roll with 2 heaping tablespoons of salsa verde.

poached gulf fish with roasted peppers and fines herbes

There's a classic dish in Louisiana called *court bouillon* that's basically fish smothered in tomato gravy and served over rice. It's a great thing to make when you've been out fishing and caught a mixture of different species and sizes, and want to serve them all up at once. The key is to place the fish in the tomato gravy to just cook through, and break up the fillets slightly when you serve them spooned over a bowl of rice.

Over the years, I've put more and more herbs into my version, and eventually, between that and the tomato, this recipe has taken on a southern French flavor that also makes perfect sense here in Louisiana.

Preheat the oven to 400°F. Line a baking sheet with parchment paper.

Place the bell and poblano peppers in a large mixing bowl with the olive oil. Use your hands to coat each pepper evenly with the olive oil. Place the peppers on the prepared baking sheet and place in the oven. Check after 15 minutes, flipping the peppers and rotating the pan 180 degrees if the peppers aren't cooking evenly. They are done when their skins are puffy, dark, and blistered, about 25 minutes.

Using tongs, place the peppers in a mixing bowl and cover tightly with plastic wrap. Set aside to steam as they cool, making the skin easier to remove, about 45 minutes. When cool, carefully remove the plastic wrap and place the peppers on a clean work surface. It's helpful to have a damp paper towel nearby to wipe your fingers as you go. Using your fingers, peel off the skin in strips. Gently split open each pepper with your thumb and wipe away all the seeds. Remove and discard the stems. Lay the peppers across the cutting board and double-check that all seeds have been removed. With your knife, cut each pepper lengthwise into ¼-inch strips, moving from the stem end to the tip.

In a medium heavy-bottomed pot, make a brown roux with the peanut oil and flour, following the detailed instructions on pages 45 and 46. When the roux is complete, stir in the onion, garlic, and celery, and cook for about 5 minutes, which will darken the roux. Add the stock and bring to a boil, whisking to work out any lumps or clumps.

makes 4 to 6 servings

2 red bell peppers

2 poblano peppers

2 tablespoons extra-virgin olive oil

⅔ cup peanut oil

1 cup all-purpose flour

1 cup diced onion

2 tablespoons finely chopped garlic

½ cup diced celery

1 quart light chicken stock (see page 49)

1 quart high-quality canned diced tomatoes (such as Pomi)

½ cup tomato paste

2 dried bay leaves

Kosher salt

Freshly cracked black pepper

1 tablespoon sweet paprika

2 pounds Gulf fish fillets, such as redfish, speckled trout, black drum, or sheepshead

1 cup fines herbes (equal parts chives, tarragon, and flat-leaf parsley leaves, plus chervil, if available), finely chopped

Hot, freshly cooked white rice (see page 369) for serving

CONTINUED

Add the tomatoes and tomato paste, decrease the heat to low, and simmer until the vegetables are tender and beginning to fall apart, about 20 minutes. Turn off the heat.

Using an immersion blender, puree the tomato mixture until smooth and all lumps are worked out (like a gravy). Or process in small batches in a blender, and return the mixture to the same pot. Add the bay leaves and simmer over low heat for 20 minutes. Season with salt and pepper, then add the paprika and stir in the roasted peppers. Gently place the fish fillets in the sauce and cook over low heat until done, about 15 minutes. The fish may break apart slightly during this process, which is totally fine.

Remove the bay leaves and gently fold in the fines herbes. Put the rice in shallow bowls, if using, and spoon the fish on top. Serve immediately.

seared tuna with red wine jus

I love the idea of treating fish like red meat—of course it doesn't work with all fish, but a hearty tuna loin is fine. The technique is similar to how you'd cook a steak—searing it, basting it, resting it, then serving it with a wine jus, or a sauce made from meat juices, which adds the complexity and richness of meat to a fish that's meaty in flavor. It's a subtle play on a beefsteak with bordelaise sauce, using a lighter, more acidic red wine–based sauce, which pairs well with tuna. This dish just goes to show that you can take classic old-school French techniques, like making demi-glace, and apply them to a simple piece of seared fish.

Tuna, unlike a delicate white fish, is fairly forgiving, and when you cook it medium-rare as instructed, it won't fall apart when you flip or plate it. Try to get a cylindrical loin piece, as opposed to a flat, wide tuna steak, though in a pinch, a tuna steak will work. To complete the steakhouse vibe, you can serve this with crispy, buttery Pommes Anna-ish (page 134), but it's just as good with a simple side salad or steamed rice.

makes 4 to 6 servings

SEARED TUNA

2 pounds yellowfin tuna loin

1 tablespoon kosher salt

Freshly cracked black pepper

3 tablespoons vegetable oil

2 tablespoons unsalted butter

2 shallots, coarsely chopped

3 cloves garlic, peeled

RED WINE JUS

1 cup dry red wine, such as Burgundy

2 shallots, coarsely chopped

5 sprigs thyme

5 black peppercorns

3 cups demi-glace (see page 50)

1 tablespoon freshly squeezed lemon juice

Kosher salt

Freshly cracked black pepper

2 tablespoons unsalted butter

¼ cup minced chives

To sear the tuna: Dry the surface of the fish by patting it with paper towels. Season with the salt and a few grinds of pepper. Heat a large cast-iron or nonstick skillet over high heat, add the oil, and heat until shimmering, but not smoking. Place the tuna in the pan; it should audibly sizzle and pop, which means the pan is at the right temperature—if not much happens when the fish goes in, chances are the pan isn't hot enough yet. In that case, quickly remove the fish and let the pan heat for another minute before you return the steak to the pan.

Once the tuna is searing, decrease the heat to medium-high and continue to sear until golden brown on the bottom, about 2 minutes. Gently flip the tuna, and, securing it in the pan with your spatula, pour the hot oil into a heatproof glass or metal container and return the pan to the stove.

Add the butter, shallots, and garlic to the pan. As the butter quickly melts, use a metal spoon to repeatedly collect the butter and distribute it over the fish, basting the tuna until it is cooked medium-rare and feels slightly springy to the touch, 2 to 3 minutes.

Transfer the tuna to a serving plate and set aside to rest for about 5 minutes, while you make the jus.

To make the jus: In a medium saucepan over high heat, combine the wine, shallots, thyme, and peppercorns. Bring to a boil, then decrease the heat to medium and slow to a slight boil. Reduce the wine to about

¼ cup, then stir in the demi-glace and reduce the sauce by two-thirds, so it's slightly viscous and coats the back of a spoon. Whisk in the lemon juice and season with salt and pepper. Taste and then strain through a fine-mesh strainer into a small saucepan. Whisk in the butter over low heat and stir in the chives.

Slice the tuna into 1-inch-thick medallions, spoon the jus over the fish, and serve.

poultry

Poultry is one of my favorite proteins. I really enjoy the process of cleaning, preparing, and eating birds—there's something almost ceremonial about picking through their parts, getting into all of the nooks and crannies to extract every last bit of meat, and then using the leftover bones to make stocks and broths.

Chicken is probably the most popular protein in America, though some people avoid it because they think it's boring. That's a shame, because chicken has a lot to offer home cooks. It has several different textures of meat—a lean, succulent breast; collagen-heavy wings and thighs; nice cartilage in some areas, which gives you braised crunchy bits; and, of course, amazingly flavorful bones to roast and make stock with. On top of that, there are so many ways to prepare it, whether slow-roasted over a fire, braised in its own jus, fried, or cooked and chilled. Plus, the quality of birds available in supermarkets has skyrocketed over the years.

Delicate, individually portioned quail, which I like to stuff with cornbread and serve with smothered field peas (see page 263), is becoming increasingly popular at butchers and gourmet shops across the country; it's also often available at international markets. There are also high-quality farm-raised ducks available across the country. But I'm a big fan of wild-harvested duck, which is very popular in my neck of the woods. I'm a duck hunter myself, and in early winter, I like to spend as much time as possible duck hunting in the Rigolets, a passage of water just east of New Orleans. As for turkey, it is all too often reserved for the Thanksgiving table (or the deli aisle), but once you try the turkey pastrami on page 270, you'll be eating it a lot more often.

I cover a lot of technical ground in this chapter. Beyond the brining and slow-roasting in the aforementioned turkey pastrami, this chapter also features Sticky Chicken (page 252), which involves caramelizing, building a deeply flavored fond, deglazing the pan, and releasing collagen from the meat to form an addictive sauce. And the success of the stuffed quail relies on searing and basting, techniques I rely on time and time again for all kinds of proteins. As you work your way through this chapter, you will develop a skill set that's useful for cooking other meats, too.

pan-roasted chicken thighs with tangerine marmalade and thyme

I like chicken thighs and wings for with their crunchy cartilage-y bites, melty collagen bits, and crispy skin. (Thighs and wings have the most collagen.) They may be common parts on a common bird, but if done right, they are outstanding.

This recipe is inspired by our Southern citrus season; I can't get enough of the crispy roasted chicken with sweet tangy marmalade, velvety butter, and acidic wine. It's a nod to duck à l'orange, but more American—a fancy chicken nugget dipped in sweet-and-sour sauce.

makes 4 to 6 servings

6 bone-in, skin-on chicken thighs

Kosher salt

Freshly cracked black pepper

¼ cup plus 2 tablespoons grapeseed oil

1 cup dry white wine

2 tablespoons finely minced shallot

¼ cup plus 2 tablespoons tangerine marmalade (see page 359) or orange marmalade

1 to 3 teaspoons water (optional)

½ cup cold unsalted butter, cut into ½-inch cubes

2 tablespoons thyme leaves

Preheat the oven to 375°F.

Season the chicken on all sides with salt and pepper.

In a large heavy-bottomed ovenproof skillet, heat the oil over high heat until shimmering. Add the chicken thighs, skin-side down. They should immediately sizzle and start frying. Decrease the heat to medium-low and cook, undisturbed, until the skin is golden brown and beginning to crisp, about 10 minutes. Using a pan lid the approximate size of the pan to keep the chicken in the pan, carefully pour out the excess oil into a glass or metal container and discard.

Leaving the chicken skin-side down, transfer the pan to the oven. Roast for 15 minutes, then flip the chicken onto the other side and roast until golden brown, an additional 5 to 7 minutes.

Remove the pan from the oven and place the chicken on a cooling rack set over a plate. With the pan over medium-high heat, add the wine and shallot and reduce the wine until almost evaporated, about 10 minutes. Stir in the marmalade and any juices or drippings that may have collected under the resting chicken. Adjust the viscosity of the sauce with a few teaspoons of water, if needed.

Decrease the heat to low and stir in the butter, three to four cubes at a time. The idea here is to allow the butter to melt and form a warm, emulsified sauce that doesn't separate. Once all of the butter has been incorporated, taste, season with salt and pepper, and add the thyme.

Return the chicken to the pan and baste the chicken using a metal spoon to collect the marmalade butter and distribute it over the chicken repeatedly. Roll over the thighs, if necessary, to evenly coat.

Transfer the chicken to a serving platter. Top with any remaining sauce from the pan and serve immediately. Store leftovers covered in the refrigerator for up to 3 days.

grilled chicken wings with white bbq sauce

As much as I love a good fried or baked chicken wing, taking the extra time to barbecue them really pays off. The process of charring them, rendering their fat, and basting them in that fat while they cook tenderizes the meat and makes these wings insanely delicious. A lot of people judge chicken on the crispiness of its skin, which is great for fried chicken, but here, I'm going for releasing the collagen to create a lip-smacking result.

White BBQ sauce is an Alabama specialty, which I was introduced to by my friend Adam Evans. What I love about it is the way it transforms in the fire—at first, it looks like the mayo-based sauce that it is, but after some time on the grill, it breaks down into a glossy, sticky coating with a ton of flavor. I like to serve the extra sauce on the side for dipping, and leftovers can be used any time you'd reach for Ranch or mayo. The recipe makes about 3 cups, so you'll have plenty for dipping and repurposing.

I like to use the whole chicken wing here, without separating its three parts: the drumette, the flat middle wingette, and the pointy tip at the end. Cooking them together helps keep the skin intact, ensuring better insulation, and it makes them much easier to handle on the grill.

makes 2 to 4 servings

12 whole chicken wings

Kosher salt

Freshly cracked black pepper

WHITE BBQ SAUCE

2 cups mayonnaise or Aioli (page 65)

1 cup apple cider vinegar

¼ cup heavy syrup (see Note)

¼ cup freshly squeezed lemon juice

2 tablespoons Worcestershire sauce

Kosher salt

Freshly cracked black pepper

NOTE
Heavy syrup is a denser, stickier, sweeter cousin to simple syrup. Combine 1 cup of sugar with ½ cup of water in a small saucepan over medium heat, bring to a boil, and cook until the sugar dissolves, 5 to 7 minutes. Once cool, store the syrup in a covered jar the refrigerator for up to 2 weeks.

Season the chicken wings with salt and pepper and set aside at room temperature for 30 minutes.

To make the sauce: Mix the mayo or aioli, vinegar, heavy syrup, lemon juice, and Worcestershire in a bowl and season with salt and a generous amount of pepper. Set aside.

If using a gas grill, heat it on high. If using charcoal or wood, build a bilevel fire by raking the hot coals so that the bed is twice as thick on one side—the hotter side—than on the other.

Test the heat level of your grill. It is ready when you can only hold your palm about 5 inches over the cooking area for 1 to 2 seconds on the hotter side. Add the chicken to the hot part of the grill, flat-side down, and cook, flipping and rearranging the wings on different hot parts of the grill every 5 minutes or so to ensure even cooking, until golden brown and slightly charred, 10 to 12 minutes in total.

Check the heat level of the lower temperature area of your grill. The temperature is right when you can hold your palm about 5 inches over the cooking area for 5 to 6 seconds. Move the chicken to this area, cover the grill, and cook until very tender and almost falling off the bone, checking every 3 to 5 minutes and rotating as needed, about 25 minutes.

Line up the wings in a row on the grill and baste them with the sauce. Flip the wings so they're sauce-side down and repeat the process. As the sauce hits the grill, it will thicken and become sticky, like a glaze. Flip and baste for another two or three times until the wings are sticky and glistening (the entire basting process should take about 5 minutes).

Transfer the wings to a serving platter and serve immediately with extra sauce on the side for dipping. Store any leftover wings covered in the refrigerator for up to 3 days. Reheat in a 300°F oven.

sticky chicken

I don't usually describe a dish as "lip-smacking good," but in this case it's well-deserved. The Cajun side of my family calls this smothered chicken "sticky" because the sauce develops so much collagen that your lips stick together as you eat it. Once you have this technique down, you can use it for other cuts of meat as well, such as pork shoulder or beef chuck. Just try to include the bone, which provides a lot of the stickiness.

Mastering this recipe involves caramelizing and deglazing a rich brown gravy several times to coax as much deep flavor out of every ingredient as possible. It's a solid afternoon of hands-on cooking, so get yourself a bottle of wine and enjoy it as you work.

This dish is great with the Roasted Turnips and Their Greens with Bacon Vinaigrette on page 119, the Savory Bread Pudding on page 151, the Braised Collards with Chopped Ham Hocks on page 120, or even just freshly made white rice (see page 369).

makes 8 servings

10 bone-in, skin-on chicken thighs

2 tablespoons kosher salt

¼ cup vegetable oil

2½ quarts water, plus more as needed

4 cups small-diced onion

1 cup small-diced poblano or other mild green pepper

1 cup small-diced celery

¼ cup finely chopped garlic

3 bunches green onion, white and green parts, chopped

1 tablespoon chopped thyme leaves, plus 2 sprigs

1½ teaspoons freshly cracked black pepper

Season the chicken on all sides with 1½ tablespoons of the salt.

Heat an extra-large heavy-bottomed Dutch oven or cast-iron pot over high heat. Add the oil and when shimmering, add the chicken thighs, one at a time, skin-side down. They should start searing immediately, signaled by the sounds of skin frying and popping. If the oil is not hot enough, wait for it to get hotter before adding the rest of the chicken.

Decrease the heat to medium-high and let the chicken continue searing and rendering its fat until the skin is heavily browned and there are browned bits sticking to the bottom of the pot, 10 to 12 minutes. The rendered fat will combine with the oil in the pan to create a delicious cooking liquid.

Flip the chicken and brown the second side for another 10 to 12 minutes. There should be no hint of a scorched or burnt smell, and the bottom of the pot should have even more beautiful bits of brown chicken stuck to it. If the browning is progressing too quickly, decrease the heat slightly. As the brown color of the chicken deepens, the aroma of caramelized chicken should smell amazing.

At this point, add about 1 cup of the water, and using a wooden spoon, scrape the bottom of the pan to release the bits of fond (caramelized bits of meat and evaporated juices on the bottom of the pan). As you continue to stir, the water will evaporate and the fond will begin re-forming on the bottom of the pan. When you have a nice rich buildup in the pan and on the meat, after about 10 minutes, deglaze again with 1 cup of water to release the buildup. Repeat this step two more times. The goal is to achieve a richer and darker caramelization each time. After the fourth deglazing, remove the chicken thighs and set aside. There should still be some liquid in the pan.

When the water has evaporated and the fond has formed on the bottom of the pan the fourth time, add the onion, poblano, celery, and garlic. The vegetables will release liquid as they cook, which will deglaze the pan, as the water did before. When that happens, allow the vegetable liquid to reduce and evaporate completely. As your vegetables continue to cook, stir them to make sure they don't scorch. The vegetables will begin to caramelize and re-form the fond, 5 to 7 minutes. Deglaze with ½ cup of water and repeat three more times. When you're done, the vegetables should be so brown and caramelized they will be almost unrecognizable.

Tuck the chicken thighs into the pot and add just enough water to cover, about 1 quart. Add the green onions and chopped thyme. Decrease the heat to low and simmer, uncovered, stirring occasionally (and gently) for 20 to 25 minutes, until the sauce has slightly thickened from the collagen in the chicken, and the chicken is so tender it's separating from the bone. Season with the remaining 1½ teaspoons of salt and the pepper.

Garnish with the thyme sprigs and serve right out of the cooking pot. Store leftovers covered in the refrigerator for up to 3 days. Reheat in a 300°F oven.

chicken and biscuits with roasted mushrooms and peas

This recipe is inspired by my love of chicken pot pie, which goes back to my childhood; it's one of the dishes I feel most nostalgic about. Instead of making a full-on pot pie with a crust topping, though, I like to use biscuits, which are a little more forgiving. And since they sit in the gravy while baking, you end up with a sort of hybrid carb: a soft, gooey dumpling on the bottom, and a golden-crisp biscuit on top.

This is a great recipe for practicing a lot of simple but important techniques, such as making a roux, making a velouté (a classic French sauce that combines roux and stock), poaching chicken, roasting mushrooms, and making biscuits. The finished product is pure comfort food, intended to be served straight from the baking dish.

makes 4 to 6 servings

POACHED CHICKEN

2 bone-in, skin-on chicken breasts (about 1 pound each)

2 cups coarsely chopped celery

1 cup coarsely chopped leeks, green parts only

2 sprigs thyme

1 head garlic, skin on, halved through the equator

1 tablespoon kosher salt

2 teaspoons black peppercorns

1½ quarts water, plus more as needed

1 pound oyster or shiitake mushrooms, stemmed and sliced ½ inch thick

3 tablespoons extra-virgin olive oil

Kosher salt

2 cups small-diced leeks, white and light green parts only

1 cup small-diced celery

2 cloves garlic, thinly sliced

¼ cup plus 2 tablespoons unsalted butter

¼ cup all-purpose flour

1 recipe Buttermilk Biscuit dough (see page 372), chilled, but not rolled out

2 cups fresh shelled peas or whole sugar snap peas

2 tablespoons freshly squeezed lemon juice

To poach the chicken: Dry off the chicken with clean paper towels and nestle in a cocotte or small cast-iron pot with a lid. Arrange the celery and leeks around the chicken and place the thyme and garlic on top. Scatter the salt and black peppercorns throughout and add about 1½ quarts of water, or enough to cover everything by ½ inch.

Heat over medium-high heat and bring to a boil. As soon as the first few bubbles appear and there's a lot of steam, decrease the heat to low and cover. Simmer for 45 minutes, or until the chicken is just cooked through. Remove the chicken from the pot and set aside until cool enough to handle, about 20 minutes; then, with your hands, pull the meat into bite-size pieces. Strain the poaching liquid into a heatproof bowl or pitcher, discarding the aromatics, and rinse the pot.

Preheat the oven to 400°F. Line a baking sheet with parchment paper.

In a mixing bowl, toss the mushrooms with 1 tablespoon of the oil and a pinch of salt. Arrange in one layer on the prepared baking sheet and roast until golden brown around the edges and slightly dry, about 25 minutes. Remove from the oven and set aside. Lower the oven temperature to 375°F.

In the same pot you poached the chicken in, heat the remaining 2 tablespoons of oil over medium heat. Add the leeks, celery, and garlic and sweat, stirring often, until the vegetables soften but don't take on any color, 5 to 7 minutes. Add the reserved chicken-poaching liquid and bring

CONTINUED

just to a boil over high heat. Decrease the heat to medium so the mixture is at a vigorous simmer.

In a small heavy-bottomed pot, make a blond roux with ¼ cup of the butter and the flour, following the detailed instructions on pages 42 and 43. Put the roux in a mixing bowl, whisk in about ¼ cup of the hot liquid from the poaching pot, and continue whisking until well combined. If the mixture looks too thick and viscous to pour, thin out with another ladleful of stock. Add the roux mixture to the poaching pot and whisk to combine. This two-step process helps make a gravy with a consistent, lump-free texture.

Increase the heat to high and bring the mixture to a boil, observing how the roux thickens the sauce, 2 to 3 minutes. At this point, it should be more like a stew than a gravy, with a velvety texture. Decrease the heat to low and cook, stirring occasionally, until all of the flour has fully dissolved and no floury taste remains, 30 minutes.

While the gravy is simmering, roll out the biscuits: Generously flour a clean work surface. Line a baking sheet with parchment paper. With your hands, pat the dough into a disk about 1½ inches thick. Using a 2-inch round biscuit cutter, or a glass or a jar, punch out five or six biscuits, without twisting the cutter as you cut them out. Place on the prepared baking sheet.

Gather up the remaining dough and, without kneading, form into another loose ball. Press this into a 1½-inch-thick disk and cut out another five or six biscuits. Don't worry about oddly shaped scraps—just gently work them together, and continue punching out biscuits until you have used all of the dough. Place the baking sheet in the refrigerator and chill for 20 to 30 minutes.

Stir the remaining 2 tablespoons of butter into the gravy, whisking to emulsify (see page 35), then stir in the pulled chicken meat, roasted mushrooms, and peas. Add the lemon juice, parsley, and thyme, and season with 2 teaspoons of salt and a few grinds of black pepper.

Pour this mixture into a large ceramic casserole or glass baking dish. Top with a single layer of biscuits. (If you have more biscuits than you can fit in your baking dish, they can be baked separately according to the directions on page 372.) Brush each biscuit with some of the egg, sprinkle with the fleur de sel, and bake until the biscuits are golden brown and flaky, about 30 minutes. Serve directly out of the baking dish. This is best eaten the day it is prepared.

½ cup finely chopped flat-leaf parsley leaves

1 tablespoon thyme leaves

Freshly cracked black pepper

1 egg, whisked

1 teaspoon fleur de sel

NOTE
It's important to use bone-in, skin-on chicken breasts to develop the flavors in the poaching liquid. But if you want to make this with leftover roasted chicken, you can; in that case, I'd recommend using chicken stock (see page 49) in place of water. I don't like to add milk or cream to the velouté; it's rich enough with the roux, though the herbs and lemon juice do provide a bright, fresh contrast to the butter and flour.

vietnola-inspired roasted chicken

Roasting a chicken is one of my favorite things to do at home, but I'm always trying to find creative things to do with it. This recipe and the three that follow showcase one roasted chicken, used three different ways). This roasted chicken recipe is inspired by the abundance of Vietnamese restaurants in New Orleans (aka VietNOLA), where I like to eat on my days off. All of these recipes can be made using just the one bird, and if you're feeling ambitious, you can make all of them at once. But it makes more sense to cook them over the course of a few days and eat your way through the leftovers.

makes 4 servings

1 (2-inch) piece ginger

1 (2½-pound) chicken (without giblets)

1 tablespoon kosher salt

Freshly cracked black pepper

5 sprigs cilantro

3 (2-inch) pieces lemongrass, split lengthwise, pale center part only

2 tablespoons unsalted butter

Preheat the oven to 425°F.

Spear the ginger with a fork. Using the open flame of a stove-top burner, gently roast the ginger, turning the fork, until the skin is black and charred, about 2 minutes. Roasting the ginger adds a richer flavor to the chicken. Set aside.

Place the chicken in a large heavy-bottomed, ovenproof sauté pan. Using a boning knife or small paring knife, cut out the wishbone at the front of the bird, where the breasts meet. Season the bird inside and out with the salt and pepper. Cut the ginger into four pieces and place inside the cavity, along with the cilantro and lemongrass. I don't truss the chicken because I want the air to flow between the thighs and body, helping that whole area get crisp.

Roast the chicken, breast-side up, until golden brown and the skin looks crispy and the internal temperature reaches about 160°F, about 70 minutes. Transfer the chicken to a cutting board, ideally one with a trough around the perimeter to catch the juices. Add the butter to the roasting pan, mix with the chicken drippings, and spoon the mixture over the bird. Let rest for 30 minutes.

Carve and serve. Alternatively, remove the meat and reserve for one of the next three recipes. To remove the meat: Pull off the leg and the thigh and, using your fingers, pull off all their meat in large pieces. Set the meat aside in a bowl and reserve the bones. Using a chef's or boning knife, remove the breasts and set aside. Remove all remaining meat from the chicken carcass, using your fingers to get into every nook and cranny. Place the meat into the bowl with the leg and thigh meat and set aside until ready to use or refrigerate covered for up to 3 days. Save all of the bones and set aside until ready to use or refrigerate for up to 5 days.

chicken noodle soup with lemongrass, fresh herbs, and jalapeño

Chock-full of aromatics, like lemongrass, ginger, and star anise, this is the most flavorful chicken noodle soup imaginable, inspired by the *pho ga* at my favorite Vietnamese restaurants in New Orleans.

Spear the ginger with a fork. Using the open flame of a stove-top burner, gently roast the ginger, turning the fork, until the skin is black and charred, about 2 minutes. Cut the charred ginger crosswise into three slices and set aside. Roasting the ginger adds a richer flavor and color to the broth.

Pick the leaves from the cilantro to accumulate ½ cup leaves. Set aside the leaves and reserve the rest of the bunch for the broth.

Break the chicken carcass into smaller parts, starting by separating the breastplate from the spine, which should be quite easy. Using a cleaver, cut the remaining bones into 3- to 4-inch pieces. Place all of the chicken bones in a medium pot and add the ginger, diced onion, star anise or cloves, cilantro stems, and lemongrass. Cover with the water. Bring to a boil over high heat, then decrease the heat to low and barely simmer the broth, undisturbed, for 2½ hours. It's important not to boil the broth or stir at all to avoid agitating the proteins, which will make it cloudy.

About 30 minutes before you're ready to serve, soak the noodles in warm water. Fill a large pot with water and bring to a boil.

While the noodles are soaking, carefully strain the broth through a fine-mesh strainer into a bowl to collect any of the impurities that might make the liquid cloudy. Wash the broth pot. Return the strained broth to the pot and add fish sauce to taste—I like to use the fish sauce in place of salt in this recipe. Decrease the heat to low to keep warm for serving.

Using a large skimmer, dip the soaked rice noodles, one handful at a time, into the boiling water and cook until soft, 1 to 2 minutes. Divide among large soup bowls. Divide the pulled chicken, green onions, thinly sliced onion, jalapeño, and reserved cilantro leaves among the bowls. Ladle the broth into the bowls, covering the chicken and noodles by ½ to 1 inch. Garnish with the mung bean sprouts and basil leaves. Pass the lime at the table for everyone to squeeze into their soup as they wish.

makes 4 servings

1 (2-inch) piece ginger, unpeeled

½ bunch cilantro

1 roasted chicken carcass (see facing page)

1 large onion, ½ medium-diced and ½ sliced into thin half-moons

3 star anise pods or 2 cloves

2 (3-inch) pieces lemongrass, split lengthwise, pale center part only

2½ quarts water

12 ounces dried narrow rice noodles

Fish sauce (preferably Three Crabs or Red Boat; see page 28) for serving

1 roasted bone-in, skin-on chicken breast (see facing page), pulled into large ribbons

½ cup thinly sliced green onions, white and green parts

1 jalapeño, thinly sliced

1 cup mung bean sprouts

8 basil leaves (preferably Thai basil), torn

1 lime, cut into wedges

cabbage salad with roasted chicken, fresh herbs, and peanuts

These seemingly humble ingredients come together in a simple salad that packs a ton of flavor. The bright notes from the lime, the crunch of the cabbage, and the umami from the fish sauce are the perfect dressing for leftover cold chicken.

makes 4 servings

2 tablespoons fish sauce (preferably Three Crabs or Red Boat; see page 28)

2 tablespoons sugar

3 tablespoons freshly squeezed lime juice

¼ cup plus 2 tablespoons water

2 cups finely shredded green cabbage

1 roasted bone-in, skin-on chicken breast (see page 258), pulled into thin shreds

¼ cup thinly sliced green onions, white and green parts

¼ cup mint leaves

¼ cup cilantro leaves

Sliced hot chiles, such as jalapeños or serranos

¼ cup coarsely chopped roasted peanuts

In a mixing bowl, combine the fish sauce, sugar, lime juice, and water and stir to blend. Let sit and dissolve at room temperature for about 30 minutes.

In a large bowl, toss the cabbage, chicken, green onions, half of the mint, half of the cilantro, and the hot chiles with the fish sauce mixture. The salad should be generously dressed.

To serve, arrange on a serving platter and garnish with the remaining mint and cilantro and the roasted peanuts.

roasted chicken rice paper rolls

Rice paper rolls are the ideal vehicle for using up all of those little bits of chicken that you can pick off the carcass after roasting or soup-making, which is, in my opinion, the entire point of cooking a whole chicken.

To make the dipping sauce: Combine the fish sauce, sugar, water, and lime juice in a bowl and let sit for 30 minutes to dissolve the sugar. Stir to blend and add the hot chile and garlic. Set aside.

Bring a medium pot of water to a boil and cook the rice noodles according to the package instructions. Drain and rinse with cool water, then chill in the refrigerator for 20 minutes.

Fill a large bowl halfway with comfortably hot water. Take one rice paper wrapper and dip it into the hot water until it softens, 20 to 30 seconds. Don't let it get too soft, or it will tear too easily once filled. Lay the rice wrap on a cutting board and, on the half closest to you, place a lettuce leaf and then layer on a bit of noodles, chicken, carrot, cucumber, basil, and cilantro. (Don't overstuff the rolls. You may not need to use all of the noodles, and that's okay.) Starting with the side closest to you, roll up the wrapper halfway, then fold in the left and right edges and finish rolling up (like a burrito). You should have a small roll, about 3 inches long and 2 inches in diameter. Place on a serving plate and repeat with the remaining wrappers and filling.

If desired, cut each roll in half crosswise, and serve with the dipping sauce. The dipping sauce, chicken, and other fillings will keep, stored separately, in the refrigerator for up to 3 days. The assembled rolls will keep covered in the refrigerator for 1 day.

makes 8 rolls

DIPPING SAUCE

2 tablespoons fish sauce (preferably Three Crabs or Red Boat; see page 28)

2 tablespoons sugar

¼ cup plus 2 tablespoons water

3 tablespoons freshly squeezed lime juice

1 teaspoon minced hot chile, such as jalapeño or serrano

½ teaspoon minced garlic

4 ounces rice noodles (see Note)

8 rice paper wrappers (see Note)

8 large pieces green-leaf lettuce

1 cup sliced roasted chicken thigh and leg meat (see page 258), with skin

1 carrot, peeled and cut into 2-inch matchsticks about ⅛ inch thick

½ cucumber, cut into 2-inch matchsticks

16 basil leaves

½ cup cilantro leaves

NOTE

Rice noodles and paper wrappers are available at most Asian markets. You can substitute butter lettuce leaves for the rice paper wrappers.

cornbread-stuffed quail over smothered field peas

I generally don't like stuffing birds, because I think you overcook all the meat before the dressing gets hot. But quail is different—because it's so small and cooks so quickly, you're able to stuff it and roast it without overcooking. And in this recipe, the stuffing is actually quite useful because it moisturizes the bird from the inside out, keeping even the smallest and most delicate quail juicy and succulent. It's a good entry-level recipe for cooking quail, too, because you won't have to worry about dry meat.

You can make just the quail if you so choose. To round out a rib-sticking Southern meal, I like to serve them over rich Field Peas in Tomato Gravy, and if I have the time and inclination, I spoon some Demi-glace–Honey-Mustard sauce over everything. The sauce is optional; the recipe is still delicious and comforting without.

To make the dressing: In a large skillet over medium-high heat, melt the butter until foamy. Add the tasso or sausage and cook until rendered and slightly crisp, 7 to 10 minutes. Add the onions and cook until soft and translucent, 6 to 8 minutes. Add the carrots and celery and cook until soft, 8 to 10 minutes. Add the stock and bring to a boil. Decrease the heat to medium and, using your hands, add the cornbread, crumbling it up into rough pieces about the size of marbles as you go. Fold the mixture together and season with the thyme, salt, and a few grinds of pepper. Cook, stirring occasionally, until the cornbread has soaked up all of the liquid, 4 to 6 minutes. Set aside to cool.

Preheat the oven to 375°F. Set a cooling rack in a baking sheet.

Season each quail, inside and out, with about 1 teaspoon of the salt and a few grinds of black pepper. Stuff each quail with about ½ cup of the dressing, or as much as will comfortably fit—you want to plump up the quail with the dressing to hold them in a nice round shape.

Heat the oil in a large cast-iron or other heavy-bottomed skillet over medium-high heat until shimmering. Working in batches, sear the quail, breast-side down, to crisp the skin, about 3 minutes. Turn the quail gently in the pan and sear on the other side for another 3 minutes. Transfer the quail, breast-side up, to the rack on the baking sheet and repeat with remaining birds. Roast the quail for 15 minutes, or until the center of the

CONTINUED

makes 8 servings

CORNBREAD DRESSING

2 tablespoons unsalted butter

¾ cup small-diced tasso, bacon, or smoked sausage (see Note)

3 cups small-diced onions

1 cup small-diced peeled carrots

1 cup small-diced celery

2 cups chicken stock (see page 49)

1 recipe Cornbread (page 371)

2 tablespoons thyme leaves

2 teaspoons kosher salt

Freshly cracked black pepper

8 semiboneless quail (see Note)

2½ tablespoons kosher salt

Freshly cracked black pepper

3 tablespoons extra-virgin olive oil

3 tablespoons unsalted butter (optional)

DEMI-GLACE–HONEY-MUSTARD SAUCE (OPTIONAL)

2 cups demi-glace (see page 50)

3 tablespoons whole-grain mustard

3 tablespoons honey

2 tablespoons unsalted butter

1 recipe Field Peas in Tomato Gravy (page 127)

cornbread-stuffed quail over smothered field peas, continued

NOTE

Tasso is South Louisiana-style cured, hot-smoked pork shoulder.

Most store-bought quail are sold semiboneless (that is, their ribs and breastplate have been removed). They are available at specialty butchers and international markets. Fresh is preferable, but frozen is also fine (just be sure to defrost it fully before stuffing).

stuffing reads 160°F on an instant-read thermometer. Set the baking sheet near the stove top.

If not making the sauce, drain the fat from the skillet (but don't wash it). Over medium heat, add the butter to the skillet and melt until foamy. Spoon the butter over the quail, and let rest for 10 minutes.

To make the sauce: In a small saucepan over medium-high heat, whisk together the demi-glace, mustard, and honey. Cook until the demi-glace has reduced in volume by half and has become noticeably sticky, with thick bubbles in it, about 7 minutes. Whisk in the butter to emulsify (see page 35) and remove from the heat.

To serve, arrange the smothered field peas in tomato gravy on a platter and top with the quail. Spoon the sauce over the birds. Leftover quail will keep covered in the refrigerator for up to 3 days. Reheat in a 300°F oven.

crispy pan-roasted duck breast with pearl onion agrodolce

Duck is common in places where duck hunting is a popular sporting activity, including Louisiana. When fall comes around, duck for dinner is a nice reminder of the season, and offers a sense of place. In this recipe, the onion agrodolce, or sweet-and-sour onion, really complements that rich, slightly iron-y tasting duck meat. It can stand up to even the most aggressive wild duck flavor, should you be lucky enough to get your hands on some. But this recipe is equally good with farm-raised duck, which tend to have larger breasts. If you are cooking wild duck breasts weighing less than the 6 ounces called for in the recipe, you may want to cook one or two extra.

Basting the duck with its own rendered fat, as I call for here, is the technique that gives you beautiful, crispy skin. The big secret is to avoid flipping the duck until the very end. I prefer to let the meat cook, skin-side down, so its fat completely renders, and then baste the meat repeatedly to make a crackling-like crust.

It's worth noting that the pearl onion agrodolce is a wonderful side for all kinds of game meats, as well as red meat such as beef or lamb, and even charcuterie.

makes 4 to 6 servings

PEARL ONION AGRODOLCE

2 tablespoons grapeseed oil

1 pound peeled pearl onions, left whole

1 cup water

1 cup sugar

½ cup dry red wine

½ cup red wine vinegar

4 (6- to 7-ounce) duck breasts

2 tablespoons plus 2 teaspoons kosher salt, plus more as needed

1 shallot, coarsely chopped

2 tablespoons thyme leaves

To make the agrodolce: Heat the oil in a large saucepan over high heat until shimmering, then add the onions. Cook until the onions are just starting to color, rolling them around a bit, about 2 minutes. Add the water and cook until it has almost entirely evaporated and the onions are becoming translucent, 8 to 10 minutes. Add the sugar, wine, and vinegar; decrease the heat to medium; and cook, stirring frequently, until the liquid thickens and coats the back of a spoon, and the onions are tender, about 15 minutes. Set aside and cool to room temperature. The onion agrodolce will keep covered for up to 1 week in the refrigerator.

Preheat the oven to 400°F.

On a clean work surface, place the duck breasts skin-side down and remove any silver skin (a fine membrane), sinew, feathers, or cartilage that may be present. Flip the breasts over and, using a sharp knife, score the skin diagonally to form a crosshatch pattern. (Be careful not to cut all the way through the skin to the meat.) Salt the skin side of each duck breast with about 1½ teaspoons of salt. The idea here is to make a very quick cure that will pull some of the moisture out of the skin, making it easier to render the duck fat and get crispier skin. Let the duck sit at room temperature for about 20 minutes.

Heat a large cast-iron or heavy-bottomed ovenproof skillet over high heat until the pan is hot, about 2 minutes. Add the duck breasts, skin-side down, and decrease the heat to medium. Cook, undisturbed, for 10 to 12 minutes. As the duck cooks, its fat will begin to render and its skin will crisp up. Use a metal spoon to collect a few tablespoons of the rendered duck fat and distribute it over the duck to baste it as it cooks. Transfer the skillet to the oven to finish cooking, until the internal temperature reaches about 135°F on a meat thermometer for medium-rare, 5 to 7 minutes. Remove the pan from the oven and add the shallot and 1 tablespoon of the thyme. Baste the meat again with its own fat.

Flip the breasts so they're skin-side up (the skin should be golden and crispy at this point), season with a pinch of salt for each breast, and continue basting for 1 minute over high heat. Remove the breasts from the pan and let rest on a cooling rack for 7 to 10 minutes. Discard the shallot and thyme and reserve any remaining duck fat.

Slice the duck into pieces about ½ inch thick and arrange on a serving platter. Spoon about 1½ teaspoons of the reserved duck fat over the duck and arrange the agrodolce over and around the meat. Garnish with the remaining 1 tablespoon of thyme and serve.

duck confit

Confit might seem fancy, but in France, this method of preserving comes from humble traditions. The idea of storing something in fat evolved from the need to feed a lot of people for a long time. In Louisiana, it's an efficient way to preserve the abundance of the wild ducks we hunt in the winter, and a nod to our French influence. Cooking the duck in fat, with the addition of salt, gives it succulence and flavor that you can't achieve by roasting or grilling.

Duck confit is endlessly versatile—you can serve the crisped legs over the Lentil Ragout on page 128; shred the meat and mix it with duck fat to make rillettes on toast points; or pull it apart into morsels and toss it with greens (like the spinach and frisée salad on page 159).

Coat each duck leg with 2 tablespoons of salt and nestle them, in a single layer, in a large casserole dish. Distribute the peppercorns and juniper berries over the top. Cover with parchment paper and weigh down with another casserole dish. Place in the refrigerator to cure for 12 hours.

When you're ready to make the confit, preheat the oven to 250°F.

Rinse the duck under cool running water to remove excess salt, and pat dry with paper towels. Place the duck in a small Dutch oven or cocotte with a lid. Tuck the thyme and garlic among the legs. Place the bay leaves on top and cover with the duck fat.

Cut a piece of parchment slightly larger than the pot, and using your fingertips, push the parchment down until it adheres to the duck fat. Cover the pot, put in the oven, and cook until the meat slips easily off the bone, about 4 hours.

Remove the duck from the oven, uncover the pot (but leave the parchment paper), and cool to room temperature, about 2 hours. It's important to cool the duck in its fat before serving to get the most succulent texture. The duck legs will keep, fully submerged in their fat (and therefore sealed), for up to 1 month.

When you're ready to serve, using tongs, remove the legs from the fat (reserve the fat for future use). Heat a large cast-iron or other heavy-bottomed pan over medium-high heat until the pan is hot, about 3 minutes. Place the duck legs, in a single layer, skin-side down (working in batches if necessary), and decrease the heat to medium. Cook, undisturbed, until the skin is golden brown, crispy, and crackling, 8 to 10 minutes. Flip to warm the other side for 1 to 2 minutes, then transfer to a serving platter.

Any leftover duck meat can be picked off the bone and resealed in leftover fat. Simply reheat the fat gently to melt it and pour over the meat.

makes 6 servings

6 duck legs

¾ cup kosher salt

2 teaspoons black peppercorns

12 juniper berries

10 sprigs thyme

6 cloves garlic

4 dried bay leaves

9 cups rendered duck fat, warmed over low heat until melted (see Note)

NOTE
The rendered duck fat you will need for this recipe is available at many specialty butchers and online. Once you have made the confit, you'll have your own. The leftover fat is a wonderful thing to have around. Cook it down over low heat for about 20 minutes, then strain through a fine-mesh strainer to remove any solids, and store it in the refrigerator for up to 1 month. Use it to cook everything from vegetables to other meats. The salty jus can be stirred into stocks or sauces.

turkey pastrami sandwiches

I love a classic Reuben sandwich, but I'm always looking for ways to do things a little differently and have some fun with the staples, which is where the idea for this turkey pastrami riff came from, featuring homemade meat and condiments. Turkey pastrami is easy to make at home, though it takes time to brine the turkey. The payoff is that it's exponentially more juicy and tasty than the deli version. And instead of standard-issue Thousand Island dressing and sauerkraut, I make my own rémoulade and choucroute, which take this glorious sandwich to the next level.

The turkey takes 2½ days from start to finish, and the choucroute takes 12 hours; plan accordingly. For more on brining and why I like to do it with leaner cuts, such as turkey breast, see the Shaved Pork Loin on Toast with Mustard Jus and Chow Chow on page 284.

makes 8 sandwiches

BRINED TURKEY

2 quarts water

½ cup kosher salt

2 tablespoons coriander seeds

2 tablespoons black peppercorns

5 garlic cloves, mashed (see page 37)

2 dried bay leaves

2 pounds boneless, skinless turkey breast

RUB

¼ cup coriander seeds

2 tablespoons black peppercorns

1 recipe Choucroute (page 355)

9 tablespoons unsalted butter, at room temperature

16 slices rye bread

½ cup whole-grain mustard

8 slices Gruyère, Emmental, or Swiss cheese, ¼ inch thick

1 cup Rémoulade (page 72)

Fleur de sel

To brine the turkey: In a large saucepan, combine the water, salt, coriander, peppercorns, garlic, and bay leaves. Bring to a boil, then remove from heat and let cool to room temperature.

Place the turkey breast in a large resealable plastic bag and pour the brine over it. Seal the bag, tuck the bag in the pot, and place in the refrigerator to brine for 2 days.

When the turkey is done brining, make the rub: In a small dry skillet over medium-high heat, combine the coriander seeds and black peppercorns. As they toast, stir and gently shake the pan, until the spices release their aromas, 3 to 5 minutes. Remove from the heat and let cool completely in the pan. Place in a clean spice grinder and grind to a medium-fine texture, similar to freshly cracked black pepper from a mill.

Preheat the oven to 325°F. Set a roasting rack in a roasting pan or on a baking sheet.

Remove the turkey from the brine, dry with paper towels, and place on the rack. Coat the turkey with a generous layer of the rub on both sides.

Wrap the turkey in foil and seal as tightly as possible. Roast for 2 to 2½ hours, until an instant-read thermometer poked straight through the foil into the thickest part of the breast reads 160°F. Remove the turkey from oven and let rest, still wrapped in foil, for about 40 minutes, at which point it should rise in temperature to about 165°F. Unwrap the turkey and slice it as thinly as possible.

Preheat the broiler to high. Set a wire rack in a baking sheet.

Drain the choucroute by gently squeezing out the liquid and drying with a clean kitchen towel.

Spread 1½ teaspoons of butter on each slice of bread. In a large cast-iron or nonstick skillet over medium-high heat, toast the bread, butter-side down, working in batches if necessary, until golden brown and crispy, 3 to 5 minutes. (Do not flip bread.) Place the toasted bread on the prepared baking sheet, buttered-side down.

Wipe the pan clean with a paper towel, and over high heat, melt the remaining 1 tablespoon of butter until foamy. Add the choucroute and cook, undisturbed, allowing it to sear on one side for 4 to 5 minutes. Using a spatula, flip as much as possible in one piece, and sear on the other side for 4 to 5 minutes, until the cabbage is partially brown and plump and juicy. Remove from the heat and set aside.

Preheat the broiler.

Arrange 8 slices of bread on the wire rack, butter-side down, and spread each slice with 1 tablespoon of the mustard. Layer about 4 ounces of thinly sliced turkey pastrami, ½ cup of seared choucroute, and 1 slice of cheese on each piece of bread. Place under the broiler and watch carefully, rotating the pan as necessary, so that the cheese melts evenly over the choucroute, 3 to 5 minutes. Remove from the oven. Spread 2 tablespoons of rémoulade on each of the remaining 8 slices of bread. Close the sandwiches and open your mouth wide. Any leftover turkey will keep covered in the refrigerator for up to 5 days.

meat

Meat is often the centerpiece of a meal, and learning to cook it properly is one of the most important skills any cook can master. This chapter features a wide range of both techniques and meats themselves, covering everything from searing to braising to brining to pounding and frying; from rabbit and pork to lamb and beef. The recipes that follow are some of my favorite things to eat, a combination of popular restaurant dishes and personal greatest hits, all adapted for the home kitchen. I hope that you'll eventually cook your way through this entire chapter.

Meat is a huge part of the cuisine of New Orleans. Our love of pork goes back generations, thanks to the Spaniards who first brought pigs to the region. Hunting and fishing are time-honored activities here (just check the motto on the Louisiana state license plate—"Sportsman's Paradise"), and game meats, like rabbit and venison, are beloved as a result. There's a distinct European influence on some of the classic New Orleans meat dishes, things like beef daube, which I've reinterpreted here in the short rib recipe on page 293. The addition of Southeast Asian flavors reflects the city's ever-evolving population.

When it comes to shopping for meat, I'm reluctant to offer hard and fast rules. I believe you should invest in the best quality that's available to you, though what that actually means is different for everyone. Personally, when it comes to beef, I'm a fan of USDA Prime, because I think they do an excellent job of grading it, and it's hard to find a better-tasting piece of meat. But some people prefer eating more naturally raised cattle, grass-fed or otherwise. You should feel good about what you're eating, and where you buy it.

I wish more people would cook rabbit at home. It's a delicious, lean protein that's very mild in texture and flavor and as easy to cook as chicken. You can find it at specialty butchers and international markets, or online, though I've been pleasantly surprised to find it in my local supermarket on occasion. The quality of domestic lamb just keeps getting better, and it's another great and underappreciated protein in American home kitchens.

While some of the recipes in this chapter are for composed dishes, most of them focus on the preparation of the meat itself. That's intentional. With the strip steak on page 302, for example, I teach you how to get a nice proper sear on the meat, baste it with aromatics, form a crust, let it rest, and finish it with a simple compound butter. You can take that same steak and add some of the sides or sauces from previous chapters and turn it into an entree. But for the sake of effective instruction, I am singling out key techniques in this chapter—pan-frying the rabbit on page 279, braising the short ribs on page 293, and grilling the skirt steak on page 301. Once you have those processes down, you'll have the freedom to decide how to build the rest of your meal around the meat.

rabbit schnitzel

Rabbit schnitzel has been on the menu at La Petite Grocery for nearly ten years. It seems adventurous, but when you eat it, it's super-mild, with very buttery, milky meat; there's nothing intense or gamy about this rabbit at all. That's part of the reason it lends itself so well to being breaded and bathed in lemony brown butter—the meat itself is so delicate, that when you add fat, acid, and crunch, it brings it all together. Normally I would braise rabbit legs (as I do in the slow-cooked recipe on page 279), but pounding them out helps tenderize the meat. The Hazelnut Spaetzle with Butternut Squash and Maple Syrup on page 143 makes a great accompaniment.

makes 6 servings

6 boneless, skinless rabbit legs

2 cups all-purpose flour

2 teaspoons kosher salt, plus more as needed

6 eggs

²/₃ cup whole milk

2 cups panko bread crumbs, finely ground in a food processor

1 cup grapeseed oil

½ cup unsalted butter

1 lemon, peeled and cut into 16 to 18 supremes (see page 36), with seeds and pith removed and rind reserved

2 tablespoons capers, drained, rinsed, and dried

2 tablespoons chopped flat-leaf parsley leaves

Freshly cracked black pepper

Working on a large, clean surface, dry the rabbit with paper towels and look it over to ensure there are no bone fragments or unwanted tendons and sinew; if there are, cut them out with a knife.

Lay out an 18- to 20-inch sheet of plastic wrap. Place two legs on the sheet and cover with another sheet of plastic wrap the same size. Use a mallet, rolling pin, or whiskey bottle to gently pound out the meat into flat, even pieces about ⅓ inch thick. Repeat with the remaining rabbit legs, replacing the plastic wrap if necessary.

Set up a dredging station. In a large flat-bottomed casserole or glass baking dish, combine the flour and 1 teaspoon of the salt. In a mixing bowl, combine the eggs and milk, whisking well, and transfer the egg wash to another flat-bottomed dish. In a final dish, combine the panko and the remaining 1 teaspoon of salt. Place a baking sheet at the end of the line.

Using one hand for the wet coating and one hand for the dry ones will result in a much tidier breading process and keep your hands from also becoming breaded. One at a time, use your right hand to dip a rabbit leg into the flour and toss it to thoroughly coat both sides, shaking off any excess. With your right hand, drop the rabbit gently into the egg wash. With your left hand, flip and swirl the leg to coat. Remove with your left hand and gently place in the panko, using your right hand again to flip and coat with the panko. Remove the rabbit with your right hand and place on the baking sheet. Repeat with the remaining rabbit and coatings.

Line a plate with paper towels. Heat ½ cup of the oil in a large cast-iron or other heavy-bottomed skillet over medium-high heat until shimmering.

CONTINUED

Place two rabbit legs in the pan; they should immediately start sizzling. Cook until golden brown, flipping once, about 3 minutes per side. Transfer the rabbit to the paper towels. Repeat with the remaining rabbit, replenishing with ½ cup of fresh oil and letting it heat until shimmering between batches.

When all the rabbit is cooked, drain the oil but don't rinse the pan. Over medium-high heat, melt and cook the butter until you smell a nutty aroma, about 3 minutes. While the butter melts, arrange the rabbit on a serving platter.

Add the lemon supremes to the pan, and squeeze in the juice from the leftover rind. Add the capers, parsley, and a few grinds of pepper to the butter and remove from the heat. Taste and add more salt if needed. Spoon the sauce over the schnitzel and serve. This dish is best made and eaten on the same day.

slow-cooked rabbit with olives, fennel, and country ham

This dish has serious European roots—braised rabbit with some combination of olives, fennel, and tomato shows up in a lot of classic French and Italian cookbooks. I've taken inspiration from those Old World flavors and adapted them to suit my Southern style. The result is basically smothered rabbit, with so much more dimension and brightness than a standard-issue gravy. The combination of white wine, tomatoes, fennel, and olives ups the acid level and makes this totally delicious. I could easily imagine cooking it at a Southern hunting camp.

In contrast to the Rabbit Schnitzel on page 276, this is a nice way to practice breaking down and cooking a whole rabbit. And flavorwise, it is significantly more rabbitcentric, thanks to the flouring, searing, and sauce-building process we go through here, which infuses every element of the dish with a rabbit flavor. If you're dying to make this but for some reason don't want to use or can't find rabbit, you can also make this with chicken thighs or legs.

Place your knife behind the front legs of the rabbit and cleanly cut them off the body. There is no joint, so they should come right off. With the cavity of the rabbit facing down, use your hands to pop out the joints of the back legs (as you would chicken thighs). Looking down, you should be able to see a clear outline of where the thighs separate from the loin. Using your knife, cut the thighs off along the spine and remove them from the body. Using a heavy knife, cut the saddle (the part of the body with the loin attached) into three equal parts. Check all pieces for bone fragments and pockets of blood, and remove with a boning knife and water, if necessary. Dry the meat well with paper towels and season on all sides with salt and pepper.

Preheat the oven to 300°F. Put the flour in a flat-bottomed casserole or glass baking dish.

Dust the rabbit pieces evenly with the flour. In a Dutch oven or another large heavy-bottomed, ovenproof pot with a lid (ideally large enough to hold all of the rabbit at once; otherwise, work in batches to avoid crowding), heat the grapeseed oil over high heat until shimmering. Gently add the rabbit in a single layer, smooth-side down. It should

makes 4 servings

1 (3- to 4-pound) rabbit

Kosher salt

Freshly cracked black pepper

½ cup all-purpose flour

½ cup grapeseed oil

1 cup small-diced dry-cured ham, such as country or Serrano

1½ cups medium-diced leek, white parts only

1½ cups medium-diced celery

1½ cups sliced peeled carrots (½-inch-thick rounds)

3 cloves garlic, finely chopped

2 cups dry white wine

3 cups chicken stock (see page 49)

1 cup cherry tomatoes

1 fennel bulb, cut into 8 wedges, fronds reserved

2 cups Castelvetrano olives, pitted

1 cup sliced fingerling potatoes (1-inch-thick rounds)

½ cup extra-virgin olive oil

1 Bouquet Garni (page 342; optional)

2 tablespoons chopped flat-leaf parsley leaves

¼ cup minced chives

CONTINUED

immediately sizzle and fry. Decrease the heat to medium-high and cook the rabbit until evenly crispy and golden brown, about 10 minutes. Flip and cook in a single layer on the other side until crispy and golden brown, another 8 to 10 minutes. Set the rabbit aside to rest.

Drain the oil from the pot, but don't wash the pot, and be sure to save any of the rabbit bits stuck to the bottom. Return the pot to medium-high heat and add the ham. Cook until the ham is slightly crisp and releasing some fat, 4 to 6 minutes, scraping the bottom of the pot with a wooden spoon to make a sticky rabbit-ham fond (caramelized bits of meat and evaporated juices on the bottom of the pan). If the meat seems close to scorching, decrease the heat slightly.

Add the leek, celery, carrots, and garlic to the pot, they should immediately start to release some liquid. Cook, stirring them with the fond and allowing them to moisten the pot, until the vegetables soften slightly and become very aromatic, about 5 minutes.

Stir in the wine to deglaze the pot, loosening the flavorful bits stuck on the bottom to flavor the sauce. Reduce the wine until the sauce is very thick, 4 to 6 minutes. Add the stock, which will thin out the sauce, and bring to a boil. Remove from the heat and return the rabbit to the pot, with any juices that have accumulated while it rested. Spoon the sauce around the rabbit. Arrange the tomatoes, fennel wedges, olives, and potatoes in one layer on top of the rabbit. Drizzle with the olive oil. Add the bouquet garni (if using) and season with salt and pepper. (Go easy on the salt, as the mixture has both ham and olives.)

Cover the pot and place in the oven for 3 hours, or until the rabbit is tender and falling off the bone. Remove from the oven and let rest, covered, for about 20 minutes.

Arrange the rabbit on a serving platter. Fold together everything remaining in the pot and spoon it on top of and around the rabbit. Garnish with the parsley, chives, and reserved fennel fronds and serve. Leftover rabbit will keep in an airtight container in the refrigerator for up to 4 days.

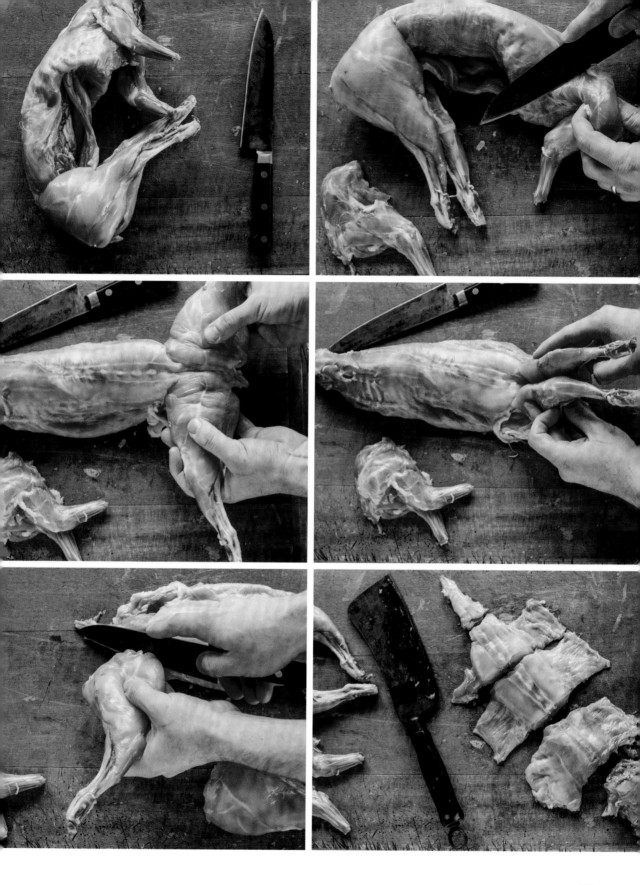

pork porterhouse steak with apple riesling jus

makes 2 or 3 servings

1 (24-ounce) pork porterhouse T-bone chop, cut double-thick, with the tenderloin

1½ tablespoons kosher salt

2 teaspoons freshly cracked black pepper

¼ cup small-diced peeled tart apple, such as Granny Smith

6 tablespoons unsalted butter, 2 tablespoons melted and 4 tablespoons cold

2 tablespoons vegetable oil

1 shallot, peeled and halved lengthwise

2 cloves garlic

1 sprig thyme

3 ounces dry Riesling or other white wine

¼ cup demi-glace (see page 50)

Just like its better-known beef cousin, pork has a porterhouse—the hefty cut of meat that contains both a strip loin and a tenderloin on either side of a T-shaped bone, making this ideal for serving two (or more). You can cook the whole thing on the stove top, basting it frequently with herb-infused butter to keep the meat juicy and flavorful and help reinforce its delicious crust.

To help cut some of the richness of the demi-glace, I like to serve this with a pile of the tangy homemade sauerkraut on page 354. Apples, pork, and sauerkraut are classic Eastern European flavors, and I think of the handful of old-school bistros in the French Quarter every time I make this recipe.

Season the pork on both sides with 1 tablespoon of the salt and 1 teaspoon of the pepper. Set the pork aside at room temperature.

Toss the diced apples with the melted butter and arrange in a single layer on a plate. Place the apples in the refrigerator and allow the butter to resolidify. This will help to keep them from oxidizing and turning brown.

Heat a large heavy-bottomed pan over high heat. Add the oil and heat until shimmering. Add the pork. The meat should begin to sear immediately; you should see it steaming at the edges and hear it sizzling and popping. If it doesn't, remove the meat and wait for the pan to heat up for a few minutes longer before returning the meat.

After 2 minutes, decrease the heat to medium-high and continue cooking the pork on the first side. After another 3 minutes, gently turn the pork over to cook the other side. Add the shallot, garlic, and thyme to the pan along with 2 tablespoons of the cold butter. As the butter melts, use a metal spoon to collect and distribute it over the pork to baste. Continue basting it every 2 minutes for the next 10 minutes, then turn the pork again and cook for about 10 minutes more, basting continually.

Remove the pork from the pan and set it aside on a plate. Spoon the remaining butter, shallot, and thyme over the top of the meat and let it rest, uncovered, for at least 8 or up to 15 minutes.

While the meat is resting, heat the same pan over medium heat and add the wine. As the wine heats it will help to release the fond—the caramelized bits of meat and evaporated juices on the bottom of the pan. With a wooden spoon, scrape all of the remaining bits from the pan into the liquid.

Cook until the wine has almost completely evaporated, about 2 minutes. Add the demi-glace, bring to a boil, and cook until it has reduced by half. You will notice the structure of the bubbles go from thin and steaming while boiling to tight and viscous once reduced.

Decrease the heat to low and add the remaining 2 tablespoons of butter, stirring for about 1 minute to emulsify (see page 35). Stir in the diced apples. The sauce should be completely smooth. Set the sauce aside and keep warm.

Cut along the T of the bone with your knife to remove the strip loin (the larger, longer side) and the tenderloin. Transfer the T bone to the serving platter. Thinly slice the strip loin and tenderloin, and nestle the meat into its original positions on bone. Spoon the sauce over the meat and serve immediately. Leftover pork will keep covered in the refrigerator for up to 3 days.

shaved pork loin on toast with mustard jus and chow chow

Some dishes just appear, fully formed, and this is one of them. It came out of the kitchen at my restaurant Balise on Day One, courtesy of the brain of our chef at the time, Paul DeMaria. We were trying to take an economical cut, like pork loin, and do something a little exciting with it. So we came up with this play on the great sliced meat and gravy dishes of the past—chipped beef on toast, Salisbury steak—done with a bit more care. There's a definite wow factor when we serve this, as it's fairly enormous—all of the meat piled up high and dripping in sauce over thick-cut toast. This is not a dainty dish.

Techniquewise, this is a good intro to brining. I use a standard ratio of 1 cup of salt to 1 gallon of water for meats, which I halved here because the recipe calls for only 1½ pounds of pork. There are so many reasons to brine meat. With a cut like loin, which isn't very fatty, a brine ensures that it will remain juicy after you roast, rest, slice, and reheat the meat to make this dish (if you did all that without brining the loin, it would become dry). Brining also allows you to impart flavor before cooking the meat, with the addition of brown sugar, pepper, and garlic.

makes 4 servings

BRINED PORK LOIN

2 quarts water

½ cup kosher salt

¼ cup lightly packed light brown sugar

2 dried bay leaves

1 tablespoon black peppercorns

2 cloves garlic, mashed (see page 37)

1½ pounds boneless pork loin (see Note)

1 teaspoon kosher salt

Freshly cracked black pepper

2 tablespoons extra-virgin olive oil

2 cups demi-glace (see page 50)

¼ cup whole-grain mustard

2 tablespoons unsalted butter

4 slices thick-cut bread, such as brioche, pan de mie, or Texas toast

¼ cup Aioli (page 65) or mayonnaise

1 recipe Chow Chow (page 356)

To brine the pork: Combine the water, salt, brown sugar, bay leaves, peppercorns, and garlic in a large pot over medium-high heat and cook until the sugar and salt are completely dissolved, 1 to 2 minutes. Let cool to room temperature.

Trim the layer of fat from the loin (it's okay to leave about ⅛ inch of fat, but no more). Place the pork in a large resealable plastic bag and pour the brine over it (the bag helps keep the pork totally submerged while it brines). Rinse and dry the brine-mixing pot, put the brining bag back in the pot or a large bowl in case it bursts and chill in the refrigerator for 18 to 24 hours. (If you want to take this all the way to ham town, you can make pork that resembles Canadian bacon in texture and flavor by brining it for 4 days, but I recommend sticking with the shorter period the first time you try it.)

After the pork has brined for 1 to 2 days, dry off the pork loin with paper towels and season with the salt and a few grinds of pepper.

Preheat the oven to 375°F.

CONTINUED

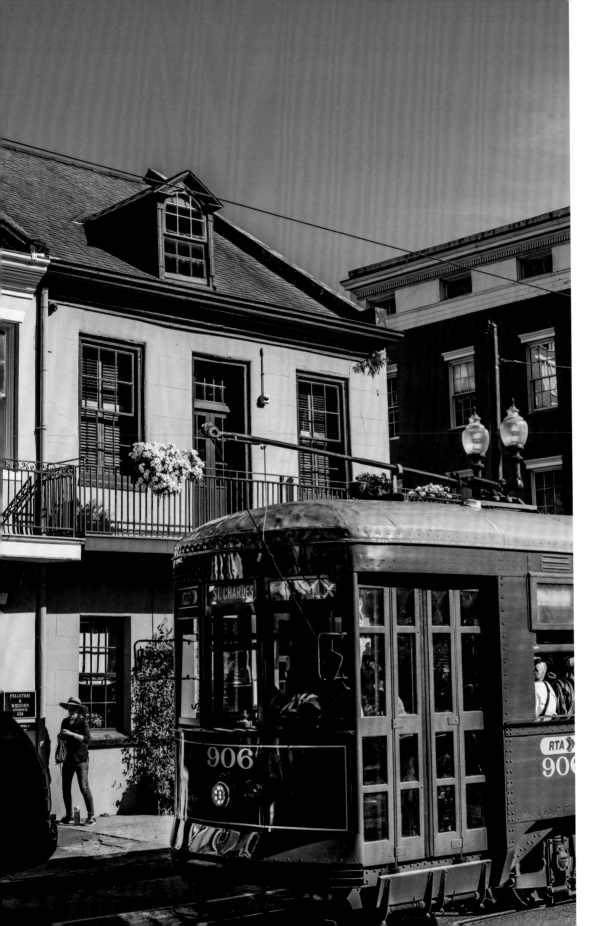

shaved pork loin on toast with mustard jus and chow chow, continued

Heat the oil in a large ovenproof, heavy-bottomed skillet over high heat until shimmering. Add the loin and sear until pale gold and crusty, 3½ to 4 minutes on each side. Place the loin, in its pan, in the oven to finish cooking, about 1 hour, turning the meat over halfway through, until an instant-read thermometer reads 150°F. Set aside on a cooling rack to rest; there's no need to tent with foil. Discard the oil, but don't rinse the pan. Leave the oven on.

In the same pan over medium-high heat, add the demi-glace, bring to a boil, and cook to reduce by half, 10 to 12 minutes. Whisk in the mustard and decrease the heat to low to simmer.

While the sauce simmers, slice the pork loin as thinly as possible and add to the sauce. Add the butter, stirring to emulsify it (see page 35) and evenly coat the pork. Leave on very low heat.

Toast the bread in the oven until slightly warm and crisp, about 5 minutes. Spread 1 tablespoon of the aioli or mayonnaise on each slice, then pile the pork slices on top—the idea is to make this completely over the top. Distribute all of the remaining sauce in the pan across the sandwiches. Top with a heaping spoonful of chow chow and serve.

NOTE
Pork loin is distinct from the tenderloin. We are referring here to the strip loin that goes down the back of the animal, which is slightly fattier than tenderloin. It's a thicker, rounder cut, which is used to make Canadian bacon.

twice-cooked oven ribs with ginger, lemongrass, and fish sauce caramel

Ribs are often associated with a lot of time and work, and people tend to avoid them for this reason, but the oven is a good way to ensure you get that low-and-slow process, without compromising the ribs' flavor. As long as you're okay without the smoky flavor from an outdoor grill, the oven is the best way to cook ribs.

The flavor profile here is reminiscent of one of my favorite dishes at Vietnamese restaurants I love in New Orleans, char-grilled pork cooked in caramel sauce. Wrapping the ribs in foil allows them to steam and tenderize; a final char-broil nails that crackly, caramelized crust. You end up with a sticky, fatty, totally delicious rib; it's ideal with the cucumber salad on page 160 on the side.

makes 4 to 6 servings

2 (3- to 3½-pound) full racks
St. Louis–cut spare ribs (ask
your butcher)

¼ cup sesame oil

2 tablespoons kosher salt

Freshly cracked black pepper

½ cup finely chopped
lemongrass, pale center
part only

½ cup finely chopped ginger

4 cloves garlic, finely
chopped

2 cups Fish Sauce Caramel
(page 61)

¼ cup finely chopped
cilantro leaves

¼ cup thinly sliced green
onions, white and green
parts

NOTE

To finish the ribs under the
broiler, the ideal setup is to
fit both racks of ribs in one
roasting pan, or use two
roasting pans. If space or
pan size is an issue, cut the
racks of ribs in half before
sealing in foil. These ribs
can also be finished on an
outdoor grill if you're so
inclined.

Preheat the oven to 225°F.

Remove the ribs from their packaging and, using paper towels, blot off any blood or water and pat dry.

Flip the ribs over so the concave side is facing up. There is a fine layer of membrane that coats the back of the ribs, which is the silver skin. Remove it with your fingers, using a clean dish towel to hold the ribs down and gently pulling the layer off the ribs. You may have to repeat this process to remove all of it.

Once the ribs are clean, lay out a sheet of foil about twice the size of the ribs. On top of the foil, lay out a piece of plastic wrap the same size. Lay one rack of ribs, concave-side up, over the plastic and rub the ribs all over with 2 tablespoons of the oil, 1 tablespoon of the salt, and few grinds of pepper. Flip the ribs over so the concave side is facing down. In one even layer, spread ¼ cup of the lemongrass, ¼ cup of the ginger, and half the garlic across the top of the ribs. Fold just the plastic over the ribs and seal tightly. Do the same with the foil, sealing as tightly as possible. If there is any area that needs more wrapping, add another piece of foil and seal tightly. Repeat the process with the second rack of ribs.

Place a rack in a wire roasting pan (set up two pans if necessary) and set the rib packets on the rack(s). Fill the pan with enough water to just touch the bottom of the foil (the goal is to keep the ribs suspended above the water).

Place the pan(s) in the oven for 4½ hours. Remove from the oven and let rest, still wrapped in foil, for 30 minutes. It's important to keep the ribs wrapped so they steam while they cool, which helps keep the meat moist. Avoid the temptation to open the foil and release that steam into the kitchen. The ribs can be cooked and stored to this point up to 2 days in advance; if doing so, once they are finished steaming and have cooled, keep the ribs wrapped in the refrigerator until ready to finish.

Preheat the broiler. Line a baking sheet with foil.

Unwrap the ribs, place them on the prepared baking sheet, and generously baste with about ½ cup of the Fish Sauce Caramel all over the tops of the ribs. Place the ribs under the broiler and broil until the sugar in the sauce starts to caramelize, about 3 minutes.

Remove the ribs from the oven, flip over, and baste the other side with another ½ cup sauce. Place under the broiler for another 3 minutes.

Remove the ribs, flip over a third time, and baste the tops with a scant ½ cup sauce. Place under the broiler for 2 minutes.

Remove the ribs, flip over a third time, and baste the top with a scant ½ cup sauce. Place under the broiler for another 2 minutes.

Remove the ribs, flip over one last time, and give a final baste with the remaining sauce. Let cool slightly and cut the rack for serving—I like to cut every two or three bones, but you can cut the rack into individual ribs, if you prefer.

Transfer the ribs to a serving platter, garnish with the cilantro and green onions, and serve. Leftover ribs will keep, well wrapped, in the refrigerator for up to 3 days. Reheat in a 300°F oven.

lamb chops basted in sage butter

Who doesn't love a lamb chop? They are intended to be eaten with your fingers—they're the perfect snack size, and ideal for groups. The technique here is all about basting the chops. When you melt the butter, it gives you another heat source, which you can infuse with extra flavor as you create a great sear. Sides like Hazelnut Spaetzle (see page 143) or turnip greens (see page 119) would be an ideal accompaniment.

makes 4 to 6 servings

3 pounds (8 to 10) lamb T-bone chops, 1½ inches thick (see Note)

8 to 14 teaspoons kosher salt

Freshly cracked black pepper

6 tablespoons extra-virgin olive oil

6 tablespoons unsalted butter

6 fresh sage leaves

2 cloves garlic, mashed (see page 37)

1 shallot, coarsely chopped

1 lemon wedge

2 tablespoons minced chives

Fleur de sel

NOTE

Look for chops that are sold with the T-bone intact (as is common; but ask your butcher if you are unsure).

Remove the chops from their packaging and, using paper towels, blot dry. Season both sides, using about 4 teaspoons salt per chop and a few grinds of black pepper. Set a wire rack in a roasting pan and place near your stove.

Heat half the oil in a large, heavy-bottomed skillet over medium-high heat until shimmering. Add the first chop—the oil should sizzle and pop vigorously when you add the meat. If you hear that, add three more chops. If you don't, the oil is not hot enough; remove the chop and allow the oil to get hot. Sear the chops until golden brown and caramelized on one side, about 5 minutes, then flip and sear for another 2 minutes. Remove from the heat and, using a spatula to secure the chops in the pan, carefully pour out the residual oil.

Nestle the chops together on one side of the pan, turn the heat to medium, and add half of the butter. Let it melt for about 1 minute. As the butter melts and the moisture evaporates into steam, you will be left with butter that's almost clarified and oily in appearance. Add 3 sage leaves and half of the garlic and half of the shallots to sweat (soften and release their aroma without browning) in the butter, about 1 minute. The butter will start to foam. Spread out the lamb chops and, with a soup spoon, baste with the butter-sage mixture constantly, for 2 to 3 minutes, until the chops are evenly brown and crusty.

Decrease the heat to low and continue basting the chops for another 2 minutes, until cooked through to medium. (As the chops are small, temperatures can vary, so it's better to go by the time here.) Transfer the chops to the rack in the roasting pan to rest. Scrape the fond (caramelized bits of meat and evaporated juices) from the skillet to incorporate into the butter and spoon the remaining sage butter over the chops while they're resting.

Wipe the skillet clean and repeat the process with the second batch of chops.

Arrange the chops on a large platter and drizzle with any remaining butter and pan drippings. Squeeze the lemon over the top, garnish with the chives and a sprinkle of sea salt, and serve. Leftover chops will keep, well wrapped, in the refrigerator for up to 3 days. Reheat in a 300°F oven.

braised lamb shanks with corn maque choux

Maque choux is a Southern Louisiana dish of smothered corn, slow-cooked with fat and aromatics, though I use the term loosely to refer to any dish made with Southern corn. This is certainly not a traditional maque choux, which is usually served by itself or with pork. So why not pair it with lamb? Many lamb shank dishes are heavy braises, but this is a little different—there's more acidity from the tomatoes, and the fresh corn crunch gives it some contrast.

The corn cooks into the sauce and thickens it with its natural starch, adding sweetness to the gravy-like stew. It's unquestionably rich and rustic; I like to double down on the corn flavor by serving it over Buttered Grits from. You could take the shanks out of the gravy and serve them over the grits, but I think it's more comforting to break it all up and eat together.

makes 6 to 8 servings

4 pounds lamb shanks

1 tablespoon kosher salt, plus more as needed

¾ teaspoon freshly cracked black pepper, plus more as needed

¼ cup vegetable oil

5 large onions, diced

1 red bell pepper, seeded and diced

1 jalapeño, minced

10 cloves garlic, finely chopped

1½ cups water

6 ears corn, kernels sliced from the cob (see page 187) to yield 4 to 5 cups

2 cups peeled, seeded tomatoes (preferably fresh, but canned will work)

5 sprigs thyme, tied with kitchen twine

1 quart chicken stock (see page 49)

1 recipe Buttered Grits (page 133)

3 bunches green onions, thinly sliced

Season the lamb on all sides with the 1 tablespoon salt and ¾ teaspoon pepper. Heat the oil in a large cast-iron or other heavy-bottomed pan over high heat until shimmering. Add the lamb and sear, turning frequently, until browned on all sides, about 10 minutes. Remove the lamb and set aside.

In the same pan, still over high heat, add the onions, bell pepper, jalapeño, and garlic and cook, stirring frequently, until the vegetables are soft and caramelized, 10 to 12 minutes. When the vegetables are soft and begin to stick to the bottom of the pan, add ½ cup of the water and simmer, scraping the pan with a wooden spoon to release the fond (caramelized bits of meat and evaporated juices on the bottom of the pan), until the water cooks off, 5 to 7 minutes. Repeat this process three times, adding a total of 1½ cups water, until the vegetables are essentially a sticky brown paste, or sofrito.

Return the lamb to the pan with the sofrito. Cover with the corn, tomatoes, thyme, and enough stock to come up to the top of the lamb. Season with salt and pepper. Bring to a boil over high heat, then turn the heat as low as possible. Cover and cook for 2½ to 3 hours, until the lamb is fork-tender and falling off the bones. You can make the grits during this time.

Place the grits in a large bowl or serving vessel. Pull the lamb off the bones and arrange over the grits, spoon the gravy over both, sprinkle the green onions over, and serve. Leftover lamb and grits will keep stored separately in the refrigerator for up to 3 days.

root beer–braised short ribs with spicy ginger dressing

I invented this many years ago as a young cook, and it's so good, it has never left the menu at my restaurants. You'd never know there's root beer in the braising liquid, but when you use Abita or a similar artisan brand with no artificial flavors, these incredible layers of spicy, earthy flavor come out as the ribs cook.

When the liquid has cooked down, the meat has a sweet-and-salty, deeply aromatic quality that reminds me of Southeast Asian food, so I like to pair this with a spicy chile and ginger sauce. This is the perfect excuse to bust out your Dutch oven. The dish can be cooked a day in advance, refrigerated overnight, and gently reheated the next day, which allows the meat to soak up even more flavor from the braising liquid. From start to finish, these take about 7 hours to cook. The oily dressing keeps well in the refrigerator, too, and is also great on grilled meats, noodles, and roasted vegetables.

Preheat the oven to 275°F.

Season the short ribs with the salt and pepper.

On the stove top, heat a large roasting pan over high heat and add the oil. When the oil is shimmering, add the meat, in batches if necessary, placing the pieces at least ½ inch apart and meat-side down in the pan. The meat should sizzle and hiss immediately when you add it to the pan and throughout cooking; if you notice excessive smoke or black spots forming on the bottom of the pan, decrease the heat to medium. Sear until a rich golden brown on the bottom, with a crispy crust. Keep the meat at least ½ inch apart while it cooks, or moisture may develop, which will steam it and prevent a good crust from forming. Flip once and sear on the bone side for 3 to 5 minutes. The goal is to caramelize both sides. Using tongs, transfer the short ribs to a plate as they're done.

Discard about half the grease from the pan. Increase the heat to high, and add the onions, celery, carrots, and garlic. Cook, stirring with a wooden spoon, until the vegetables soften, 7 to 10 minutes. As the vegetables cook, scrape up any caramelized bits of meat and evaporated juices stuck to the bottom of the pan (the fond) and stir them into the vegetables to release their flavor. Add the tomato paste and stir to coat the vegetables,

CONTINUED

makes 6 to 8 servings

4 pounds bone-in beef short ribs, cut into 4-inch square pieces

1 tablespoon kosher salt

2 teaspoons freshly cracked black pepper

¼ cup olive oil

2 cups large-diced onions

1 cup small-diced celery

1 cup small-diced peeled carrots

10 cloves garlic, mashed (see page 37)

1 cup tomato paste

1 Bouquet Garni (page 342; optional)

20 black peppercorns

2 (12-ounce) bottles all-natural root beer (I like Abita)

2 quarts chicken stock (see page 49)

1 quart demi-glace (see page 50)

SPICY GINGER DRESSING

1 tablespoon kosher salt

8 cloves garlic, smashed

2 tablespoons minced ginger

½ cup Korean dried red chile flakes (gochugaru; see page 32)

1 tablespoon fish sauce (preferably Three Crabs or Red Boat; see page 28)

1 tablespoon freshly squeezed lemon juice

1 cup canola oil

about 2 minutes. Add the bouquet garni, peppercorns, root beer, stock, and demi-glace and stir to combine.

Return the short rib meat to the pan and nestle it into the liquid and vegetable mixture. Cover the pan with a lid or foil and move the roasting pan into the oven. Cook for 5 hours.

After 5 hours, the short ribs should be extremely tender, like a perfect pot roast. Remove the roasting pan from the oven. Remove the meat from the liquid and set aside, then strain the cooking liquid into a clean pot large enough to hold all the meat, which you'll return to the liquid later.

Heat the cooking liquid over medium-high heat and maintain a low boil until it reduces by half, 45 to 60 minutes. Add the ribs to the reduced cooking liquid. Remove from the heat and let the rib meat rest in the liquid while you make the dressing.

To make the dressing: In a small bowl, whisk together the salt, garlic, ginger, chile flakes, fish sauce, and lemon juice. Slowly drizzle in the canola oil and stir briefly to combine.

Arrange the rib meat on a large platter and spoon about 1 cup of the braising liquid over the top. If you have any braising liquid left over, reserve it for another use (such as your next steak night, or to add to the brisket and kale stew on page 205).

Serve the rib meat with the dressing on the side to add more kick. Leftovers will keep in an airtight container in the refrigerator for up to 5 days.

roast beef po'boys

The roast beef version of this sandwich is a little more involved than the fried oyster version (see page 216). If you'd like to break up the workflow, the beef and garlic butter can be made up to one day in advance.

makes 8 to 10 servings

ROAST BEEF

2 large carrots, peeled and coarsely chopped

3 yellow onions, coarsely chopped

1 bunch celery, leaves and hearts removed, coarsely chopped

10 cloves garlic

6 sprigs thyme

5 bay leaves

2 to 3 pounds beef brisket

Kosher salt

Freshly ground black pepper

1 dark beer, such as brown ale

1 can crushed San Marzano tomatoes

3 quarts chicken stock (see page 29)

1 cup all-purpose flour

⅔ cup peanut oil

3 tablespoons grapeseed oil

2 yellow onions, small diced

10 cloves garlic, finely chopped

2 cups Dark Roux (page 46)

Kosher salt

Freshly ground black pepper

To make the beef: Preheat the oven to 400°F.

In a large, deep roasting pan, arrange a bed of the carrots, onions, celery, garlic, thyme, and bay leaves. Season the brisket liberally with salt and pepper and place on top of the vegetables and aromatics. Roast in the oven, uncovered, until golden brown and slightly caramelized, 30 to 40 minutes.

Decrease the oven temperature to 250°F. Pour the beer, tomatoes, and stock into the pan. Cover with parchment paper and foil. Cook for 4 hours, until the meat is tender enough to pull apart with a fork. Cool in the refrigerator for at least 4 hours or, ideally, overnight, to make the meat easier to slice.

Once fully cooled, remove the beef from the braising liquid and pat dry. Slice crosswise against the grain into ¼-inch slices and set aside. Strain the braising liquid, skimming off any fat, and set aside.

Make a dark roux with the flour and oil (see page 46 for step-by-step instructions).

In a medium saucepan, heat the oil over medium-high heat until shimmering. Add the onions and garlic and cook until slightly browned, 5 to 7 minutes. Stir in the reserved brisket braising liquid and bring to a boil over high heat. Slowly whisk in the dark roux, about ½ cup at a time, until fully dissolved, 10 to 15 minutes. Decrease the heat to low and simmer for 1 hour, until the roux is fully incorporated and no floury taste remains. (It's wise to make the garlic butter during this time.) Season with salt and pepper. Keep the gravy warm over low heat until ready to assemble the sandwiches.

Preheat the oven to 400°F.

Cut the bread into 8-inch portions (or desired lengths) and slice horizontally lengthwise. Brush the inside of the bread with the garlic butter and toast in the oven for 4 to 5 minutes, until crispy and just slightly brown.

Add the sliced beef to the pot with the gravy and simmer over medium heat until the beef is warmed through and tender, 10 to 15 minutes. Adjust the seasoning as desired. Spread the aioli on each side of the bread, about 2 tablespoons per sandwich. Arrange the sliced beef and gravy on the bottom bun, then place the cheese on top. Return the bottom half of the sandwich to the oven for 4 to 5 minutes, until cheese is nice and melted. Top with the lettuce and pickles, then place the top half of bread on top. Serve with hot sauce and extra napkins.

2 large loaves po'boy bread or French bread

3 tablespoons garlic butter (see page 216)

1 cup Aioli (page 65)

6 slices Swiss cheese

½ large head iceberg lettuce, shredded

1 cup LPG Burger Pickles (page 350)

Homemade Hot Sauce (page 62) or store-bought sauce (preferably Crystal) for serving

lpg cheeseburger

When I was a young chef just taking over at La Petite Grocery, I was hesitant to put a burger on the menu, believing them to be beneath my culinary abilities. Over time, I warmed to the idea, and eventually decided that if I was going to make burgers, I wanted them to have a similar flavor profile to a charcuterie plate, tricked out with a little something sweet (onion marmalade), something salty (pickles), and something sharp (whole-grain mustard) to balance the richness of the meat. And so the LPG burger was born and quickly became so popular we had to install a flat top in our kitchen to handle all the orders. The burger hasn't changed once in its decade-plus existence, and it never will.

This burger has developed a real cult following, and I've gotten a lot of requests for the recipe over the years; so here we go. The biggest mistake people make when cooking burgers at home are, in my opinion, buying ground beef that's too lean, and cooking it outside on a grill. The problem with a grill is that it doesn't get hot enough to form a good sear quickly; by the time you do manage to form a nice crusty exterior, the interior is overcooked. That's why I like to sear the burger in a pan over high heat, then finish it briefly under the broiler. That, combined with the high fat content in the ground beef, creates a beautifully crispy exterior and a juicy interior, the way a burger should be.

I'm sharing it here exactly as we make it in the restaurant, where we have an extensive setup of flavorful additions, such as housemade pickles and onion marmalade (which can also be used on grilled cheese, eggs, charcuterie, and more). I included this in its purest form—even though it's more cheffy than what I typically make at home—because all of this extra effort adds up to make this burger so special.

makes 4 burgers

ONION MARMALADE

2 tablespoons vegetable oil

6 large yellow onions, thinly sliced

½ cup sugar

½ cup apple cider vinegar

2 pounds freshly ground chuck (ideally 85% lean)

Kosher salt

Freshly cracked black pepper

Neutral oil

4 slices Gruyère cheese

4 brioche rolls or other soft bread buns

¼ cup whole-grain mustard

¼ cup Aioli (page 65) or mayonnaise

2 cups arugula

16 slices LPG Burger Pickles (page 350) or store-bought pickles

To make the marmalade: Heat the oil in a large deep pot over medium-high heat until shimmering. Add the onions and cook, stirring occasionally. After 30 minutes, the onions will begin to collapse and release their liquid. When the liquid has evaporated and the onions are starting to caramelize, about 15 minutes more, decrease the heat to medium-low. Continue cooking, stirring occasionally, until the onions have totally caramelized, with an amber-brown hue and soft, stringy texture, 15 to 20 minutes more.

Add the sugar to the pot and cook, stirring, to coat the onions and dissolve the sugar. Add the vinegar and cook, stirring occasionally, until the liquid has reduced to a thick and viscous coating and the onions have a jammy consistency, 25 to 30 minutes. Set aside until ready to use or store in an airtight container in the refrigerator for up to 10 days.

Preheat the broiler.

Form the ground chuck into four thin patties. The patty size is variable; it really depends on the size of your bun. I aim to make a raw patty that's about 1 inch larger in circumference than the bun, because the meat shrinks slightly as it cooks, so the finished patty fits on the bun with just a tad bit of overhang. No one wants a floppy patty, or a patty that's gotten lost in the bun.

Season the patties with salt and pepper. Lightly coat a griddle or cast-iron skillet with neutral oil to avoid sticking. Heat over medium-high heat. Cook each burger for 2 minutes per side for medium-rare (3 minutes for medium), then transfer the burgers to a baking sheet.

Smear about 2 tablespoons of the marmalade on the top of each burger, and cover with 1 slice of cheese. Set the burgers under the broiler for 45 seconds to melt the cheese. Remove from the oven.

On a clean baking sheet, lightly toast the buns under the broiler for about 1 minute. On the bottom halves, spread 1 tablespoon of the mustard. On the tops, spread 1 tablespoon of the aioli or mayonnaise. Place each burger, cheese-side up, on the bottom bun, and top with a handful of arugula and 4 pickle slices. Close with the top bun and enjoy.

grilled skirt steak with salsa verde

This is a classic flavor profile of a South American grilled steak, served with an herbaceous salsa verde, which is like a cousin to chimichurri (a sauce from Argentina). The steak is a thin cut of meat, which cooks up quickly with a bit of char, while the sauce packs a big, bright punch, helping balance the rich red meat. I find that cuts like skirt, along with hangar and flank steak, have a slightly iron-y flavor to them, which this sauce really sharpens.

Spring and fall are good grilling seasons in New Orleans, but summer is a different beast. There usually comes a point in late summer when it's too hot to cook inside because you don't want to mess with your carefully calibrated AC, but when you step outside, it's about 100 degrees with 100 percent humidity. Masochistic as it may sound, these have become my favorite grilling days; I look forward to them all year as a test of endurance.

Place the steaks into a large resealable plastic bag. In a mixing bowl, combine the oil, garlic, paprika, and parsley. Pour the oil mixture into the bag with the steaks, seal, and marinate in the refrigerator for at least 4 hours or up to 8 hours.

If using a gas grill, heat it on high. If using charcoal or wood, build a hot fire.

Remove the steaks from the marinade and place on a baking sheet or platter. Season each steak on both sides with the salt and a few grinds of pepper. Place the steak on the grill and cook until they have grill marks and are slightly charred, but reddish in the middle (for medium-rare), 3 to 5 minutes per side. Set aside to rest for 5 minutes.

Find the direction of the grain on each steak (how the muscle fibers are aligned) and slice against it on the bias, into pieces about ¼ inch thick. Slicing against the grain makes the meat more tender. Arrange the slices on a large platter, spoon the salsa verde over them, and serve.

makes 4 to 6 servings

2 pounds skirt steaks

¼ cup extra-virgin olive oil

2 tablespoons finely chopped garlic

1 tablespoon paprika, preferably smoked

¼ cup finely chopped flat-leaf parsley leaves

1 tablespoon kosher salt

Freshly cracked black pepper

1½ cups Salsa Verde (see page 56)

seared new york strip steak with herbed pimento butter

New York strip is my favorite steak cut—it packs a ton of flavor and has a nice balance of lean meat to fat. When it comes to cooking steak, I generally think that simpler is better. I'm a big fan of salt and pepper for seasoning, quickly searing or grilling, and concentrating on the cooking method more than how many ingredients I put on the outside or in the marinade.

This is a very basic but technique-driven pan-roasted steak, basted in an aromatic butter to create a beautifully crusty exterior. It's also a great showcase for a flavorful compound butter. When used on a steak, you don't need to apply a rub or marinate before cooking, or finish it with a sauce. The end result is still incredibly flavorful. The butter, infused with the sweetness of bell pepper and the bright flavors of a ton of fresh herbs, gives the steak a handsome finish. For more on compound butters, see page 364.

makes 6 servings

4 New York strip steaks (about 3½ pounds total)

¼ cup kosher salt

Freshly cracked black pepper

6 tablespoons extra-virgin olive oil

4 tablespoons unsalted butter

2 sprigs rosemary

2 cloves garlic, mashed (see page 37)

1 shallot, coarsely chopped

1 recipe Herbed Pimento Butter (page 368), chilled

Fleur de sel

Remove the steaks from their packaging and, using paper towels, blot and pat dry. Season on all sides with about 1 tablespoon of the kosher salt per steak and a few grinds of black pepper. Set a rack inside a roasting pan.

Heat half the oil in a large cast-iron skillet or other heavy-bottomed pan over medium-high heat until shimmering. Add two of the steaks and sear on one side until golden brown and caramelized, about 5 minutes. Flip and sear on the second sides for 1½ minutes. Add half each of the unsalted butter, rosemary, garlic, and shallot. The butter will start to foam. With a soup spoon, collect the butter and spoon it over the steaks repeatedly to baste until the steaks are evenly brown and crusty, 4 to 5 minutes.

Decrease the heat to medium-low and continue basting the steaks for another 2 minutes, flipping once after 1 minute. Transfer the steaks to the roasting pan to rest, and spoon the remaining butter from the pan over the top.

Wipe the pan clean and repeat with the remaining steaks. While the steaks rest, remove the Herbed-Pimento Butter from the refrigerator and cut into six medallions, each about ⅓ inch wide, and set aside to warm up slightly before serving.

Cut each steak in thirds, for a total of twelve rectangular pieces. Arrange on a platter and place one medallion of butter on top of every two pieces, allowing it to melt into the hot steak. (If necessary, place the platter in a hot oven for 30 seconds to encourage melting.) Sprinkle with fleur de sel and serve.

dessert

Desserts are a big part of the food culture in New Orleans; we have a passion for sugary things. I love dessert and think it plays an important role in the arc of a meal. It's the finishing touch before friends or family part ways. That said, I tend to favor desserts that are a little salty, a little savory, and have some texture to them. That's why you'll see recipes with burnt sugar, whole-wheat flour, salt, and dark chocolate in this chapter.

When I started out at La Petite Grocery in 2007, we didn't have a dedicated pastry chef, and wouldn't for another five years. I was responsible for making desserts, and I gained a huge appreciation for the craft during that time. A lot of these recipes are from then. The S'mores Tarts on page 335 and the Spiced Citrus Pound Cake on page 327 were developed by chef Lennon Clotiaux-Fitzgerald and me in the midst of a full-on experimental mode while also running other departments in the kitchen. But for the past several years, I have been fortunate to have pastry chefs assigned to that specific role, primarily Bronwen Wyatt and Austin Breckenridge. Many of their contributions are represented here as well, including the Butterscotch Pudding on page 316 and the ice creams on pages 308 to 313.

Some techniques in this chapter have appeared in savory recipes, such as browning butter, but many of them are specific to pastry (for example, making shortbread dough, custards, and mousses, and working with gelatin). That's part of what makes dessert so special, and so delicious.

café au lait ice cream

There's something equally big-city and country about making ice cream. Ice cream base—milk, cream, sugar, and egg yolks—is a blank canvas. The true secret to making the best ice cream is using the best ingredients, so it's worth seeking out farm-fresh milk, cream, and eggs. Once you have the basic technique down, experiment with flavorings—start with herbal or aromatic infusions, such as lemongrass, herbs, and spices. Dry add-ins don't affect the liquid content much, whereas adding ingredients that have a lot of moisture is more complicated.

The yolk-heavy base is rich, creamy, and almost fluffy in texture, and should scoop out easily after churning. If it's too loose, the finished ice cream will become frosty and hard in the freezer; if it's too thick, it may be overbeaten and have a greasy texture when frozen. It should look like perfect soft-serve when you pack it into a container to freeze.

makes about 2 quarts

2 cups whole milk

1 quart heavy cream

2 tablespoons brewed dark-roast chicory and coffee blend, grinds strained out

1½ cups sugar

12 egg yolks

In a saucepan over medium-high heat, bring the milk, 2 cups of the cream, and the chicory coffee to just below a boil. Meanwhile, in a large mixing bowl, whisk the sugar and egg yolks until light yellow, smooth ribbons with a bit of froth form.

Whisk the scalding milk mixture into the egg mixture, a few tablespoons at a time, until about 1 cup has been added, and then add the remainder and whisk until the mixture is smooth and combined. This technique of gradually mixing hot liquid into raw eggs, to slowly increase the temperature of the eggs without cooking them into unappealing scrambled bits, is called tempering. Stir in the remaining 2 cups cream.

Pour the mixture back into the pot, decrease the heat to low, and cook, stirring, until it is slightly thickened and coats the back of a spoon, 3 to 5 minutes.

Transfer the mixture to a bowl, cover, and refrigerate until completely chilled, 4 to 6 hours.

Pour the chilled base into an ice cream maker and churn according to the manufacturer's directions, until it resembles soft-serve ice cream and is smooth and creamy. Watch to be sure the paddle keeps moving during this process—if it stops, the ice cream is too stiff.

Transfer the ice cream from the machine to a plastic container with a lid, smoothing it out as you go to remove any air bubbles. Freeze for 4 to 6 hours, scoop, and serve. Leftover ice cream will keep in the freezer for up to 2 months.

rum raisin ice cream

Rum raisin is a favorite flavor of New Orleans, from tipsy grandmas to little kids. Maybe it's our Caribbean connection and fondness for all things sugarcane. Soaking the raisins in rum overnight ensures they won't freeze into teeth-chipping little pebbles, and makes for a deliciously creamy old-school scoop.

makes about 2 quarts

1 cup raisins

1 cup dark rum

2 cups whole milk

1 quart heavy cream

1½ cups sugar

12 egg yolks

In a small bowl, soak the raisins in the rum overnight, covered, at room temperature. Drain the raisins and reserve the rum for another use.

In a saucepan over medium-high heat, bring the milk and 2 cups of the cream to just below a boil. Meanwhile, in a large mixing bowl, whisk the sugar and egg yolks until light yellow, smooth ribbons with a bit of froth form.

Whisk the scalding milk mixture into the egg mixture, a few tablespoons at a time, until about 1 cup has been added, and then add the remainder and whisk until the mixture is smooth and well combined. This technique of gradually mixing hot liquid into raw eggs, to slowly increase the temperature of the eggs without cooking them into unappealing scrambled bits, is called tempering. Stir in the remaining 2 cups cream.

Pour the mixture back into the pot, decrease the heat to low, and cook, stirring, until it is slightly thickened and coats the back of a spoon, 3 to 5 minutes.

Transfer the mixture to a bowl, stir in the raisins, cover, and refrigerate until completely chilled, 4 to 6 hours.

Pour the chilled base into an ice cream maker and churn according to the manufacturer's directions, until it resembles soft-serve ice cream and is smooth and creamy. Watch to be sure the paddle keeps moving during this process—if it stops, that means the ice cream is too hard.

Remove the ice cream from the machine and pack it into a plastic container with a lid, smoothing it out as you go to remove any air bubbles. Freeze for 4 to 6 hours, scoop, and serve. Leftover ice cream will keep in the freezer for up to 2 months.

sea salt ice cream

This ice cream is fairly neutral, so I like to serve it with things that are light in flavor and could use a bit of salt, like the cornbread financiers on page 322. The idea here is to have a sweet, cold, slightly briny ice cream that goes down smooth and easy.

makes about 2 quarts

2 cups whole milk

1 quart heavy cream

1½ cups sugar

12 egg yolks

1 tablespoon flaky sea salt (such as Maldon), plus more for serving

In a saucepan over medium-high heat, bring the milk and 2 cups of the cream to just below a boil. Meanwhile, in a large mixing bowl, whisk the sugar and egg yolks until light yellow, smooth ribbons with a bit of froth form.

Whisk the scalding milk mixture into the egg mixture, a few tablespoons at a time, until about 1 cup has been added, and then add the remainder and whisk until the mixture is smooth and well combined. This technique of gradually mixing hot liquid into raw eggs, to slowly increase the temperature of the eggs without cooking them into unappealing scrambled bits, is called tempering. Stir in the remaining 2 cups cream.

Pour the mixture back into the pot, decrease the heat to low, and cook, stirring until it is slightly thickened and coats the back of a spoon, 3 to 5 minutes.

Transfer the mixture to a bowl, add the salt, cover, and refrigerate until completely chilled, 4 to 6 hours.

Pour the chilled base into an ice cream maker and churn according to the manufacturer's directions, until it resembles soft-serve ice cream and is smooth and creamy. Watch to be sure the paddle keeps moving during this process—if it stops, that means the ice cream is too hard.

Remove the ice cream from the machine and pack it into a plastic container with a lid, smoothing it out as you go to remove any air bubbles. Freeze for 4 to 6 hours, scoop, sprinkle with salt, and serve. Leftover ice cream will keep in the freezer for up to 2 months.

sage ice cream

For this ice cream, you warm the sage and release its essential oils into the base, creating a light aroma of sage—just enough to barely flavor the cream. Be sure to strain the leaves after chilling, before spinning the base in the machine.

makes about 2 quarts

2 cups whole milk

1 quart heavy cream

1½ cups sugar

12 egg yolks

8 sage leaves

In a saucepan over medium-high heat, bring the milk and 2 cups of the cream to just below a boil. Meanwhile, in a large mixing bowl, whisk the sugar and egg yolks until light yellow, smooth ribbons with a bit of froth form.

Whisk the scalding milk mixture into the egg mixture, a few tablespoons at a time, until about 1 cup has been added, and then add the remainder and whisk until the mixture is smooth and well combined. This technique of gradually mixing hot liquid into raw eggs, to slowly increase the temperature of the eggs without cooking them into unappealing scrambled bits, is called tempering. Stir in the remaining 2 cups cream.

Pour the mixture back into the pot, add the sage leaves, decrease the heat to low, and cook, stirring until it is slightly thickened and coats the back of a spoon, 3 to 5 minutes.

Transfer the mixture to a bowl, cover and refrigerate, until completely chilled, 4 to 6 hours. Remove and discard the sage.

Pour the chilled base into an ice cream maker and churn according to the manufacturer's directions, until it resembles soft-serve ice cream and is smooth and creamy. Watch to be sure the paddle keeps moving during this process—if it stops, that means the ice cream is too hard.

Remove the ice cream from the machine and pack it into a plastic container with a lid, smoothing it out as you go to remove any air bubbles. Freeze for 4 to 6 hours, scoop, and serve. Leftover ice cream will keep in the freezer for up to 2 months.

goat cheese mousse

Once you know how to make this sweet-tart goat cheese recipe, you'll be able to tackle any recipe for mousse. Juicy strawberries are a great topping when they're in season, but you can use other berries or fruit throughout the year.

makes 8 to 10 servings

1 tablespoon plus 1 teaspoon water

1½ teaspoons gelatin powder

½ cup plus 1 tablespoon crème fraîche (see page 363)

1 pound goat cheese

2 cups heavy cream

½ cup plus 1 tablespoon whole milk

1 cup plus 2 tablespoons sugar

1 pint fresh strawberries, hulled and quartered, or other seasonal fruit

Pour the water into a bowl and sprinkle the gelatin powder over it to bloom.

In a mixing bowl, combine the crème fraîche and goat cheese with a sturdy spoon, mixing until completely blended.

In a second bowl, whip the cream until it forms medium peaks and takes 3 to 4 seconds to fall off the whisk when you lift it out of the bowl, 3 to 5 minutes. Set aside, covered, in the refrigerator.

Combine the milk and sugar in a small saucepan over medium heat. Cook, stirring often, until the mixture reaches 190°F on an instant-read thermometer, 5 to 6 minutes. When the temperature approaches 190°F, the mixture will start to puff steam, which is a sign that it is almost at the right temperature—you want to turn off the heat before it begins simmering or boiling outright.

Whisk the gelatin into the hot milk and sugar mixture to dissolve. Let the bloomed mixture cool to room temperature.

Stir the milk mixture into the crème fraîche and goat cheese. Gently but quickly fold in the whipped cream.

Pour the unset mousse into a large casserole dish or serving vessel (a parfait bowl is nice, if you have one). Chill, loosely covered with plastic wrap, in the refrigerator for 4 hours to allow the mousse to set.

Serve directly out of the dish, spooning the strawberries over the top of each serving.

butterscotch pudding

I need to credit my former pastry chef Bronwen Wyatt for putting this on the menu at LPG, where it has remained ever since. It's the epitome of butterscotch pudding, and it makes people close their eyes in bliss. I've been a fan of butterscotch pudding since I was a kid and fancy myself something of a connoisseur—so it says a lot when I tell you this is the best you'll ever have.

Anytime you're working with sugar over high heat to make caramel, it's important to stay focused. If something does go wrong (for example, your sugar crystallizes or burns), just start over—don't try to fix it by adding cream or another liquid, because you will only make a bigger mess.

makes 4 to 6 servings

PUDDING

3 tablespoons unsalted butter

1½ teaspoons cane syrup or molasses

½ cup firmly packed light brown sugar

2 cups plus 2 tablespoons heavy cream

1 large vanilla bean, split open

¼ cup plus 2 tablespoons granulated sugar

¼ cup water

1 teaspoon gelatin powder

3 egg yolks

¾ teaspoon amber or dark rum

Pinch of salt

VANILLA BEAN CREAM

1 cup heavy cream

2 teaspoons powdered sugar

1 vanilla bean, split open

To make the pudding: In a medium saucepan over medium heat, combine the butter and cane syrup. When the butter is melted, add the brown sugar and cook, stirring, until bubbling, just beginning to smoke, and copper in color, 5 to 10 minutes. Add 2 cups of the cream and whisk until the caramel is dissolved, making sure the sugar does not crystallize, 3 to 5 minutes. Scrape the vanilla bean seeds into the cream mixture, and drop in the pod. Remove from the heat, cover, and let steep for 1 hour.

Meanwhile, combine the granulated sugar and 2 tablespoons of the water in a small heavy-bottomed, nonreactive saucepan. Cover and bring to a boil (when the steam begins to escape from under the lid, remove the lid). Let the sugar caramelize, undisturbed, until it reaches a deep amber color and has a burnt sugar aroma (like crème brûlée), about 5 minutes.

Immediately remove from the heat and whisk in the remaining 2 tablespoons of heavy cream. Add this caramel mixture to the cream mixture over low heat, and whisk thoroughly until the caramel is totally dissolved, 2 to 3 minutes. Remove from the heat.

Pour the remaining 2 tablespoons of water into a small bowl and sprinkle the gelatin powder over it to bloom.

Whisk the egg yolks in a stainless-steel mixing bowl. Whisk the warm caramel-cream mixture into the egg yolks, a few tablespoons at a time, until ½ cup has been added, and then add the remainder and whisk until the mixture is smooth and well combined. This technique of gradually

CONTINUED

mixing hot liquid into raw eggs, to slowly increase the temperature of the eggs without cooking them into unappealing scrambled bits, is called tempering.

Return the custard to the saucepan, and cook, stirring, over low heat until the mixture thickly coats the back of a spoon, about 10 minutes. Remove from the heat and immediately whisk in the bloomed gelatin until dissolved. Fill a mixing bowl with ice and place another mixing bowl over the ice. Strain the custard through a fine-mesh strainer into the top bowl. Add the dark rum and salt. Let cool for 1 hour, stirring occasionally. The mixture will thicken as it cools. Pour into a large serving bowl, cover, and refrigerate for at least 6 hours or up to 12 hours to completely set.

Just before serving, make the vanilla bean cream: Combine the cream and powdered sugar in a metal mixing bowl. Scrape the vanilla bean seeds into the bowl and whisk until medium-stiff peaks form (just stiff enough to stand up firmly with a slight curl at the tip), about 5 minutes.

Spoon the pudding into bowls and top with a dollop of whipped cream, or pass the bowl of whipped cream at the table. Leftover pudding will keep, covered, in the refrigerator for up to 3 days.

chocolate–chicory coffee pots de crème

Pots de crème is a classic French bistro dessert; this version pays homage to New Orleans' coffee heritage. During the Civil War, a Union naval blockade cut off the port, so locals started cutting their dwindling supply of coffee beans with the baked and ground roots of chicory plants. People got used to the bitter flavor and even started to enjoy it. Today, any traditional New Orleans coffee shop will have chicory coffee—and chicory, coffee, and dessert go together like, well, chicory, coffee, and dessert. The pots should be luscious and creamy when they set, and topped liberally with whipped cream.

makes 6 to 8 servings

3 eggs, plus 2 egg yolks

½ cup chopped 65% cacao bittersweet chocolate

¼ cup chopped milk chocolate

1½ cups whole milk

2 cups heavy cream

¼ cup granulated sugar

½ teaspoon ground dark-roast chicory and coffee blend, grounds strained out

2 teaspoons powdered sugar

Place the eggs and egg yolks in a medium stainless-steel mixing bowl and whisk to combine until smooth and falling off the whisk in ribbons when it's lifted out of the bowl. Add both chocolates. Nestle the bowl into a kitchen towel on the countertop for stability, as you will need both hands for mixing.

In a medium saucepan over high heat, bring the milk, 1 cup of the cream, and the granulated sugar just to a boil. Immediately remove from the heat.

Whisk a few tablespoons of the warm cream mixture into the egg and chocolate mixture, a few tablespoons at a time, until ½ cup has been added and the chocolate has melted. Add the remaining cream mixture and whisk until smooth and well combined. This technique of gradually mixing hot liquid into raw eggs, to slowly increase the temperature of the eggs without cooking them into unappealing scrambled bits, is called tempering. Stir in the coffee and chill the mixture, covered, in the refrigerator for at least 2 hours or up to overnight.

Strain the chilled base through a fine-mesh strainer to remove any residual coffee grounds.

Fill a 9 x 13-inch baking or casserole dish halfway with water to create a water bath. Place the dish in the oven and preheat to 350°F.

While the oven preheats, fill six to eight 4-ounce ramekins or canning jars one-half to three-quarters full with the custard mixture. Slide out the oven rack with the water bath on it, and place the custards into the water bath, about 1 inch apart. Bake until they are set but still jiggle slightly when tapped, 30 to 35 minutes.

Remove the whole water bath, being careful not to spill, and set on the counter. Line a baking sheet with a kitchen towel and transfer the ramekins or jars onto it. Transfer the baking sheet to the refrigerator and chill until the puddings are fully set, 6 to 8 hours.

Just before serving, combine the remaining 1 cup of cream and the powdered sugar in a metal mixing bowl and whisk until soft peaks form, about 3 minutes.

To serve, dollop each ramekin or jar with whipped cream, or pass the whipped cream at the table.

cornbread financiers with sea salt ice cream

If you cook from this book often, you'll notice that one of my favorite flavor profiles for corn is basically butter and salt, inspired by my love for movie-theater popcorn (see also Buttered Grits, page 133). These financiers take that same principle and apply it to dessert, in the form of a buttery, sugary, crispy cornbread cookie, served with salty, creamy ice cream.

This is one of the few times that I do call for a special piece of equipment. A financier baking pan is thin, with a lot of surface area, so you get all of that butter-sugar crispiness in each bar. I prefer metal to silicone pans because they form a crispier exterior. If you want to make these without a financier pan, you can use a mini cupcake pan, or even pour a thin layer of batter into a 9-inch square cake pan and cut the pastry into 1½ x 3½-inch bars, about 1 inch thick. The goal is to maximize surface area to get the best crust. You can even crisp the bars up on a buttered griddle just before serving.

makes 12 financiers

7 tablespoons unsalted butter, plus more, at room temperature, for greasing the pan

½ cup plus 1 tablespoon sugar

¼ cup plus 3 tablespoons fine cornmeal

3 tablespoons all-purpose flour

2 tablespoons almond meal

1 teaspoon kosher salt

3 egg whites

1 recipe Sea Salt Ice Cream (page 312)

Preheat the oven to 425°F. Lightly grease a financier pan with butter.

In a large bowl, whisk the sugar with the cornmeal, flour, almond meal, and salt. In another bowl, with a whisk or handheld mixer on medium-high, vigorously whip the egg whites until slightly frothy and foamy, 2 to 3 minutes, then slowly fold the egg whites into the dry ingredients until just combined. This helps create a light, airy texture.

In a small skillet, melt the 7 tablespoons butter over medium heat and cook, stirring, until the butter begins to brown and smell nutty, 6 to 8 minutes. Remove from the heat and pour the hot butter into the batter, whisking until smooth. The batter should be thicker than pancake batter, but thinner than cookie dough.

Spoon a large dollop of batter into each indentation in the financier pan, filling about halfway. Place the pan in the oven, decrease the temperature to 350°F, and bake until the financiers are light gold, about 10 minutes. Rotate the pan and bake until golden brown, about 5 minutes more.

Remove the pan from the oven and, using a fork, gently flip the financiers over in the pan so the bottom side cools faster. Unmold when cool enough to touch, but still warm.

Serve warm with the ice cream. When completely cool, leftover financiers will keep in an airtight container at room temperature for up to 2 days.

brown butter crepes with rum raisin ice cream

Crepes are one of those things that seem super-fancy, but this recipe squashes the idea that they have to be fussy. Use a blender to make a quick batter out of basic pantry staples. Brown butter is easy to make, and adds a rich, complex flavor of nutty toasted butter, so why not?

The crepes themselves are something of a blank canvas, and equally good for sweet or savory uses. You can eat them like pancakes with maple syrup and powdered sugar or fill them with Nutella or smoked salmon, cream cheese, and dill; or stuff with roasted chicken and mayo.

makes about 16 crepes

9 tablespoons unsalted butter, plus more, at room temperature, for greasing the pan

2 cups all-purpose flour

1 teaspoon kosher salt

6 eggs, beaten

2¼ cups whole milk

Fleur de sel

1 recipe Rum Raisin Ice Cream (page 311)

In a small saucepan or skillet over medium-high heat, melt the 9 tablespoons butter, then decrease the heat to medium and allow the butter to gently toast, turning from a pale whitish–yellow to bright yellow, 6 to 8 minutes. Steam will rise off as the water evaporates. Once the water has evaporated completely, the butter will toast quickly, turning from a clear yellow to a nutty brown color, and will develop a toasted aroma in another 2 to 4 minutes. Remove from the heat and divide the brown butter evenly between two separate bowls.

Combine the flour, salt, eggs, and milk in a blender and blend on medium speed until smooth, about 45 seconds. Decrease the speed to low and, with the blender running, drizzle in half of the brown butter. Let the batter rest for 10 to 15 minutes before cooking.

In a large nonstick skillet over medium heat, wipe about ½ teaspoon of room-temperature butter across the hot surface, then wipe the pan with another paper towel.

Working with ¼ cup at a time, pour the batter into the pan, swirl around into a large circle, and cook until the batter starts to solidify and looks light gold, about 90 seconds. Gently pick up one side of the crepe with a spatula and flip, then cook on the other side for 20 to 30 seconds. Fold the crepe in half. Fold the half in half (to make one-quarter of a circle) and fold that wedge in half again so you make a narrow triangular pocket. Repeat with the remaining batter, greasing the pan as needed and stacking the crepes on top of each other as you go.

Arrange the folded crepes on a platter, spoon the remaining brown butter over the top, and sprinkle with fleur de sel. Serve with the ice cream scooped on top or in a separate bowl alongside. When completely cool, leftover crepes will keep in an airtight container at room temperature for up to 1 day.

spiced citrus pound cake with sage ice cream

This is a simple, elegant dessert with fall flavors; it's both forgiving and easy to execute, giving you that classic dense, buttery texture. Much like the ice creams on pages 308 to 313, this is a base recipe that can be tweaked according to the season or your preferences. If you have leftover cake, slice it thick and toast it in a buttered pan for breakfast.

Preheat the oven to 325°F. Coat the inside of a 9 x 5-inch loaf pan evenly with 1 tablespoon of the butter. Dust the surface of the pan with 1 tablespoon of the flour.

In a stand mixer fitted with a paddle attachment, mix the remaining 1 cup of butter on medium speed until light and creamy, about 30 seconds. Add the sugar, 2 tablespoons at a time, about 10 seconds apart, while continuing to cream the butter. Mix for 3 minutes more, or until very airy and creamy. Add one egg at a time (I like to crack them into a small bowl first and add from the bowl to avoid any shells), mixing each for about 30 seconds, until fully incorporated, before adding the next. The batter will be fluffier and voluminous at this point.

Remove the bowl from the mixer. Whisk together the remaining 1¾ cups of flour, the baking powder, and salt in a small bowl and fold into the batter, half at a time, using a spatula (doing this gently by hand will make for a nicer texture). Add the vanilla, marmalade, ginger, and nutmeg and gently fold to combine.

Pour the batter into the prepared cake pan and bake for 45 minutes to 1 hour, rotating the pan halfway through, until a toothpick inserted in the middle comes out dry. I recommend testing several times, starting at the 45-minute mark, and removing as soon as the batter no longer clings to the toothpick.

Let the cake cool in the pan for 30 minutes, then gently turn the pan over to release the cake. Cut into 2-inch slices and serve with the ice cream. Leftover cake will keep, covered, at room temperature for up to 5 days.

makes one 9-inch loaf cake

1 cup unsalted butter, plus 1 tablespoon, at room temperature, for greasing the pan

1¾ cups all-purpose flour, plus 1 tablespoon for dusting the pan

½ cup sugar

7 eggs, at room temperature

1 teaspoon baking powder

½ teaspoon kosher salt

½ teaspoon vanilla extract

2 tablespoons tangerine marmalade (see page 359)

2 teaspoons grated ginger

¼ teaspoon freshly grated nutmeg

1 recipe Sage Ice Cream (page 313)

date and toffee pudding cake

This dessert is a perennial favorite in our restaurants. One of the reasons I like it so much is because it comes out looking like a bread pudding—gooey, custardy, and scoopable—but it's not an actual bread pudding, which you see on almost every menu in New Orleans. This cake pays homage to the original, but it's a little more technically demanding, while still delivering a lot of the same warm, sticky pleasure.

The soft, gooey texture comes partially from the baking, but also from soaking the finished cake in the bourbon toffee sauce, making it extra gooey and delicious. The dark, rich, slightly toasty flavors make this a favorite for fall or winter gatherings. It can be eaten at room temperature, or briefly reheated before serving with the sweet-and-salty buttered pecans and Cafe au Lait Ice Cream.

makes 6 to 8 servings

DATE PUDDING CAKE

1½ cups (16 to 18) Medjool dates, split and seeds removed

2 cups water

1½ teaspoons baking soda

6 tablespoons unsalted butter, at room temperature

1 cup granulated sugar

3 eggs, at room temperature

2 cups all-purpose flour

½ teaspoon kosher salt

1½ teaspoons baking powder

TOFFEE SAUCE

1½ teaspoons vanilla extract

½ cup bourbon

1 vanilla bean, split open

1 cup unsalted butter, cut into cubes

1¼ cups firmly packed light brown sugar

1 cup heavy cream

SWEET-AND-SALTY BUTTERED PECANS

8 ounces pecan halves

2 tablespoons unsalted butter, melted

1 tablespoon kosher salt

1 tablespoon granulated sugar

1 recipe Café au Lait Ice Cream (page 308)

To make the cake: Preheat the oven to 325°F.

Place the dates and water in a medium saucepan over high heat and bring almost to a boil, about 15 minutes. Remove from the heat and add the baking soda. Cover and let sit for 20 minutes to allow the baking soda to dissolve and help break down the skin of the dates.

In the bowl of a stand mixer fitted with a paddle attachment, combine the butter and granulated sugar. Mix on medium speed until airy and creamy, 3 to 5 minutes.

With the mixer on medium speed, add the eggs, one at a time (I like to crack them into a small bowl first and add from the bowl to avoid any shells), mixing each for about 30 seconds (or until fully incorporated) before adding the next. In a separate bowl, whisk together the flour, salt, and baking powder. Slow the mixer to low speed and add the flour, salt, and baking powder. Mix for about 2 minutes, until all the ingredients are incorporated but the dough still looks shaggy.

Add the date-water mixture to the mixer bowl and mix on medium speed for about 2 minutes, until the batter is smooth and falls off the beater in ribbons as you lift it out of the bowl. Scrape down the sides of the bowl with a spatula and give one more quick 30-second mix to combine. The dates should be broken down slightly due to the mixing, but still in visible pieces throughout the batter.

Pour the batter into a 2-quart round ungreased baking or souffle dish with 3- to 4-inch-high sides.

Prepare a water bath by placing the cake pan in a deep baking or roasting pan. Add enough water to reach halfway up the outside of the cake pan.

Bake the cake in its water bath for 30 to 35 minutes, until it's puffed at the edges, a toothpick inserted toward the edge comes out clean, and the center is slightly jiggly. While the cake is baking, make the toffee sauce.

To make the sauce: Combine the vanilla extract and bourbon in a bowl, scrape in the vanilla seeds, and whisk to combine. Set aside.

In a medium heavy-bottomed saucepan over medium-high heat, melt the butter, 5 to 7 minutes. Add the brown sugar and whisk to dissolve, about 5 minutes. Remove from the heat (to avoid a flare-up) and carefully pour in the bourbon, whisking to combine.

Return the pot to low heat and cook until the sauce is slightly thickened and the alcohol has cooked off, about 5 minutes. Increase the heat to medium-high and cook for another 5 minutes, or until the liquid has reduced by about half. Add the cream and cook for 5 minutes more, or until the sauce is viscous but not gummy, and smooth but not runny— you're looking for the consistency in between.

When the cake comes out of the oven, pour all of the toffee sauce over the top while the cake is hot and set aside to rest and soak at room temperature for 1 hour.

Just before serving, make the pecans: Preheat the oven to 325°F. Line a baking sheet with parchment paper.

In a large bowl, toss the pecans with the melted butter to coat evenly, and season with the salt and granulated sugar. Place the buttered pecans on the prepared baking sheet and bake for 7 to 10 minutes, until lightly toasted and aromatic. (There is no need to move or shake the pecans while they toast.) If you would like to eat the cake warm, leave the oven at 325°F and return the cake to the oven for 5 minutes.

Serve the cake straight out of the pan with a scoop of the ice cream and a spoonful of the pecans scattered across the top. Leftover cake will keep, covered, at room temperature for up to 2 days.

pecan tart

In the Deep South, there's nothing more nostalgic than pecan pie. Every family has a recipe, and at every family get-together, there's at least one pecan pie in the mix. Pecan season peaks in the fall, so they're often associated with Thanksgiving and Christmas.

This is a slightly more delicate version of that quintessential pie, perfect to go alongside a morning coffee or as a dainty end to a rich meal. It makes use of my beloved brown butter, which pairs so well with nutty, aromatic pecans. The pie is enriched with cane syrup, a thick, sweet, molasses-like Southern ingredient that adds a distinctive malty richness.

makes one 11-inch tart

SHORTBREAD DOUGH

1 cup unsalted butter

½ cup sugar

2 cups all-purpose flour

¼ teaspoon kosher salt

FILLING

¼ cup unsalted butter

2 cups pecan halves

1 cup sugar

1½ teaspoons all-purpose flour

¼ teaspoon sea salt

1 teaspoon vanilla extract

1 cup cane syrup

3 eggs, plus 2 egg yolks

NOTE

If you have leftover dough, freeze it for later use. It makes very tasty shortbread cookies. Roll it out until ¼ inch thick, cut out shapes with a cookie cutter, and bake at 350°F for 8 to 10 minutes.

To make the shortbread dough: In a small saucepan over medium heat, melt the butter.

Whisk together the sugar, flour, and kosher salt in a mixing bowl and, using a wooden spoon, stir in the melted butter, and continue stirring until the mixture resembles cookie dough.

Using your hands, press the dough into an 11-inch round tart pan. Make sure the dough is evenly distributed around the fluted sides of the pan. Use leftover scraps to fill in any bare spots.

Wrap the tart shell in plastic wrap and refrigerate for 30 minutes while you make the filling.

To make the filling: Preheat the oven to 350°F. Line a baking sheet with parchment paper.

Melt the butter in a small saucepan or skillet over medium-high heat, then decrease the heat to medium and let the butter gently toast until its color turns from a pale whitish-yellow to bright yellow, 6 to 8 minutes. Steam will rise off of it as water evaporates. Once the water has evaporated, the butter will toast quickly, turning from a clear yellow to a nutty brown color, and will develop the aroma of toasted butter, another 2 to 4 minutes. Set the brown butter aside.

Spread out the pecans on the prepared baking sheet and toast in the oven until slightly darkened and aromatic, about 15 minutes. Toasting the pecans activates their natural oil to help bring out their flavor.

CONTINUED

In a large mixing bowl, whisk together the sugar, flour, and sea salt. In a separate bowl, mix together the vanilla, cane syrup, eggs and egg yolks, and brown butter. Slowly whisk the wet mixture into the dry mixture, and fold in the pecans. Set aside at room temperature while you bake the tart shell.

Remove the shell from the refrigerator. Cut a piece of parchment paper about 2 inches bigger than the pan and lay it across the top of the dough. Weigh down the paper with a large handful of dried beans or ceramic pie weights in an even layer and bake until the dough is slightly toasted and dry to the touch, about 15 minutes. Remove the parchment and beans and let the shell cool to room temperature.

Spoon the filling into the tart shell and bake until the pecans have risen to the top and formed a dry, crispy top that doesn't move when tapped, about 30 minutes. Let cool on a wire rack for 1 hour. Serve slightly warm or at room temperature. Leftover tart will keep at room temperature for up to 3 days.

s'mores tarts

There's the s'mores you had as a kid, and then there's this—a buttery whole-wheat graham cracker crust with a molten brownie filling and a gooey toasted homemade-marshmallow top. It's on the sweet side, as we tend to like it in New Orleans.

To make the dough: In a mixing bowl, whisk together the all-purpose flour, whole-wheat flour, salt, baking soda, and cinnamon and set aside.

Place the butter, both sugars, and honey in the bowl of a stand mixer fitted with a paddle attachment. Mix on medium-high speed until completely blended and the mixture sticks to the sides of the bowl.

On low speed, gradually add the dry ingredients to the wet ingredients, turning off the machine and scraping down the sides of the bowl now and then, until everything is incorporated. Form the dough into a ball with your hands, wrap in plastic wrap, and freeze for 30 minutes.

Preheat the oven to 325°F. Line a baking sheet with parchment paper.

On a clean floured surface, roll out the dough into a ¼-inch-thick sheet, about 12 x 24 inches. Cut out a 4⅜-inch circle from parchment paper or a paper bag. Using the paper circle as a guide, cut out six circles.

Using a spatula, place the dough in 3⅛-inch ring molds, where it should hang over the sides slightly. Using your fingers, press the dough into the molds and trim off any excess that extends beyond the rim.

Place the molds on the prepared baking sheet and bake until dry to the touch and slightly toasted, about 10 minutes. Using a shot glass, lightly press the dough down to make a flat, even bottom and edge. Set aside to cool in the molds. (Leave the oven on.)

To make the filling: Fill a medium pot with 3 cups of water and bring to a simmer over medium heat. Suspend a metal bowl in the pot (the bottom should not touch the water). Add the chocolate and butter to the bowl, decrease the heat to medium-low, and stir with a heatproof spatula until the chocolate is melted and blended with the butter, about 2 minutes. Set aside to cool slightly so as not to cook the eggs in the next step.

In a separate bowl, whisk together the eggs and granulated sugar. Add the chocolate to the egg mixture and gently whisk to combine. In another bowl, whisk together the flour, baking powder, and salt. Whisk the dry ingredients into the chocolate-egg mixture until smooth and well combined.

makes 6 tarts

GRAHAM CRACKER DOUGH

1 cup all-purpose flour

¼ cup whole-wheat flour

½ teaspoon kosher salt

¼ teaspoon baking soda

¼ teaspoon ground cinnamon

½ cup unsalted butter, cut into ½-inch cubes

2 tablespoons firmly packed light brown sugar

2 tablespoons granulated sugar

2 tablespoons honey

CHOCOLATE FILLING

½ cup chopped 65% cacao bittersweet chocolate

½ cup cubed unsalted butter (½-inch cubes)

2 eggs

1 cup granulated sugar

½ cup plus 2 tablespoons all-purpose flour

½ teaspoon baking powder

¼ teaspoon kosher salt

CONTINUED

MARSHMALLOWS

3½ cups water

¼ cup powdered gelatin

About ¼ cup canola oil for greasing

2¼ cups granulated sugar

½ cup plus 2 tablespoons corn syrup

2¼ cups powdered sugar

NOTE

You'll need 3⅛-inch ring molds to make these. The graham cracker tarts and chocolate filling can be made a day in advance, but the marshmallows are best in this recipe on the day they're made. However, the recipe makes double the amount needed for the tarts, so you have leftovers for hot chocolate (or snacking) later.

Fill each pastry shell with about 2 tablespoons of filling.

Bake in the oven until just barely set, about 10 minutes. The filling should look undercooked at this point, not cakey or firm.

Remove the tarts from the oven and gently tamp down the tops with a spoon, ensuring that the center and sides form an even surface for the marshmallow layer. Set aside to cool to room temperature. At this point, you can store the tarts, covered, in the refrigerator for up to 1 day.

To make the marshmallows: Pour 3 cups of the water into a small bowl and sprinkle the gelatin powder over it to bloom.

Grease an 18 x 13-inch baking sheet with some of the oil. Top the baking sheet with a sheet of plastic wrap and press it onto the oil so it sticks. Grease the top of the plastic with more oil. Wipe the paddle end of a rubber spatula with oil and set aside with the oiled pan.

In a medium saucepan, combine the granulated sugar, remaining ½ cup of water, and the corn syrup and bring to a boil. Add the gelatin and stir gently to dissolve. Pour the hot mixture into the bowl of a stand mixer fitted with whisk attachment. Starting on low speed, begin whisking, and gradually increase the speed every 10 seconds until you reach high. Mix on high speed until fluffy and glossy, about 7 minutes. Mixing this way aerates the proteins in the gelatin, creating that signature marshmallow fluff.

Working as quickly as possible, pour the marshmallow fluff onto the prepared pan in a layer about 1½ inches thick, and smooth it out using the oiled rubber spatula. Chill in the refrigerator until set, about 1 hour.

Sift 1 cup of the powdered sugar onto work surface and smooth out to roughly the same dimensions as the marshmallow pan. Invert the entire marshmallow from the pan over the powdered sugar. Peel off the plastic wrap and dust the top with 1 cup of powdered sugar. Cut the marshmallows into 3- to 4-inch squares. Dust the sides of each square with the remaining ¼ cup of powdered sugar to keep them from sticking together. Transfer half of the marshmallows to an airtight container and store in a cool place for 2 to 3 days for another use.

Preheat the oven to 325°F. Line a baking sheet with parchment paper.

Place the chocolate-filled shells on the prepared baking sheet and reheat in the oven for 3 to 5 minutes, until hot to the touch.

Remove the rings from the tarts and top each shell with a marshmallow square. Using a culinary torch or your broiler set to high, toast the tops of the marshmallows until deep golden brown, about 5 seconds with a torch, or 10 to 15 seconds under a broiler, watching closely. Serve warm.

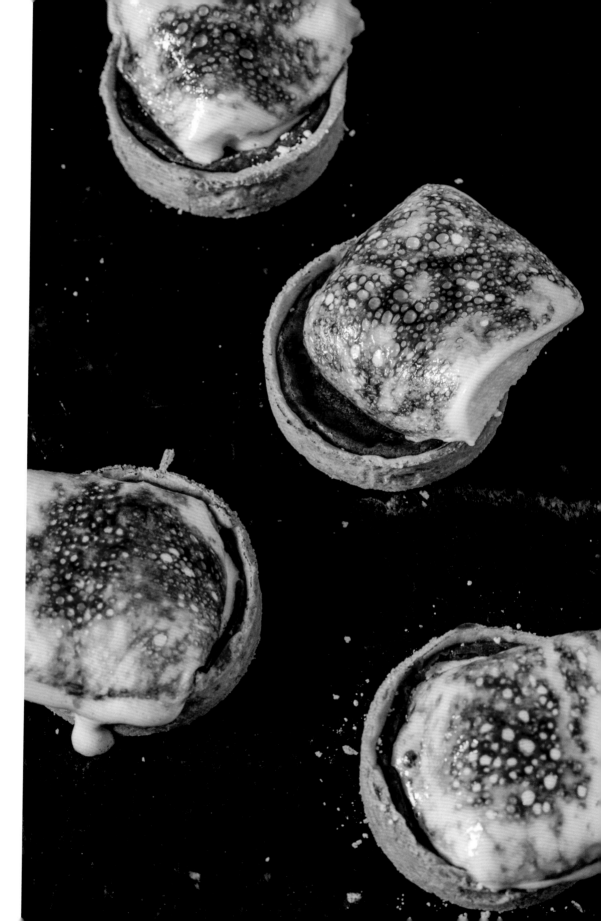

basics

This chapter consists of recipes that you can make and keep on hand to enhance others, building a foundation of flavors and textures. I like to make a lot of pantry staples myself—components like jam, pickles, hot sauce, cured pork, and more—because I find the process very satisfying and the taste far better than what I can buy from a store.

bouquet garni

This is one of those things—a little bundle of aromatic herbs—that we make a lot at my restaurants, where we have leftover bits and bobs lying around. It's rarely essential for a recipe, but it's a good way to introduce a larger range of herbs without having them chopped up and scattered throughout. Bouquets garnis are typically added to a liquid while cooking and pulled out before serving, leaving the dish with a subtle aroma from the herbal infusion.

makes 1 bouquet

3 sprigs thyme

5 sprigs flat-leaf parsley

1 sprig sage

2 bay leaves

1 sprig rosemary

Roll the thyme, parsley, sage, bay leaves, and rosemary into a cheesecloth sachet and secure with kitchen twine. Use as directed in a recipe.

preserved lemon peel

I've always been fascinated by preserved lemons, because it's a way to take something that normally gets tossed—lemon rind—and transform it into a versatile ingredient. Preserved peels work less like lemons do and more like a seasoning, imparting a subtle, salty, lemony pop. I stir them into sauces as they finish, mince and whisk into mayonnaise or Aioli (page 65), or toss them into a salad with olives and cucumber for contrast.

You're probably used to seeing recipes for whole preserved lemons. I prefer to preserve just the peels because it's quicker and they have a more subtle presence in the finished dish than whole preserved lemon.

makes about 2 cups

10 lemons

1 cup kosher salt

Scrub the lemons to remove any wax, then peel with a peeler and juice the lemons. Pack the lemon peels into a clean 1-quart canning jar. In a 1-quart measuring cup, combine the juice and salt and pour over the lemon peels. Cure in the refrigerator for a minimum of 5 days or up to 10 days. Rinse well before using. Store in an airtight container in the refrigerator for up to 3 months.

preserved lemon gremolata

Gremolata is a classic Italian condiment, traditionally made with grated lemon zest, but I like to use preserved lemon to give it a boost of salty cured flavor. I find it helps cut through the richness of many New Orleans dishes. Use it on braised meats, roasted vegetables, grilled fish, or anything that needs a hit of bright freshness.

makes about ½ cup

1 cup finely chopped flat-leaf parsley leaves

1 clove garlic, finely minced

2 tablespoons finely chopped Preserved Lemon Peel (facing page)

In a mixing bowl, combine the parsley, garlic, and lemon peel. Store in an airtight container in the refrigerator for up to 2 days.

oven-dried tomatoes

Just a tiny bit of work and some time is all it takes to transform ordinary tomatoes into something exciting and complex. A simple process of dehydration and warming gives you a rich, sweet, acidic, concentrated tomato. I scatter these across braised meats and stir them into cooked stews, scrambled eggs, and more.

makes about 2 cups

Extra-virgin olive oil
for coating the pan and
tomatoes

5 Roma tomatoes

1 tablespoon kosher salt

5 sprigs thyme

Preheat the oven to 225°F. Line a baking sheet with parchment paper and coat with oil.

Cut the tomatoes into quarters and place, cut-side up, on the prepared baking sheet. Drizzle the tomatoes with more oil and season with the salt. Scatter the thyme sprigs across the tops of the tomatoes and place in the oven. Roast until the tomatoes are curled up and dry to the touch, about 2½ hours, checking periodically to ensure they have not completely shriveled up and overdried. Store in an airtight container in the refrigerator for up to 1 week.

roasted tomato relish

This is a great way to prepare a sauce or vinaigrette after you've made Oven-Dried Tomatoes, to give it another dimension. The tomato doesn't really change, but you add other flavors to give it more complexity. Eat this with grilled fish (like the Garlic-and-Herb-Crusted Snapper with Oven-Dried Tomatoes and Pistou on page 231), on seared meats, or spread it across a sandwich—it's versatile like that.

makes 2 cups

¼ cup extra-virgin olive oil

1 teaspoon finely
minced garlic

2 tablespoons thinly
sliced shallots

1 tablespoon capers, drained,
rinsed, and dried

1 tablespoon freshly
squeezed lemon juice

2 teaspoons thyme leaves

1 teaspoon minced chives

½ teaspoon kosher salt

Freshly cracked black pepper

2 cups Oven-Dried Tomatoes
(page 344)

In a medium mixing bowl, combine the oil, garlic, shallots, capers, lemon juice, thyme, and chives. Season with the salt and a few grinds of pepper. Add the tomatoes and toss to coat and combine. Let stand at room temperature for 30 to 45 minutes to let the flavors meld, or store in the refrigerator for up to 8 hours. Serve at room temperature.

violet mustard

Use this any time mustard is needed, for an alternative that's a little more acidic and brighter than yellow mustard. The addition of reduced red wine provides a tannic, fruity dimension. I use it on cold meat or with charcuterie, all kinds of sandwiches, and even as a dressing for steak tartare.

makes 1 cup

1 (750-ml bottle) red wine

1 cup Dijon mustard

In a medium saucepan over medium heat, bring the red wine to a boil. Cook at a low boil, undisturbed, until reduced to ¼ cup, about 45 minutes. Remove from the heat and transfer to a mixing bowl, using a heatproof rubber spatula to get everything out of the pan.

Whisk in the Dijon and continue whisking until well combined. Transfer to a small bowl or storage container and chill for 30 minutes. Store in an airtight container in the refrigerator indefinitely.

basic pickles

I eat pickles all the time, and am endlessly enthusiastic about them. From a cooking standpoint, keeping a variety of pickles in your pantry is a great way to give that last boost to a dish that feels almost-but-not-quite finished. And they're just a good thing to have on hand, in the event that a guest stops by unannounced—pretty much everyone loves a homemade pickle.

This pickle brine is a general formula for all kinds of quick pickles. You can make this brine and pour it over just about any washed and prepared vegetable, then marinate it in the refrigerator for a few days, and your pickles are ready to go. Quick pickles won't be as sour or funky as their fermented counterparts—they'll be a little sweet, more like bread-and-butter pickles.

The best vegetables to pickle are those that are naturally crunchy, such as carrots, radishes, celery, cucumbers, cauliflower, zucchini, and fennel. Other strong contenders include the parts of vegetables you'd normally throw out—the stems of collard greens, kale, or broccoli and watermelon rinds. If you pickle something grassy and vegetal, like green beans, blanch them first, to avoid an unpleasant raw flavor.

You can also add herbs and spices to the brine, such as coriander, cardamom, and basil, as well as sliced jalapeños or other chiles. Add spices to the brine when heating it, and add herbs to the jar when packing in the pickles. This basic recipe can be doubled.

makes about 1 quart

1 cup vinegar

½ cup sugar

½ cup water

2 tablespoons kosher salt

About 1 cup washed, chopped vegetables, such as carrots, fennel, cucumber, and/or celery

In a small saucepan over medium heat, combine the vinegar, sugar, water, and salt and stir until the sugar and salt dissolve. Remove from the heat and let cool to room temperature. Place the vegetables in a glass jar or plastic container with a tight-fitting lid and pour the brine over to cover. Seal and cure in the refrigerator for 48 hours. Store in the refrigerator for up to 3 weeks.

lpg burger pickles

This is the first pickle we made at La Petite Grocery, and we developed it specifically for the burger on page 298. These super-simple, acid-forward pickles have apple cider vinegar for sweetness. And they have other delicious possibilities beyond the burger—try them with any charcuterie plate or grilled meat to balance the richness.

makes about 1 quart

2 large cucumbers, thickly sliced

1 tablespoon kosher salt

2⅔ cups apple cider vinegar

1 cup water

1⅓ cups sugar

1 tablespoon black peppercorns

1 tablespoon coriander seeds

1 tablespoon juniper berries

Peel of 1 lemon

In a bowl, toss the cucumbers with the salt, then cover with ice water. Let sit for 2 hours to draw out excess moisture.

Prepare an ice bath by filling another bowl with ice and adding just enough water to loosen (see page 35).

In a large saucepan, combine the vinegar, 1 cup water, sugar, peppercorns, coriander seeds, juniper berries, and lemon peel and bring to a boil. Place the pan in the ice bath and cool the pickling liquid until it reads 40°F or lower on an instant-read thermometer.

Drain the cucumbers and place in a glass jar or plastic container with a tight-fitting lid. When the liquid has cooled, strain through a fine-mesh strainer and pour over the cucumbers. Seal and cure in the refrigerator for 48 hours. Store in the brine in the refrigerator for up to 2 weeks.

half-sour pickles

These are the opposite of the burger pickles on the facing page; they contain less vinegar and rely on a slightly more complicated fermentation process to develop that classic sour pickle flavor. The important thing here is the quality of your cukes—low-quality specimens will get mushy as they brine. If possible, buy yours from the farmers' market and store unrefrigerated, which will give the best crunch. If using store-bought, buy individually wrapped English cucumbers. As the pickles ferment, you will start to see them transform—the liquid will become slightly cloudy and smoky-looking, but if it looks too weird, like there's mold growing on top (which can occur if the vegetables are not fully submerged in the brine), toss out the whole batch and start again.

makes about 2 quarts

¼ cup plus 1 tablespoon kosher salt

5 cups cold water

2 cucumbers
(or 1, if using English)

½ white onion, thinly sliced

3 cloves garlic, mashed
(see page 37)

1 tablespoon black peppercorns

4 to 5 sprigs dill

½ cup white wine vinegar

Combine the salt and water in a pitcher and stir gently to help dissolve the salt. Pour 2 cups of this brine into a resealable plastic bag. Release the air from the bag by gently pressing on the bag. Seal it and set aside. This will be used later for weighing down the cucumbers.

Cut the cucumbers crosswise into four equal pieces (eight if using English cucumber), and trim the ends to speed up the brining process. Place the cucumbers in a large nonreactive bowl, such as glass or stainless steel. Add the onion, garlic, peppercorns, and dill, and pour in the remaining 3 cups of brine. Place the plastic brine bag on top of the cucumbers.

Cure at room temperature for 48 hours. When the water is cloudy and the cucumbers have fermented, remove ½ cup of the brine from the vegetables and stir in the white wine vinegar. Transfer the pickles and brine to a glass jar or plastic container with a tight-fitting lid. Store in the refrigerator for up to 4 weeks.

pickled shallots

Pickled shallots are one of my favorite all-purpose condiments. I like to have them on hand for adding to everything from sandwiches to grilled seafood, raw seafood, scrambled eggs, and more. I like the way the fruity orange peel and coriander seeds brighten the shallots, which are called for in the charred cucumber-mint salad on page 160, along with the warm spinach and frisée salad on page 159.

makes about 1 quart

2 tablespoons kosher salt

2 cups water

2 cups white wine vinegar

10 strips orange peel (no pith)

2 teaspoons coriander seeds

2 teaspoons white peppercorns

12 shallots, very thinly sliced

In a medium saucepan, combine 1 tablespoon of the salt, the water, vinegar, orange peel, coriander seeds, and peppercorns and bring to a boil. Immediately remove from the heat and set this brine aside to cool to room temperature.

While the brine cools, in a nonreactive bowl, such as glass or stainless steel, toss the shallots with the remaining 1 tablespoon of salt. Set aside for a minimum of 20 minutes or up to 30 minutes (no longer, to avoid oversalting). Briefly rinse the shallots under cool running water (don't soak them, as you want some of the salt to remain for seasoning) and drain in a colander until most of the water is gone.

Arrange the shallots in a glass jar or plastic container with a tight-fitting lid. Pour the brine, with its spices, directly over the shallots. Seal and cure in the refrigerator for 12 hours. Store, covered, in the refrigerator for up to 4 weeks.

pickled jalapeños

I love pickled jalapeños and eat them on everything from eggs to sandwiches to pizza, or sometimes just snack on them plain. The pickling liquid is also great for seasoning sauces, soups, greens, and, last but certainly not least, Bloody Marys, with a bright, peppery kick.

In a small saucepan over medium heat, combine the vinegar, sugar, water, salt, garlic, and coriander seeds and stir until the sugar and salt dissolve. Let cool to room temperature.

Place the jalapeños in a glass jar or plastic container with a tight-fitting lid. Pour the brine over it to cover. Seal and cure in the refrigerator for 12 hours. Store in the refrigerator for up to 2 weeks.

makes about 1 pint

¼ cup apple cider vinegar

1½ teaspoons sugar

¼ cup water

3 tablespoons kosher salt

1 clove garlic

1 teaspoon coriander seeds

6 jalapeños, julienned

sauerkraut

True sauerkraut takes a while to make due to the fermenting process, so I'm giving you two options: this classic sour cabbage version, which is fermented for several days to sour the cabbage, and a faster alternative, the Choucroute on the facing page, using vinegar, which has already been fermented and gives a similar taste to the cabbage. Experiment and make whichever one you have time for.

I like to keep these in my refrigerator at home to eat as a snack, and I feel virtuous about the natural probiotics that come with the fermentation of the cabbage. Use them any time with classic options, such as hot dogs and bratwurst, but also with hamburgers, pork chops, grilled meats, and even grain salads.

makes about 1 quart

½ teaspoon caraway seeds

1 large head cabbage

1 tablespoon kosher salt

In a small saucepan or skillet over medium-high heat, toast the caraway seeds until they begin to give off a rye-smelling aroma, 3 to 5 minutes. Remove from the heat and allow to cool.

Quarter the cabbage head and remove the core. Slice the cabbage ¼ inch thick and transfer to a nonreactive bowl, such as glass or stainless steel. Add the salt and toss. Let sit at room temperature for 30 minutes. At this point, the salt should have pulled out much of the moisture and wilted the cabbage, making it more pliable. Drain any excess liquid, and using your hands, squeeze the cabbage to release and drain as much remaining liquid as possible. Stir in the caraway seeds.

Transfer the cabbage to a 2-quart glass jar and cover with a clean piece of cheesecloth, sealed around the mouth of the jar with a rubber band. Let sit at room temperature for 48 to 60 hours, until the color has gone from green to muted green-yellow, and the brine is slightly cloudy. Seal with a loose-fitting lid or plastic wrap with small holes poked in it and ferment in the refrigerator for 2 hours. Store, covered, in the refrigerator for up to 6 weeks.

choucroute

The quicker version of sauerkraut, choucroute tastes more vinegary and pickled, while sauerkraut is more sour, similar to kimchee or a true fermented product.

makes about 1 quart

1 large head cabbage

¼ cup kosher salt

2 cups apple cider vinegar

2 cloves garlic, sliced

Quarter the cabbage head and remove the core. Slice the cabbage ¼ inch thick and transfer to a nonreactive bowl, such as glass or stainless steel. Add the salt and toss. Let sit at room temperature for 30 minutes. At this point, the salt should have pulled out much of the moisture and wilted the cabbage, making it more pliable. Drain any excess liquid, and using your hands, squeeze the cabbage to release and drain as much remaining liquid as possible.

Transfer the cabbage to a colander and rinse under cool running water to remove excess salt. Transfer the cabbage to a large storage container with a tight-fitting lid, cover with the apple cider vinegar and garlic, and toss to combine. Cover the container and place in the refrigerator. The cabbage may not be completely submerged, and that's okay—it will continue to break down as it pickles. Every few hours, submerge the cabbage with a spoon, or weight down with a jar of water. Cure for 8 to 12 hours. Store, covered, in the refrigerator for up to 6 weeks.

chow chow

I think of chow chow as a kind of Southern giardiniera (the Italian condiment made from assorted finely chopped pickled veggies)—it's crunchy, acidic, sweet, sour, and a little spicy. I put it on a lot of sandwiches, or any type of barbecued or fried chicken thing, and I use it as a hot dog relish. Chow chow keeps best when its contents are submerged in a lot of liquid. If green tomatoes are difficult to find, try using fennel, celery, apple, or more cabbage.

makes about 3 cups

2 red bell peppers

3 teaspoons extra-virgin olive oil

5 green tomatoes

⅔ cup apple cider vinegar

⅔ cup sugar

2 cloves garlic

1 shallot, diced

1 cup chopped cabbage

2 teaspoons mustard seeds

Kosher salt

Preheat the oven to 375°F. Line a baking sheet with parchment paper.

Brush the bell peppers with the oil and place on the prepared baking sheet. Roast, turning once, until the skin is visibly blistered and separating from the flesh, about 20 minutes. Place the peppers in a bowl and cover tightly with plastic wrap. Set aside to steam as they cool, about 45 minutes, making the skin easier to remove. When cool, carefully remove the plastic wrap and place the peppers on a clean work surface. It's helpful to have a damp paper towel nearby to wipe your fingers as you go. Using your fingers, peel off the skin in strips.

Once all the skin is removed, gently split open the peppers with your thumb and wipe away all the seeds and membrane. Chop the peppers into a very small dice. Let cool to room temperature.

Bring a stockpot filled with water to a boil. In a large bowl, make an ice water bath (page 35). Drop the tomatoes into the boiling water and cook for 1 minute to blanch. Using tongs, transfer the tomatoes to the ice water bath. When cool enough to handle, peel and dice the tomatoes. Transfer the juicy inner flesh and seeds to a blender.

Add the vinegar, sugar, and garlic to the blender and puree. Transfer to a medium saucepan over high heat and add the diced tomatoes, shallot, cabbage, and mustard seeds. Bring to a boil, then decrease the heat to low and simmer until the mixture is reduced by half and thickens to a slightly syrupy consistency, about 1 hour. Add the bell peppers and continue to cook until thick and jammy, 25 to 30 minutes more. Season with salt. Remove from the heat, let cool to room temperature, and transfer to a glass jar or plastic container with a tight-fitting lid. Store, covered, in the refrigerator for up to 4 weeks.

strawberry-tarragon jam

Jam, like crème fraîche (see page 363) and cured pork belly (see page 375), is one of those things that you can certainly buy in the store, but making it at home pays off in quality and self-confidence. If you like cooking, you're going to like it even more when you learn how to make things like jam. And once you make one jam, you'll want to make others, because it's a straightforward process, which just changes a bit depending on the type of fruit you use.

This is a fancy jam that I like to serve with the Country Pork Pâté on page 103. Strawberries are acidic, but they have a nice floral under-tone, and I find that tarragon helps bring out their natural aroma. Beyond the pâté, this is perfect with most other types of charcuterie as well as scones and biscuits.

makes about ½ cup

1 pound strawberries, hulled and quartered

1⅔ cups sugar

2 sprigs tarragon, plus 1 tablespoon chopped tarragon leaves

In a mixing bowl, toss the strawberries with the sugar and the sprigs of tarragon. Let sit at room temperature for 20 to 30 minutes to macerate—the sugar will start to dissolve, and the moisture from the berries will start to leach out.

Transfer everything to a small saucepan and heat over medium-high heat until the mixture reaches a light boil. Decrease the heat to medium-low and let the mixture gently simmer until thick, about 20 minutes. To test, dip a spoon in the jam, let cool slightly, and then run your finger down the back of the spoon—the line you form with your finger shouldn't fill in.

Transfer the jam to a shallow proof dish—something with a large base, to speed cooling. Let cool completely, about 1½ hours, then transfer to a sterilized jam jar (see Note, page 84) or other glass container with a tight-fitting lid. Store, covered, in the refrigerator for up to 3 months.

watermelon-ginger jam

This is a rendition of the way my grandmother used to preserve watermelon. Her reason for doing so, which I'm still fascinated by today, is because everyone throws away the rinds and she didn't like to waste them. This jam goes well with soft-rind triple-crème cheeses, grilled meats, and the twice-cooked ribs on page 288, or on a bagel with cream cheese.

makes about 2 cups

1 (8- to 10-pound) watermelon

1 cup sugar

2 tablespoons freshly squeezed lemon juice

3 slices peeled ginger

Cut the watermelon crosswise into 1-inch slices so you have 1-inch rounds and then cut those into half-moons. Using a peeler, peel off the green skin and discard. Separate the red meat from the white rind. Juice the meat by removing the seeds, pureeing in the blender, and passing through a fine-mesh strainer. You should have about 2 cups of watermelon juice. Split the rind into ½-inch pieces, then cut those into ½-inch cubes. You should have about 5 cups of rinds.

Combine the watermelon rinds, watermelon juice, sugar, and lemon juice in a stainless-steel saucepan. Bring to a boil over high heat, then decrease the heat to medium-low and simmer for 1 hour. The watermelon rind should look translucent but still be slightly crunchy, as its water is being cooked out and replaced by the sugar. Remove from the heat, stir in the ginger, and pour into a shallow heatproof dish—something with a large base, to speed cooling. Let cool at room temperature for 15 minutes, then transfer to a sterilized jam jar (see page 84) or other glass container with a tight-fitting lid. Place in the refrigerator to cool completely. Store, covered, in the refrigerator for up to 3 months.

tangerine marmalade

In New Orleans, we have a very prolific, highly anticipated satsuma season from early fall into winter. If you have access to fleeting satsumas, use them for this recipe, but otherwise, tangerines make a fine substitute. This marmalade is integral to the pan-roasted chicken thighs on page 248, but can also be served with charcuterie or on scones, biscuits, or toast.

makes about 2 cups

16 tangerines

1¼ cups sugar

Peel the tangerines, ideally leaving the peels as large and intact as possible. Push all of the fruit through a colander with fine holes, squeezing and mushing the flesh to extract all of the juice. You should be able to reserve 1¾ to 2 cups. Cut the peels into matchsticks, being careful not to include any green stems. You should have about 3 cups of peels.

Place the peels in a large pot and cover with about 1 inch of cold water. Place the pot over high heat and bring just to a boil. Immediately remove from the heat and drain through a colander. Return the peels to the empty pot, cover again with cold water, and repeat the process. After the second time, taste the rinds—the goal is to cook out that unpleasant pithy, bitter flavor until the peels are palatable. This can take anywhere from three to five boil-and-rinse cycles.

Once complete, return the peels to the empty pot and combine with the reserved tangerine juice and sugar. Bring to a boil, then decrease the heat to low, and cook for 1½ to 2 hours, stirring very occasionally, until the juice and sugar form a thick syrup—not so thick that it hardens when cool, but thick enough to separate when you drag a spoon through it. Let cool to room temperature, then transfer to a sterilized jam jar (see page 84) with a tight-fitting lid. Store, covered, in the refrigerator for up to 2 weeks.

onion marmalade

This rich, savory caramelized onion jam is called for in the famous LPG Cheeseburger on page 298, but it can also be used on grilled cheese, eggs, charcuterie, and more. Be patient when caramelizing the onions; they take time to cook all the way down, but the end result is worth it.

makes about 2 cups

2 tablespoons vegetable oil

6 large yellow onions, very thinly sliced

½ cup sugar

½ cup apple cider vinegar

Heat the oil in a large, deep pot over medium-high heat until shimmering. Add the onions and cook, stirring occasionally, until they start to collapse on themselves and release their liquid, about 30 minutes. Continue cooking until all of the liquid has evaporated and the onions are starting to caramelize, about 15 minutes more. Decrease the heat to medium-low and continue cooking, stirring occasionally, until the onions have totally caramelized, and have an amber-brown hue and soft, stringy texture, another 15 to 20 minutes.

Add the sugar and stir until the onions are coated and the sugar has dissolved. Add the vinegar and cook, stirring occasionally, until the liquid has reduced into a thick and viscous coating and the onions have a jammy consistency, 25 to 30 minutes. Set aside to cool. Use right away, or transfer to a glass jar with a tight-fitting lid. Store in the refrigerator for up to 10 days.

crème fraîche

You can buy crème fraîche in most grocery stores, but it's easy to make your own, and to customize it according to your preferences. You can tweak the cream's thickness, for example, by straining out more or less liquid after letting it stand. It's fun to make because you can get creative with the final result, which I find very satisfying.

makes 1 cup

1 cup heavy cream

2 tablespoons buttermilk

In a small saucepan over medium heat, bring the cream to 110°F on an instant-read themometer, 3 to 5 minutes. Remove from the heat and stir in the buttermilk. Let stand at room temperature until thick and creamy, 12 to 24 hours. Strain through cheesecloth if want yours thicker. Transfer to a container with a tight-fitting lid. Store covered in the refrigerator for up to 1 week.

basic compound butter

Compound butters are a really clever way to add flavor to a dish and can be used in so many ways—as a sauce, condiment, spread, or even as a crust (as in the garlic-and-herb-crusted snapper on page 231). Compound butters store well, too. And when you're thinking about flavor profiles, and using butter as the vehicle for those flavors, the sky is the limit. Here's a simple recipe for a compound butter base, to which you can add additional flavors as you see fit. (See the recipes that follow for more ideas for what to add to this basic recipe.)

makes about 1 cup

1 cup unsalted butter, at room temperature

1 clove garlic, mashed (see page 37)

2 teaspoons freshly squeezed lemon juice

1 teaspoon kosher salt

In a mixing bowl, whisk the butter, garlic, lemon juice, and salt until everything is evenly combined, creamy, and smooth. (If adding other ingredients, fold them in after whisking the base together.)

Cut an 18-inch sheet of plastic wrap and spread the butter in a long line lengthwise across the middle, leaving about 4 inches from either end of the wrap. The line of butter should be about 10 inches long and 1¼ inches in diameter.

Fold the plastic over the butter and press the butter into a log, pushing out any air bubbles. You should have a tight, even log. Roll the plastic over itself like an old-fashioned candy wrapper, and twist the ends closed. Tuck the ends underneath the log, put on a plate, and chill in the refrigerator for 20 minutes before using. Alternatively, you can cut the butter into cubes and freeze them in a resealable plastic bag indefinitely.

preserved lemon and olive butter

This butter has an earthy, briny Mediterranean flavor profile, which lends itself well to pastas, seafood, or roasted chicken (just smear it all over).

makes about 1 cup

1 cup unsalted butter, at room temperature

1 clove garlic, mashed (see page 37)

2 teaspoons freshly squeezed lemon juice

1 teaspoon kosher salt

2 teaspoons finely chopped oregano leaves

¼ cup finely chopped flat-leaf parsley leaves

1 shallot, finely minced

½ cup finely chopped pitted small black olives, such as Nicoise or Arbequina

1 tablespoon finely chopped Preserved Lemon Peel (page 342)

1 anchovy fillet, finely chopped

In a mixing bowl, whisk the butter, garlic, lemon juice, salt, oregano, parsley, shallot, olives, lemon peel, and anchovy until everything is evenly combined, creamy, and smooth. (If adding other ingredients, fold them in after whisking the base together.)

Cut an 18-inch sheet of plastic wrap and spread the butter in a long line lengthwise across the middle, leaving about 4 inches from either end of the wrap. The line of butter should be about 10 inches long and 1¼ inches in diameter.

Fold the plastic over the butter and press the butter into a log, pushing out any air bubbles. You should have a tight, even log. Roll the plastic over itself like an old-fashioned candy wrapper, and twist the ends closed. Tuck the ends underneath the log, put on a plate, and chill in the refrigerator for 20 minutes before using. Alternatively, you can cut the butter into cubes and freeze them in a resealable plastic bag indefinitely.

korean chile butter

This is a classic chile butter that we've been using for a long time in the restaurant. You can emulsify it into warm water or stock and make a nice sauce for fish or shellfish, or use it as butter to baste roasted cabbage or grilled vegetables.

Gochugaru is a seedless chile flake available in many Asian markets and online—it's spicy, but very fragrant, and that's why I prefer it instead of red pepper flakes. Combined with fish sauce, which has a distinctly fermented fragrance, the two blend together and make a funky, peppery chile butter that goes well on almost anything.

makes about 1 cup

1 cup unsalted butter, at room temperature

2 cloves garlic, mashed (see page 37)

1 tablespoon freshly squeezed lemon juice

1 teaspoon kosher salt

3 tablespoons Korean dried red chile flakes (gochugaru; see page 32)

1 tablespoon fish sauce

In a mixing bowl, whisk the butter, garlic, lemon juice, salt, chile flakes, and fish sauce until everything is evenly combined, creamy, and smooth. (If adding other ingredients, fold them in after whisking the base together.)

Cut an 18-inch sheet of plastic wrap and spread the butter in a long line lengthwise across the middle, leaving about 4 inches from either end of the wrap. The line of butter should be about 10 inches long and 1¼ inches in diameter.

Fold the plastic over the butter and press the butter into a log, pushing out any air bubbles. You should have a tight, even log. Roll the plastic over itself like an old-fashioned candy wrapper, and twist the ends closed. Tuck the ends under the log, put on plate, and chill in the refrigerator for 20 minutes before using. Alternatively, you can cut the butter into cubes and freeze them in a resealable plastic bag indefinitely.

herbed pimento butter

This started out as me trying to come up with a butter condiment that would mimic pimento cheese, but I quickly realized that the biggest part of pimento cheese is the cheese. So it didn't really work out the way I had hoped, but I'm still happy with the unexpectedly delightful results, and turned this into a nice butter that goes marvelously with grilled meats.

makes about 1 cup

1 red bell pepper

3 teaspoons extra-virgin olive oil

1 cup unsalted butter, at room temperature

1 tablespoon kosher salt

1 shallot, finely minced

2 cloves garlic, mashed (see page 37)

¼ cup finely chopped flat-leaf parsley leaves

¼ cup finely chopped chives

1 tablespoon chopped thyme leaves

Freshly cracked black pepper

3 tablespoons freshly squeezed lemon juice

Preheat the oven to 375°F. Line a baking sheet with parchment paper.

Brush the bell pepper with 1 teaspoon of the oil and place on the prepared baking sheet. Place in the oven. Check after 15 minutes, flipping the bell pepper, and rotate the pan 180 degrees if the pepper is not cooking evenly. It's done when its skin is puffy, dark, and blistered, about 25 minutes.

Using tongs, place the bell pepper in a bowl and cover tightly with plastic wrap. Set aside to steam as it cools, which makes the skin easier to remove, about 45 minutes.

When cool, carefully remove the plastic wrap and place the bell pepper on a clean work surface. It's helpful to have a damp paper towel nearby to wipe your fingers as you go. Using your fingers, peel off the skin in strips. Once all the skin has been removed, gently split the bell pepper open with your thumb. Remove and discard the stem, seeds, and white membrane. Chop the bell pepper into a very small dice and let cool to room temperature.

In a bowl, combine the bell pepper, butter, remaining 2 teaspoons oil, salt, shallot, garlic, parsley, chives, thyme, black pepper, and lemon juice. Fold together using a spatula until well combined and the butter is very creamy and totally smooth.

Cut an 18-inch sheet of plastic wrap and spread the butter in a long line lengthwise across the middle, leaving 4 inches from either end of the paper. The line of butter should be about 10 inches long and 1½ inches in diameter

Fold the plastic wrap over the butter and press it under the log, pushing out any air bubbles. You should have a tight, even log. Roll up the wrap over itself—like an old-fashioned candy wrapper—and twist the ends closed. Tuck the ends under the log, put on a plate, and chill in the refrigerator for 20 minutes before using. Alternatively, you can cut the butter into cubes and freeze them in a resealable plastic bag indefinitely.

foolproof rice

When I started cooking, making rice was intimidating, but this is a way to get it right every time. Rice is foundational to Cajun cooking. So many recipes in this book—gumbo, butter beans, field peas, poached fish, and more—could easily be served in true Louisiana fashion, over rice.

In a covered saucepan over high heat, bring the water and salt to a boil. Add the rice, stir, and return to a boil. Cover, decrease the heat to low, and simmer for 15 minutes. Then set aside, covered, for 10 minutes. Uncover, fluff with a fork, and serve.

makes about 4 cups

1 quart water

½ teaspoon kosher salt

2 cups long-grain rice (see Note)

NOTE

If using short-grain rice, follow the instructions on the package to adjust the water-to-rice ratio.

torn croutons

Add these compulsively snackable croutons to the broccoli Caesar on page 165 or any other salad that would benefit from some extra crunch.

makes about 2 cups

1 small baguette

½ cup extra-virgin olive oil

2 teaspoons kosher salt

Preheat the oven to 350°F. Line a baking sheet with parchment paper.

Break the baguette into pieces. Tear each piece into ¾-inch chunks (a great group activity). Place all the chunks in a mixing bowl and toss with the oil to coat evenly. Sprinkle with the salt and spread out in a single layer on the prepared baking sheet. Bake until golden and dry, 15 to 20 minutes. Let cool to room temperature before adding to salads. Store in an airtight container at room temperature for up to 1 week.

cornbread

This recipe comes with a caveat: I love this version of cornbread for what we use it for, which is making crumbs for the mac-and-cheese on page 146 and as stuffing for the quail on page 263. But it's not necessarily what I'd make as a side dish. I'm not convinced the world needs another cornbread recipe, and New Orleans isn't really a cornbread town. Feel free to make this as a stand-alone side if you so desire, but know that this is sweeter and more cakey than the classic Southern versions you might be thinking of.

Preheat the oven to 400°F.

In a large mixing bowl, whisk together the cornmeal, flour, baking powder, sugar, and salt. In a separate bowl, gently whisk together the milk, butter, and egg to combine. Pour the wet ingredients into the dry and stir to combine. Let rest for at least 10 minutes or up to 1 hour to activate the baking powder.

Butter a 9 x 13-inch baking dish. Pour in the batter (it should be a thin layer, which will help make for crispy crumbs) and bake until brown and slightly puffy, 20 to 25 minutes. Let cool in the pan, then cut and serve. Store leftovers in an airtight container at room temperature for up to 2 days.

makes one 9 x 13-inch cornbread

½ cup fine cornmeal

½ cup all-purpose flour

1 teaspoon baking powder

¼ cup sugar

½ teaspoon kosher salt

¾ cup whole milk

2 tablespoons unsalted butter, melted, plus more for greasing the pan

1 egg

buttermilk biscuits

The biscuits at La Petite Grocery are laminated and folded, which is great when you have a professional kitchen; but at home, when you just want a nice classic biscuit, this is the one to do.

A big part of achieving that perfectly fluffy, airy buttermilk biscuit is not overworking the dough, which happens if you more than barely handle it as you work in the butter. If you freeze your butter and quickly grate it directly into the flour instead of cutting it in, you can save a lot of time and the butter will be the perfect size to make those little pockets of moisture that are integral to the fluffiness of a biscuit. You can even keep grated butter in the freezer for this purpose.

makes 10 to 12 biscuits

3 cups all-purpose flour

1½ teaspoons kosher salt

3 teaspoons baking powder

1 cup unsalted butter (in stick form), frozen for 1 hour, plus ½ cup unsalted butter, melted

2 cups chilled buttermilk

2 tablespoons fleur de sel

In a large mixing bowl, whisk the flour, kosher salt, and baking powder.

Using the large holes on a box grater, grate the frozen butter into the flour mixture and gently toss to coat the butter with flour. It's important to keep everything cold. Put the bowl of flour mixture in the freezer to chill for 15 to 20 minutes.

Add the buttermilk to the flour and lift and pull with your fingertips (avoid kneading the dough) to form a shaggy ball. It's okay if the dough isn't perfectly smooth and even. Cover the bowl with plastic wrap and chill for 20 minutes in the refrigerator.

Preheat the oven to 400°F. Line a baking sheet with parchment paper.

Generously flour a clean work surface and transfer the dough to the work surface. Pat the dough into a disk about 12 inches long and 1½ inches thick. Using a 2-inch round cutter (or a glass or jar), punch out five or six biscuits and transfer to the prepared baking sheet.

Gather the dough scraps, and without kneading, form into another loose ball. Press this into a 1½-inch-thick disk and cut out another five or six biscuits. Don't worry about oddly shaped scraps—just gently work them back into a disk, and this will allow you to use all of the dough.

Chill the baking sheet full of biscuits for 5 minutes in the freezer or 10 minutes in the refrigerator.

Place the baking sheet in the oven and bake until the biscuits are golden brown and have risen and gently puffed up, and the edges are toasted, 15 to 20 minutes. Remove from the oven and gently spoon the melted butter over the top of each biscuit, then return to the oven for 2 minutes.

Sprinkle each biscuit with the fleur de sel and let rest for 5 to 10 minutes before serving. Store in an airtight container at room temperature, if you're restrained enough to have any left over.

cured pork belly (pancetta)

We use salted pork so much as a seasoning at the restaurants that it makes sense for us to cure our own. But cured pork isn't just for pros—as a home cook, it's important and fun to learn how to do these things on a smaller scale. Curing pork is one of those techniques that will enable you to add your own signature touch to your cooking, taking you one step further toward owning your personal style in the kitchen.

You can use this in any recipe in this book that calls for a cured pork product, bacon, sausage, just remember that the flavor will be slightly different because this pork isn't smoked. But you'll still get a delicious porkiness, which in some cases might work even better than a smoky flavor.

makes about 1¾ pounds

2 pounds fresh pork belly, skin removed

⅓ cup sugar

¼ cup kosher salt

2 cloves garlic, chopped

2 tablespoons thyme leaves

1 tablespoon freshly cracked black pepper

2 tablespoons red wine

Dry the pork belly with paper towels and place in a baking dish. Combine the sugar, salt, garlic, thyme, and pepper in a mixing bowl. Add the pork belly and coat evenly with a thin layer of the spice mixture. Using your fingertips, sprinkle the red wine over the meat. Cover with parchment paper and place in the refrigerator for 10 days, flipping and re-covering every 24 to 36 hours. The pork will lose some moisture as it cures, will feel slightly stiff to the touch, and look slightly oxidized (darker) on the surface.

Rinse the pork under cool running water and dry very well with clean paper towels. Cut the pork into thirds. Use immediately or wrap in plastic and store in the freezer for up to 12 weeks. To use the frozen cured pork, partially thaw in the refrigerator just until still firm and you can cut through it with a knife (it cuts more easily and cleanly when it's partially thawed than when fully thawed). Use as directed in a recipe.

ALUMACRAFT

acknowledgments

To the book team:

Jamie Feldmar

Lorena Jones, Lizzie Allen, Emma Campion, Jane Chinn, Doug Ogan, Kristin Casemore, Allison Renzulli, and the rest of the Ten Speed Press team

David Black and everyone at the David Black Agency

Denny Culbert

Amanda Medsger

Joe Vidrine

Erin Zimmer Strenio

And to my work family:

Anne Kearney

Austin Breckenridge

Blake Sherere

Brian Rivlin

Bronwen Wyatt

Colin Lawson

Daniel Causgrove

Erin Hollis

Jessica Stokes

Joe Bruno

Joseph Tiedmann

Lennon Clotiaux-Fitzgerald

Matt Mayeda

Nicelle Harrington

Patrick Dunn

Paul DiMaria

Phil Hamilton

Sausage Steve

Stephanie Bruno

TG Harrington

Tom Gunn

index

Published in the United States by Lorena Jones Books, an imprint
of Random House, a division of Penguin Random House LLC, New York.
www.tenspeed.com

Lorena Jones Books and the Lorena Jones Books colophon are trademarks of
Penguin Random House, LLC.

Library of Congress Cataloging-in-Publication Data
 Names: Devillier, Justin, 1981–author. | Feldmar, Jamie, author. | Culbert,
   Denny, photographer.
 Title: The New Orleans kitchen : classic recipes and modern techniques for
   an unrivaled cuisine / Justin Devillier with Jamie Feldmar ; photographs by
   Denny Culbert.
 Description: New York : Lorena Jones Books [2019] | Includes bibliographical
   references and index.
 Identifiers: LCCN 2019009413 (print) | LCCN 2019015681 (ebook) |
   ISBN 9780399582301 (ebook) | ISBN 9780399582295 (hardcover : alk. paper)
 Subjects: LCSH: Cooking, American—Louisiana style. | Cooking—Louisiana—
   New Orleans. | LCGFT: Cookbooks.
 Classification: LCC TX715.2.L68 (ebook) | LCC TX715.2.L68 D49 2019 (print) |
   DDC 641.59763/35—dc23
 LC record available at https://lccn.loc.gov/2019009413

Hardcover ISBN: 978-0-399-58229-5
Ebook ISBN: 978-0-399-58230-1

Design by Lizzie Allen
Prop styling by Amanda Medsger
Food styling by Joseph Tiedmann
Printed in China

10 9 8 7 6 5 4 3 2 1

First Edition